Social Policy for Welfare Practice in Wales

Third Edition

Edited by
Hefin Gwilym and Charlotte Williams

© British Association of Social Workers Ltd, 2021

All rights reserved. No part of this publication may be reproduced, stored in a retrieval system, or transmitted, in any form or by any means, electronic, mechanical, photocopying, recording or otherwise, without the prior permission of the British Association of Social Workers.

Published by
British Association of Social Workers
Wellesley House
37 Waterloo Street
Birmingham B2 5PP

www.basw.co.uk

British Library Cataloguing-in-Publication Data
A catalogue record for this book is available from the British Library

ISBN: 978-1-86178-090-4 (paperback)

Printed by:
Hobbs the Printers Ltd
Brunel Road
Totton
SO40 3WX

Printed in Great Britain

Contents

List of figures and tables	viii	Editors	xi
List of abbreviations	ix	Notes on contributors	xii
Acknowledgements	x	Foreword : Rt Hon Mark Drakeford	xv

EDITORS' INTRODUCTION — 1
Hefin Gwilym & Charlotte Williams

Introduction — 1
Modern Wales — 2
Chapter overview — 4
Conclusions — 7

1 WALES 20 YEARS ON: THE RECORD AND NEW GOALS — 9
Hefin Gwilym

Introduction — 9
Background — 9
Notable achievements and challenges — 12
New goals — 15
Conclusions — 17
References — 17

2 SOCIAL CARE: RESEARCH, POLICY AND PRACTICE IN WALES — 19
Diane Seddon, Gill Toms and Fiona Verity

Introduction — 19
Vision for social care policy, practice, and research in Wales — 20
Realising the vision — 22
   Number of stakeholders — 22
   The nature of social care research — 23
      Its funding and practice context — *23*
      Its common methodologies — *24*
      Its chief investigators — *25*
      Its opportunity to achieve impact — *26*
Taking forward the social care research vision in Wales — 27
   Research support landscape — 28
   Social care innovations lab — 29
   Developing evidence enriched practice — 30
   Research networks — 31
      Enabling research in care homes Cymru — *31*
      The Wales Institute for Social Prescribing — *31*
Summary and conclusions — 32
References — 32

3 TACKLING POVERTY AND INEQUALITY — 35
David Beck

Introduction	35
What is 'poverty'?	36
Poverty inside and outside of Wales	36
Current structural drivers	37
Geographical considerations	38
Families and in-work poverty	39
Food poverty and food banks: An identification of modern poverty	41
The radical shake-up: Conditionality and eligibility	42
What gets measured gets mended	44
The future well-being of Wales	45
Future challenges	46
Conclusions	46
References	46

4 ENDING CHILD POVERTY IN 2020 IN WALES? — 51
Martin Elliott

Introduction	51
Timeline and key events	53
Definitions, measures, and the scale of child poverty	54
Not just about the money: understanding poverty in all its forms	55
From worklessness to in work poverty	56
A focus on inequalities	57
The UN rapporteur report	58
The tensions between UK and Welsh Government policies	58
The response to child poverty in Wales	59
Conclusions: A charter for change?	61
References	63

5 HEALTH POLICY IN WALES: TWO DECADES OF DEVOLUTION — 67
David Matthews

Introduction	67
The policy context	67
Collaboration, localism and participation	68
Public health and well-being	71
Public provision and ownership	74
Conclusions	76
References	77

6 HOUSING AS A SOCIAL ISSUE — 81
Edith England and Helen Taylor

Introduction	81
Homelessness in Wales	83
Social rental sector in Wales	85
Private rental sector	87
The impact of home on health	89
Conclusions	90
References	91

7 THE ROLE OF LANGUAGE POLICY, PLANNING AND LEGISLATION IN SOCIAL WELFARE IN WALES — 95
Rhian Hodges

Introduction	95
Background – The Welsh language	96
Key Welsh language legislative developments	97
Language policy and planning and social welfare	99
Devolution, the Welsh language, and social welfare provision	101
Legislation and policies versus daily practicalities	104
The way forward and conclusions	107
References	108

8 CLIMATE CHANGE AND SOCIAL WELFARE: EXPLORING ENVIRONMENTAL SOCIAL WORK — 113
Holly Gordon

Introduction	113
Environmental social work	114
Environmental policy and social welfare professions	117
Environmental social work education	120
Action for change	122
Conclusion	126
References	127

9 SOCIAL WELFARE AND THE SCOPE OF HUMAN RIGHTS — 131
Gideon Calder

Prelude: Bethan's choices — 131
Introduction: approaching human rights in Wales — 131
The very idea of human rights — 133
Forms of human rights — 134
Neoliberalism and the place of human rights — 136
A 'Welsh' approach to human rights? — 138
Conclusions: human rights work in an unequal society — 141
References — 141

10 ADVANCING EQUALITIES AND SOCIAL JUSTICE POST 2010 — 145
Charlotte Williams and Teresa Crew

Introduction — 145
The equalities challenge in Wales — 147
Women — 147
Disabled citizens — 149
Ethnic minorities — 149
LGBTIQ — 150
Religion and belief — 151
Age — 152
One step forward, two steps back? — 152
Advancing equality – everybody's business — 153
Conclusions — 155
References — 156

11 CHILD AND FAMILY SERVICES: WELSH POLICY DEVELOPMENTS 2010-2020 — 161
Jen Lyttleton-Smith

Introduction — 161
Policy context and strategic development — 162
The Children and Families (Wales) Measure 2010 — 163
Rights of Children and Young Persons (Wales) Measure 2011 — 163
Sustainable Social Services: A framework for Action 2011 — 164
Key legislative developments — 164
Social Services and Well-being (Wales) Act 2014 — 165
The Well-being of Future Generations (Wales) Act 2015 — 166
Policy themes of the 2010s for child and family services — 166
A rights-based conceptual understanding of childhood — 166
Mandatory advocacy and participation — 167
Family support and early intervention services — 168
The improvement of placement quality and capacity for looked-after children — 170

A 'well-being' centred approach and outcomes-focussed practice	171
Broad child and family population measures	171
Curtailed marketization in favour of partnership working	172
Conclusions	173
References	174

12   CRIMINAL JUSTICE IN WALES   179
Iolo Madoc-Jones and Karen Washington-Dyer

Introduction	179
Devolution	179
The political priorities of Wales	180
Particular criminal justice needs of Wales	184
Criminal justice and Welsh nationhood	185
The jagged edge	186
Conclusions	188
References	190

13   SOCIAL SERVICES   193
Jo Redcliffe

Introduction	193
The demography of Wales	194
Legislation and policy in Wales	195
Older citizens	198
Citizens with physical disabilities	200
Citizens with learning disabilities	201
Conclusions – a way forward?	203
References	205

List of figures and tables

Figures

2.1	Schematic overview of #SCIL	29
8.1	Principles of the Future Generations (Wales) Act 2015	119
11.1	Welsh Government Approach to Family Services	169

Tables

8.1	Number of articles that state attributes	116

List of abbreviations

AHC	After Housing Costs	**LGBTQ+**	Lesbian Gay Bisexual Transgender Queer (or Questioning)
BAME	Black Asian and Minority Ethnic	**LHB**	Local Health Board
BHC	Before Housing Costs	**NAW**	National Assembly for Wales
CADR	Wales Centre for Ageing and Dementia Research	**NGO**	Non-governmental Organisation
CCG	Clinical Commission Group	**NHS**	National Health Service
CIH	Chartered Institute of Housing	**NICE**	National Institute for Health and Care Excellence
CPEL	Continuing Professional Education and Learning	**OECD**	Organisation for Economic Co-operation and Development
CRC	Community Rehabilitation Companies	**ONS**	Office for National Statistics
DEEP	Developing Evidence Enriched Practice	**PRS**	Private Rental Sector
DWP	Department for Work and Pensions	**PSB**	Public Service Board
		RPB	Regional Partnership Board
EHRC	Equalities and Human Rights Commission	**SCIE**	Social Care Institute for Excellence
ENRICH	Enable Research in Care Homes	**#SCIL**	Social Care Innovations Lab
FSM	Free School Meals	**SHEP**	School Holiday Enrichment Programme
HCRW	Health Care Research Wales	**SSWB**	Social Services and Wellbeing (Wales) Act 2014
HWB	Health and Wellbeing Board		
IFFS	Integrated Family Support Services	**UC**	Universal Credit
IJB	Integration Joint Board	**WFG**	Wellbeing and Future Generations (Wales) Act 2015
IR-ESA	Income-related Employment and Support Allowance	**WG**	Welsh Government
JRF	Joseph Rowntree Foundation	**WIMD**	Welsh Index of Multiple Deprivation
JSA	Jobseeker's Allowance	**WSSCR**	Wales School for Social Care Research
LA	Local Authority		
LGBTI	Lesbian Gay Bisexual Transgender Intersex		

Acknowledgements

Our thanks to all the contributors to this volume who found time under the very difficult circumstances of the Covid-19 pandemic to work on this edition.

Thanks also to BASW and Venture Press for supporting this project in its third iteration.

Editors

Hefin Gwilym is Lecturer in Social Policy in the School of History, Philosophy, and Social Sciences, Bangor University since 2012. Previously he had been a lecturer in social work at the same institution from 2006 to 2012. He has published peer-reviewed articles in academic journals on social work and neoliberalism. His doctoral thesis completed in 2016 is on social work biographies within a neoliberal era. He teaches on social policy modules at undergraduate and postgraduate levels at Bangor. He also supervises PhD students in social policy in areas including food banking, carers' resilience and the link between social welfare and public transport in Wales. He regularly contributes to BBC Radio Cymru and BBC Radio Wales news programmes.

Charlotte Williams OBE is Honorary Professor in the School of History, Philosophy and Social Sciences, Bangor University. She holds Honorary Fellow appointments at Wrexham Glyndŵr University and University of South Wales. Charlotte has researched and published extensively on issues of migration, race/ethnicity, and multiculturalism with particular reference to professional practice. The ground-breaking and multidisciplinary work *A Tolerant Nation?* University of Wales Press (Ed. with Evans and O'Leary, 2003 and 2015) remains the foundational work for race studies in Wales. Charlotte was responsible for the design and editing of the two previous editions of *Social Policy for Social Welfare Practice* (BASW, 2007 and 2011). Charlotte was awarded an OBE in the Queen's New Year's Honours List (2007) for services to ethnic minorities and equal opportunities in Wales.

Notes on contributors

David Beck is a lecturer in social policy at the University of Salford. His teaching and research centres on food poverty and the growth of emergency food aid provisions. David completed his PhD on the growth of food banking at Bangor University in 2018. It looked at the impact of poverty following the Welfare Reform Act (2012) and how this created instability for the people of Wales, especially in the precarity of food sourcing. Identifying the growth of the food banking landscape, David's work also focused on mapping food banks, and bringing clarity to the exact numbers of food banks across Wales. His current research is looking at the influence of Universal Credit and people's use of food banks across Greater Manchester.

Gideon Calder is Associate Professor of Sociology and Social Policy at Swansea University. His main current research interests lie in three areas, which sometimes overlap: inequalities and social justice in childhood; ethics, including in research; and co-production. His ten books include, most recently, *How Inequality Runs in Families* (Policy Press, 2016) and the *Routledge Handbook of the Philosophy of Childhood and Children* (2018). He is co-editor of the journal *Ethics and Social Welfare*, director of Swansea's Research Institute of Ethics and Law, and Chair of the Newport Fairness Commission.

Teresa Crew is a Senior Lecturer in Social Policy at Bangor University and a Senior HEA Fellow. She recently published a book on working-class academics entitled *Higher Education and Working-Class Academics: Precarity and Diversity in Academia* (Palgrave Macmillan, 2020) Her research and teaching interests centre around the broad area of inequalities. She has previously written about graduate outcomes in relation to class, gender and place, as well as local employability skills. Prior to this, she coordinated a Gypsy Traveller Accommodation Assessment and has published in this area. Teresa has also managed projects relating to young people who are not in education, employment or training (NEETs) and gender inequalities in employment. Teresa has previously worked on the housing strategy for her local council, as a researcher for a regional equality network, and as a communications officer for the Welsh Assembly Government.

Martin Elliott is a research associate in the Children's Social Care Research and Development Centre (CASCADE) at Cardiff University. An ex-social worker with 17 years' experience in statutory children's services, including front-line practice and team management, in both Wales and England, his research interests include: children and young people in and out of home care; children on the edge of care; social inequalities and poverty; and services for disabled children and young people. He has a methodological interest in the use of routinely collected administrative data.

Edith England is a lecturer at the Department of Social Policy at Cardiff Metropolitan University. Edith's research background is in social policy and access to housing justice, and is currently completing a PhD at Cardiff University, examining the implementation of the Housing (Wales) Act 2014 with particular attention to its implications for citizenship. Edith is especially interested in the relationship between bureaucracy and access to justice, especially for often-overlooked groups, and has worked with Shelter Cymru and End Youth Homelessness Cymru to produce specific research into LGBTQ+ youth homelessness and trans people's experiences of homelessness.

Holly Gordon is Senior Manager of Safeguarding and Quality Assurance in Powys Children's Services'. She is a qualified social worker with 14 years post qualifying experience in Wales. She has previously developed child sexual exploitation services across the UK for the NSPCC and has managed Local Authority looked after and care leaving services. She has an academic interest in green and environmental social work and has completed her doctoral research and published on this subject.

Rhian Hodges is a Senior Lecturer in Sociology and Social Policy at the School of History, Philosophy and Social Sciences, Bangor University. She is Programme Lead for the MA Language Policy and Planning, and has published widely within this field. Dr Hodges' research interests include key language planning topics such as, new speakers of minoritized languages, minority language education, language transmission and language use within the community.

Jen Lyttleton-Smith is a researcher specialising in care-experienced childhoods, co-production, and well-being. A sociologist by background, her research spans issues around gender, agency, relationality, and power. Jen works in the CASCADE Children's Social Care Research and Development Centre within the Cardiff University School of Social Sciences and is a Health and Care Research Wales Post-Doctoral Fellow. Her work is driven by a passionate belief in the value of listening to children and young people on the issues that affect them and in centralising their views in decision-making. She holds an ongoing research interest in the subjectivities and lived experiences of childhood and how early social interaction shapes identity later in life.

Iolo Madoc-Jones is Professor in Social and Criminal Justice at Wrexham Glyndwr University. His practice background is in probation and prison and he has worked as a senior probation officer as well as an Inspector for both HMI Probation and HMI Prisons. His PhD obtained in 2010 explored criminal justice in Wales and in particular the experiences of Welsh speakers. Since that time he has undertaken funded research and published extensively on issues related to justice in Wales, more recently exploring how substance misuse policies and homelessness policies in Wales have been developed and applied to meet the needs of prison leavers.

David Matthews received his BA (Hons), MA, and PhD in sociology and social policy from Bangor University. He is a lecturer in health and social care at Coleg Llandrillo, and programme leader for its FdA Health and Social Care, and CertHE Social Care, awarded by Bangor University. His research interests, and publications, focus on critical and materialist understandings of the welfare state and social policy, with a particular emphasis on the impact of neoliberalism and capitalism for physical health and mental health.

Jo Redcliffe worked in statutory mental health services in South Wales following a BSc (Hons) in Psychology at Bangor University. Upon completion of the Diploma in Social Work and MSc in Applied Social Sciences at Swansea University Jo practised as a social worker in a variety of settings, primarily adult substance misuse. Jo has worked in social work education at Swansea University since 1988, and is currently the Swansea University lead for post-qualifying social work education and social work internationalisation link. Jo is a visiting professor at the University of Houston, Texas, United States of America and at Zhongyuan University of Technology, Zhengzhou, People's Republic of China. Jo's research interests include post-qualifying social work, disability, citizen involvement and substance misuse. Her PhD examined the inclusion of disability issues within social work education in Wales, United Kingdom, and Texas, United States of America. Jo is currently Associate Professor of Social Work at Swansea University.

Diane Seddon is Reader in Social Care, Wales Centre for Ageing and Dementia Research, School of Health Sciences, Bangor University. Diane has taken a leading role in developing a social care research programme, attracting research grants totalling over £10 million. With an established reputation for completing policy relevant research that has impact, Diane has advised on national policy development and led reviews of national policy implementation. Diane contributes to the delivery of the Welsh Government Research Infrastructure Support and she leads initiatives to integrate research, policy and practice, including the new Social Care Innovations Labs (#SCIL).

Helen Taylor is a lecturer in Housing Studies in the Department of Social Policy at Cardiff Metropolitan University. Her research background is in applied philosophy, and she has a particular interest in issues around homelessness and social justice. In 2019 she completed a National Assembly Research Service Academic Fellowship looking at the experience of individuals who are homeless or who have experienced homelessness in engaging with the priority need process. She is the Vice Chair of the Housing Studies Association and is on the board of Cymorth Cymru.

Gill Toms is Research and Development Officer, Wales School for Social Care Research (WSSCR), School of Health Sciences, Bangor University. Gill has a social care research capacity building role and works to support practitioners who want to engage in research. Recent research interests in social care have included alternative short breaks, integrated health and social care services, as well as care and support at home and in care homes.

Fiona Verity is Professor in the School of Human and Health Sciences, Swansea University. She is a sociologist with a background in social work in Australia working in community development and social planning. Her research expertise is in community development, prevention and community-based interventions, using participatory methods. She held the position of Dean, School of Social and Policy Studies at Flinders University, South Australia (2011-2013) and Director of the Wales School for Social Care Research (2016-2020).

Karen Washington-Dyer is Senior Lecturer in Criminal Justice at Wrexham Glyndwr University. Karen began her career as a sessional youth worker and youth work coordinator where she supported families and young people who were at risk of being excluded from mainstream education. Following on from this, Karen worked in a range of settings with young people and adults who have offended, delivering services that could help those being released from custody reintegrate into society. Based on her experiences in custodial settings, Karen's PhD, obtained in 2016, explored 'New' terrorism and the implications of this construct for perceptions about followers of Islam in Wales. This research underpins a continued interest in how issues of UK wide significance are experienced in devolved contexts like Wales.

Foreword

Rt Hon Mark Drakeford, First Minister of Wales

It is a great pleasure to provide this foreword to the third edition of *Social Policy for Welfare Practice in Wales*.

It is now over twenty years since the National Assembly for Wales, as it then was, was elected for the first time. Right at the start of the devolution journey, a group of far sighted individuals, led by the indefatigable Charlotte Williams, decided that students at home and beyond needed and deserved a book which would draw together the latest information, analysis and explanation of the social policy landscape in a radically different Wales.

In those earliest days I remember there were some hesitations: would there be a story to tell? Was there anything distinctive enough about Welsh social policy? Would anyone be interested, even if there were? It is a tribute to the editors of the series that these questions were very soon answered. As someone who has written, read and taught from this volume, I know myself just how valuable it has been. Along the way the contributors to the different editions read as a roll call of those who have been at the forefront of Welsh scholarship in the devolution era. I just want to take a moment to mention my great friend, Professor Mike Sullivan, a great democratic socialist. He would have worn, as a badge of honour, the term 'academic activist', even as the present UK Prime Minister casts activism in social policy as a term of condemnation. This book is full of writers who regard the relationship between the academy and the reality of people's lives not as two hermetically sealed spheres, but as two sides of a single coin. For Mike, the point of social policy scholarship was to help make a difference in the lives of Welsh people. This book lives on in that great tradition.

And, what a great deal it has to cover. The Senedd, at the start of the third decade of devolution is a very different place to the institution reflected in the first edition. Its powers have been deepened and extended. Its confidence in the independent exercise of those powers far more mature. And, as a result of the coronavirus crisis, its place in the understanding of the Welsh population far more secure.

One of the great things about this edition is that it sees a new generation of Welsh academics writing in this area. There is a handful of survivors from the first two editions, written in a time when the number of people involved in research and writing about social policy in Wales was far smaller. This edition includes contributions from no fewer than 19 different researchers. It is a sign of just how far and how positively the discipline and its subject matter have evolved during the devolution era.

At the same time the essential focus of the earlier editions has been strongly sustained here. The case for the first publication was never to be a text for academics only. The emphasis on social welfare practice was integral from the start – theoretically informed, empirically grounded practice certainly, but rooted firmly in the everyday realities of front line practice.

In promoting the second edition of the book in 2011, BASW said that 'devolution in Wales has come of age'. The decade which has followed has, in some ways, been the mirror image of the first ten years. The 2011 text reflected a devolution settlement of limited powers but expanding spending power. The budget available to the Welsh Government saw real terms growth in every year to 2011. It has reduced in real terms every year since. At the same time, the scope of the Senedd – its legislative powers, its fiscal responsibilities – is of an entirely different order to its earliest years.

Readers would expect me to have a particular view of the use which has been made of these powers over the last two decades. As someone who has been lucky enough to play a part in every Welsh Government, I believe that the strongest thread in social policy making has been the strength of the great Welsh radical tradition: a belief in the power of government to craft solutions which reach deepest into the lives who need that help the most.

17th November 2020

Editors' Introduction

Hefin Gwilym and Charlotte Williams

Introduction

Since the creation of the Welsh Assembly in 1999, Wales has matured as a devolved democratic entity exercising ever-increasing powers and responsibilities in the task of governing Wales. In September 2019 a Festival of Democracy was held at Pier Head the location of the iconic Assembly (Senedd) building to mark the occasion of the anniversary and to celebrate the successes. The successes of the Assembly since 1999 are obvious to identify. The eye-catching and arguably distinctively *Made-in-Wales* initiatives are the opt-out system for organ donation, the smoking ban, free public transport for the over sixties, free prescriptions, plastic carrier-bag charge, cheaper tuition fees, the Welsh Baccalaureate, no free schools and academies and dissention from privatising the NHS. The offices of the Children and Older People Commissioners have been created, with important reports emanating, such as on child poverty. On the legislative front, the Welsh Government has used legislative powers devolved during the first twenty years of the Assembly to pass the standout Social Services and Wellbeing Act 2014 providing the legal framework for social services in Wales. Other pre-eminent acts of significance for welfare and social policy are the ground-breaking Wellbeing of Future Generations Act 2015.

Thus, at a time of celebrating the Welsh Assembly's successes it is an appropriate time to publish the third edition of *Social Policy for Welfare Practice in Wales* to reflect on its undoubted achievements and identify the future challenges to the Made-in-Wales approach to welfare and social policy. These include how Wales continues to resist the tide of privatisation and austerity – often referred to as the ideology of neoliberalism, which is particularly strong in anglophile states, including England. Unfortunately, Wales has a poor record in tackling poverty with little change over the past twenty years with just under a third of Welsh children living in poverty (in households living below 60 per cent of median income) and a total of 24 per cent of Welsh families living in poverty. Allied to the poverty challenge is the challenge of low-income jobs, social insecurity, precarious employment and zero-hour contracts. Post Communities First, the Welsh Government's former flag-ship anti-poverty initiative, a reinvigorated debate requiring new research is in progress in Wales, such as the Welsh Government's recent consultations on food poverty and fuel poverty.

Students of social welfare and social policy in Wales need a reflective and critical account of these developments over the past twenty years of the Welsh Assembly, both positive and negative. They need to understand what has happened, what has and has not worked, and how legislative changes put into effect in the most recent years are expected to bring results in the middle-range future. However, there are difficulties to address too, such as does the Welsh Assembly have enough powers regarding the economy and fiscal and tax policies to bring about meaningful change in the poverty rates? Will the Assembly be able to resist the tide of privatisation and neoliberalism in the face of the international crises in capitalism? How can long waiting times for hospital consultations in Wales be addressed? Overall, they need an understanding of where Wales is headed for in the next ten years or so and what it will look like when we get there.

Modern Wales

It has been said that devolution in the form of the Welsh Assembly and Welsh Government is a process rather than an event. Since its creation in 1999 the Welsh Assembly has certainly seen a process of gradual growth in responsibilities and powers. But the history of Welsh governance starts much earlier than that so this introduction will continue with a brief overview of the political and constitutional history of Wales which will we hope situate devolution in a wider historical context.

Wales became a constituent part of the Kingdom of England with the Laws in Wales Acts of 1536 and 1542. Once it had been an independent Principality (at least for some of the time) and had its own Hywel Dda (d. 950) laws in the medieval era. The castles of Edward I in Caernarfon (1284) and Conwy (1287) are symbols of English conquest and domination following the defeat of the Welsh princes. Various rebellions followed, most famously those led by the insurgent Owain Glyndwr (c1359-1415), the last Welshman to hold the title Prince of Wales. Since the Tudor era (1485-1603) and the enthronement of Welshman Henry VII in 1485, Wales has been intrinsically and intimately enmeshed in the British state. Its people have been engaged in British tasks such as the building of an Empire and industrialisation. For most of the period following the accession of the Tudors until the Victorian era, welfare support in Wales like England was provided under a system of poor laws renowned for their harsh conditions of deserving and undeserving poor and their iconic institution of the workhouse.

Largely as a result of industrialisation the British State expanded over the decades and centuries as government took on new functions, such as working conditions and public health. Consequently, the State became increasingly centralised in London. Local government which had been strong in the UK and viewed as a counter to the threat of the kind of dictatorships that had happened elsewhere in Europe, such as the Napoleonic years in France (1799-1815), became much weaker as the modern central State grew. Arguably this led to shortcomings in the governance of Wales and a longing for more autonomy. This was exemplified in the modern industrial era with the Cymru Fydd Movement (1886) and the Welsh Liberal Party's (founded 1898) support for Welsh self-government, enthusiastically supported by a young David Lloyd-George (1863-1945), who would later abandon such ideals and become British Prime Minister (1916-22).

What followed was a slow process of administrative devolution, starting in 1954 with the appointment of a minister with responsibility for Wales based in the Home Office. Then the creation of the UK Cabinet post of Secretary of State for Wales in 1964 and the establishment of the Welsh Office in 1965. An unsuccessful devolution referendum was held in 1979 which was followed almost immediately by the election of Margaret Thatcher's Conservative Government with policies that were resented in a Wales dominated by the Labour Party. Following the election of Tony Blair's Labour Government in 1997, a second devolution referendum was held in 1998, which this time was successful and in 1999 the Welsh Assembly was created. A further referendum was held in 2011 on the question of granting law-making powers to Wales. The outcome was positive and for the first time since the laws of Hywel Dda Wales was able to create laws again. Further powers have been gradually granted to the Welsh Assembly in recent times, by far the most important of these being the introduction of tax raising powers in 2019 allowing Welsh Government to adjust income tax by 10 pence in every pound. This gives the Assembly very considerable tax raising powers which could be used exclusively on Welsh public services.

The establishment of the Assembly in 1999 heralded a new era of autonomy in social policy in Wales as health services and social services became devolved areas. It is because of this that Made-in-Wales policies emerged in these and other devolved areas as policy packages were honed-in on specific Wales circumstances. It also enabled the development of an ideological approach to Made-in-Wales policy that varied from England with less emphasis on privatisation and more on a collective public service approach to welfare such as in the Welsh National Health Service (NHS) and statutory social work services in local authorities. These developments were discussed in the two previous editions of this book in 2007 and 2011 and which was widely welcomed by academics, students and practitioners alike.

So, after twenty years of the Welsh Assembly marked by celebratory commemorations during 2019, it is a good time to re-examine the achievements and failings of devolution in Wales over these past twenty years. To reflect on the Made-in-Wales policy and legislative agenda and eye-catching initiatives which in some instances have been innovative on a UK and international level. But also, to reflect on the aspirations that have not yet been met, none more important than the challenge of poverty in Wales and the scourge of child poverty. The purpose of this third edition is to fulfil such a task and provide a resource that is easily accessible for all. It is primarily intended for the academic and professional community in Wales – a resource on Welsh social policy for undergraduate and postgraduate students alike. It is relevant for all those engaged in professional courses in social work, social welfare and public sector management – both at initial qualifying level and in continuous professional development. Furthermore, it is accessible for all those in the UK and beyond who look to Welsh social policy for new ideas and inspiration.

The next section contains a brief summary of chapters contained in the book.

Chapter overview

The chapters in this volume engage with the theme of 'made in Wales' distinctiveness, addressing the issue of a divergence in the value base underpinning Welsh policy making. They identify key opportunities emerging within a more confident Welsh policy making arena but acknowledge the critical issue of lack of control over fiscal and social security powers. Taken together, the chapters suggest a strong endorsement of an approach that valorises social justice concerns of citizen rights, representation and participation and redistributive mechanisms.

In Chapter 1 Hefin Gwilym reflects on the developments in welfare since the establishment of the Welsh Assembly (Senedd) in 1999. Wales has always made an innovative contribution to social welfare and there have been further notable developments since 1999 but there remain major challenges, amongst them persistent poverty and Brexit. On the Assembly's anniversary, the chapter looks ahead to the future and what policy goals need to be identified and addressed for the next twenty years.

The Social Services and Well-being (Wales) Act (Welsh Government, 2014) has established a robust and integrated framework for the delivery of social care in Wales. The policy ambitions of the Act signal the important role of research evidence to the achievement of improved citizen wellbeing. In Chapter 2, Seddon, Toms and Verity outline the trajectory for the development of research informed policy and practice, looking at the infrastructure, the capacity and initiatives that have emerged to support innovative practices. They argue that what is emerging is unique support landscape that enables collaboration between academia, practitioners and policy makers as well as giving voice to users of social services. Much, of course, will depend on the effective translation and use of research messages in practice if the policy vision of the government is to be realised. Notwithstanding, the opportunities are now immense for a coordinated and inclusive approach to the development of social care research as the bedrock of Welsh policy making.

It is worth reading the chapters by Beck and Elliott on aspects of poverty in conjunction. All the evidence suggests that Wales includes some of the poorest regions in Europe, and that socio-economic factors underpin profound and sustained inequalities. Beck in Chapter 3 addresses the broad sweep of government policy aimed at tackling poverty and inequality and points to some of the key obstacles to progress on this front. His approach focuses on the the lived experience of poverty, reflecting on the subjective nature of *felt* poverty rather than poverty as a statistical artefact. He demonstrates that the impact of poverty is both long-term and intergenerational and damaging to the economy as a whole. He is optimistic, however, that new policies and new ways of working that suggest a developmental approach involving more than just policy makers, will bring dividends. Elliott, in Chapter 4, focusing on child poverty, notes along with Beck that the Welsh Government is critically restricted through a limited devolution of policy making powers, as social security decisions remain with the UK Government. The year 2020 was to be a key social policy milestone in the eradication of child poverty. The shocking statistic that we live with in Wales is that currently 28 per cent of the nation's children live in poverty and it is estimated that it will increase to closer to 40 per cent of children by 2021-22. Elliott takes us through a timeline of key milestones of the UK wide agenda on tackling child poverty and the specific measures taken in Wales. He concludes with the argument that the national policy has lost its way and draws on the call by the Welsh Children's Commissioner for a new and reinvigorated Strategy on child poverty.

By contrast, health policy, where the Welsh Government has near full powers, is a policy sphere where academic commentators have documented some of the most significant expressions of divergence from elsewhere in the UK. David Matthews examines this trajectory in Chapter 5, exploring the claim that Wales offers a radical health agenda, with distinctive organisational characteristics, themes, policy developments, and most significantly in the central values which underpin the organisation of healthcare. Matthews evaluates the principle values of collaboration, localism, participation, public health and well-being, and public provision, demonstrating how these have shaped the agenda over the last twenty years. He argues, the intellectual and policy acceptance to focus attention on macro social and economic inequalities as fundamental to good health and to infusing the whole agenda with the need to enhance democratic accountability marks out a distinctive approach. Interestingly, Matthews acknowledges that it is nevertheless the case that Covid-19 has illustrated one of the most significant weaknesses in the Welsh approach. The unequal impact of the virus on the Welsh population has illustrated that despite this policy orientation, the Government's lack of authority over fiscal policy and social security, has meant that efforts in Wales to combat those very social and economic inequalities contributing to this unequal experience, have been severely constrained.

England and Taylor pursue the theme of a distinctive 'made in Wales' approach to the field of housing policy in Chapter 6. Housing in their analysis has both a physical and emotional resonance as spaces that we call 'home'. Their chapter explores the different ways in which issues relating to housing, home, and homelessness are responded to by the Welsh Government and how this relates to broader issues of equality and social justice. They note housing as a social issue as experienced by individuals and impacted upon by a variety of factors such as socio-economic status, health status, household size and type. In their concluding evaluation of the claimed *'progressive universalism'* of the Welsh approach, their signal is that much more needs to be done. They argue that there are clear areas where policy divergence has not been as effective as planned, and crucially where divergence can be seen to undermine the Welsh Government's broader approach to social justice.

In Chapter 7 Rhian Hodges also points to the issue of values in her consideration of the development of Welsh language policy and culture. Hodges points to the often-uneasy relationships between language policy and planning efforts, legislation and the provision of bilingual social welfare in Wales. She seeks to tease out critical language policy and legislative junctures that highlight the disconnect between the strategies adopted and the realities of implementation, and regulations and the reality of delivering bilingual social welfare services in Wales. Hodges illustrates the complexities of providing a comprehensive and substantial provision, arguing that regardless of demand, the onus is on providers to ensure the language needs of service users are met across different localities. Hodges suggests that despite the strengthening of legislative powers relating to the Welsh language within the social welfare sector, the daily reality is that service users do not always have their language needs met within this sector. Her proposal is that language policy and planning strategies at different levels needs to be utilised to create more joined-up-thinking in terms of bilingual social welfare provision in Wales. In particular, she puts out the call for more holistic language planning that mobilizes a workforce sufficiently language competent to meet the needs of bilingual services users across Wales.

An area of increasing importance to social welfare is that of climate change and in Chapter 8 Holly Gordon takes up the climate emergency challenge declared by Welsh Government to view the history of environmental social work which previously has had a lack of status and priority. Gordon explores ways forward linked to the important concepts of wellbeing and sustainability in Wales. Asking questions such as what can social work education do to contribute, Gordon concludes with a list of practical and wide-ranging recommendations for social welfare practice to address the threat of global warming on Wales.

Social work is often termed a human rights profession and in Chapter 9 Gideon Calder looks at the complex area of applying universal human rights to 'small places' or the locality in which we all live and work. Calder engages with a theoretical overview of human rights before exploring a distinctive Wales approach to human rights.

Since its inception, the devolved legislature has prioritised a commitment to equalities and has embedded in its constitution a unique cross-cutting architecture for advancing the ambition to *mainstream* equalities across all public service provision. It is a testament to this commitment that the Welsh Government's equalities framework is considered world leading. Williams and Crew in Chapter 10 take as a starting point the new departure in approach to equalities established under the Equality Act 2010. They seek to review developments over the ensuing decade that has witnessed the Welsh Government seeking to tackle the complex task of implementing this bold piece of legislation and strengthening its integration via complementary legislation, namely, the Welsh Act 2017, which gave the Welsh Government added powers to promote human rights, and the Well-being and Future Generations (Wales) Act 2015 with the overarching goal of "a more equal Wales" (2019). They find that there has been much progress, yet there remain sustained and deepening inequalities in Wales, exacerbated not least by the Covid-19 pandemic.

In Chapter 11, Jen Lyttleton-Smith looks at the broad vista of child and family services in Wales by considering the considerable ambitions in Wales and the restrictions posed by UK wide austerity policies. She covers the wide-scope policy and legislative initiatives in Wales since 2010 and examines some of the key themes that have guided action in Wales, including rights, voice, prevention and wellbeing.

In Chapter 12 Madoc-Jones and Washington-Dyer address what is described as the 'jagged edge' of criminal justice in Wales, an uneasy relationship between a non-devolved criminal justice system and the ambitions of the Welsh Government to do more to support those who find themselves at the wrong end of the system. Reflecting ideological divides between a neoliberal England and a social democratic Wales they navigate through a complex criminal justice system which may be devolved to Wales going forward. Interestingly, they raise concerns about the high prison population in Wales and apparent increasing sympathy amongst the public for punitive neoliberal policies.

In the concluding Chapter 13 Jo Redcliffe comprehensively maps out the current state of play with adult social services in Wales reflecting on meeting the needs of a postmodern society with all its diversity and complexities. While recognising the constraints of austere times, Redcliffe explores current definitions of disabilities and the legislative and policy frameworks in place in Wales to address the demographic challenges of an ageing and progressively diverse population in Wales.

Conclusions

We hope that this third edition will, as did the previous two editions, provide a valuable and informative resource for students and practitioners alike in Wales. The contributors demonstrate in their chapters that Wales has an imagination for innovative practice and for creating new policy ideas. Wales' social policy over the years has been of interest internationally. With devolution progressing forwards with increasing powers and responsibilities to Wales, Wales has potential to achieve even more in the future. It has the chance to build a strong, inclusive and fair society for all the people living in this part of the world.

Chapter 1

Wales 20 Years On: The Record and New Goals

Hefin Gwilym

Introduction

This chapter explores and discusses the process of devolution in Wales since the creation of the Welsh Assembly in 1999. At the time of writing the Welsh Assembly has been renamed the Welsh Parliament but the term Welsh Assembly is used in this chapter and the others in this volume since it is the accurate term for the period covered in the book. The creation of the Welsh Assembly had its modern day roots in the economic crises of the 1980s and the desire for greater political protection form the consequences of deindustrialisation and globalisation which have been a feature of Welsh society in recent times (see Chapter 3). The chapter describes the setting up of the Welsh Assembly and the process of evolution with increasing powers and scope since its establishment. It will explore some of the noteworthy achievements of Welsh Government and of the Assembly and the challenges that it faces going forward. At the time of writing there are mixed processes occurring, on the one hand the effects of Brexit and on the other the response in Wales to the Covid-19 pandemic. Brexit poses many challenges to the governance and to the economy of Wales and the consequences are not yet clear. Covid-19 will remain a major concern for some time to come but the role of Welsh Government in protecting the people of Wales may highlight like nothing else before that Wales is different and the governance of Wales is now in so many areas centred in Cardiff rather than London.

Background

The process of devolution that started in Wales in 1997 with the referendum had a sketchy start. The referendum result was a narrow win for the setting up of a national assembly with limited powers and indeed resembling nothing much more than a glorified council though on an all-Wales level. The referendum saw 50 per cent of the Welsh electorate participate and the narrow outcome of 50.3 per cent to 49.7 per cent would influence the work of the Assembly for the following five years since gaining the trust and support of the Welsh people became a priority in the face of such a narrow result. The new Assembly could not afford to attract the same level of criticism and cynicism of the Westminster Parliament at that time which had been embroiled in various financial and personal scandals involving politicians (Shortridge, 2010). Public support and acceptance was not the only challenge. The framework of the devolution settlement itself was criticised for being less than fit-for-purpose. There had been little preparation for the Assembly and there were design flaws, not least the absence of sufficient separation of powers between the executive and the legislature which had to be addressed later on as the Assembly gained greater legislative powers (Shortridge, 2010). However, in 2002 the second First Minister, Rhodri Morgan, used a stroke of rhetorical brilliance by his phrase 'clear red water' to distinguish Wales as a Social Democratic country, different from neo-liberal England, thus giving the impression at least that the Welsh Labour Government was 'standing up for Wales' (Evans, 2018: 498).

The evolution of the Welsh Assembly over twenty years reflects the incremental and asymmetrical nature of the devolution process in the UK, with significant differences between Wales, Scotland and Northern Ireland. The Assembly consisted of sixty members, forty were directly elected and twenty were drawn from a list based on proportional representation. The design was deliberate to ensure no persistent Labour Party overall control of devolution with the likelihood of coalitions designed into the system. To begin with the Assembly had powers only to make secondary legislation in areas ranging from health and social care to housing and economic development. It had a budget of £7bn allocated from Westminster through the block-grant and had no tax raising powers of its own in those early years.

In 2002 the Assembly was reformed to create clearer separation between the legislature and the executive with the creation of a Cabinet of Ministers who became collectively known as the Welsh Assembly Government, later Welsh Government, and the creation of departmental select committees. Despite all the early challenges it is argued that the Assembly has been successful in agreeing a budget since the process is detailed and thoughtful involving all the Assembly's sixty members. Furthermore, it is argued that its decision-making processes are better than what existed before since the Assembly is able to listen to a wide range of advice from many sectors in Wales and not just take advice from civil servants (Shortridge, 2010). There is also some evidence that devolution in the UK has initiated policy innovation, such as regarding organ donations and the smoking bans. Both high profile initiatives were taken up by the UK Government for implementation in England. However, there is still room for improvement in policy exchange between the devolved parliaments since to a very significant degree each parliament is acting independently of each other (Coutts. 2019).

Since its inception in 1999 there have been five Assemblies elected each lasting for a fixed-term of five years. With the passing of the Government of Wales Act 2006 the Assembly was able for the first time to seek powers from the UK government to pass legislation. This was the first time Wales had been able to create its own laws in centuries and marked a significant step along the devolution journey. It was a step that made the Assembly look more like a parliament than a talking shop. The new Welsh laws were known as Measures and to be created there was a complicated and slow process of receiving permission form Westminster known as Legislative Competence Orders. Such a process was in effect a sop to anti-devolutionists in Wales who were very wary of the devolution process and where it might lead. Although the anti-devolutionists were becoming less influential there remained significant groups amongst Labour MPs at Westminster and the Welsh Conservative Party. The 2006 Act also made it possible for the Assembly to move in the direction of making its own laws independent of Westminster but only after such development would be approved by another referendum. Another referendum was a further concession to anti-devolutionists and firmly established the principle that any additional significant steps on the devolution journey would require a further referendum. Such a check and balance was designed to slow the devolution process since a referendum victory for further devolutionary steps is always far from guaranteed. The referendum was held in 2011 with 63.5 per cent of those people that voted voting for the Assembly to be given full law-making powers. This was a significant victory for pro-devolutionists since it seemed to show increasing support and acceptance in Wales amongst the public for devolution. However, it also has to be seen within the context of very weak organised support by the anti-devolutionists at this time and a very poor turnout of just 35 per cent of the Welsh electorate.

The Wales Act 2014 strengthened the Welsh Assembly further with certain tax raising powers. The Act gave the Welsh Assembly the powers to raise taxes and to borrow money from the UK government for certain limited purposes. The taxes cover areas such as land fill and taxes to replace stamp duty in Wales (Law Wales, 2020). From 2019 onwards Wales has had the ability to vary income tax by 10 pence in every pound but there is no sign of this power being used at least not before the next Welsh general election in 2021 (Welsh Government, 2020a). The Tax Collection and Management (Wales) Act 2016 creates the Welsh Revenue Authority (WRA) which has the responsibility for the management and collection of devolved taxes. The WRA looks like an organisation that could evolve in future with more Welsh taxes and expenditure to resemble the Treasury in Whitehall which has been for centuries the most powerful financial institution in the UK. More tax raising powers might be contested since it would necessitate a progression of the devolution process in the direction of further self-government and even towards independence. At the time of writing the support for Welsh independence has risen to about 30 per cent, far higher than the traditional levels in Wales of about 9 per cent (Evans, 2020).

Moreover, the Wales Act 2017 strengthened the Assembly by moving from a conferred powers model which had been introduced in the 2006 Act to a reserved powers model for legislation which means the Assembly can now legislate in all areas except for those specifically reserved for Westminster, such as in the area of national defence. New areas for legislation include the controversial area of fracking which has produced significant public opposition throughout the United Kingdom in recent years. At the time of writing the latest step in the Assembly's evolution is the Senedd and Elections (Wales) Act 2020 which gives sixteen to eighteen-year olds in Wales the right to vote in future Assembly and local government elections and renames the Assembly the Welsh Parliament. A point worth recording is that the Welsh name for the Assembly, namely Senedd, has always been translated as parliament. The naming of the Assembly as parliament in English is a further sign of confidence that the Assembly has rooted itself in Welsh society and culture and is here to stay.

One of the notable achievements of the Assembly since its inception in 1999 has been the increased representation of women compared to Westminster and the other assemblies and parliaments of the UK. The increase in women members, during the first Assembly there were more women than men, has resulted from women only constituency short-lists by the Labour and Plaid Cymru parties. The number of women in the Assembly has consistently remained high and is certain to continue to remain high. However, in the Assembly's lifetime to date there have only been two women party leaders, namely Leanne Wood of Plaid Cymru and Kirsty Williams of the Welsh Liberal Democrats.

Notable achievements and challenges

It has been argued that the acquiring of legislative powers has been transformative to devolution and has embedded the institutions of devolution in the governance of Wales and in the minds of the Welsh people. One of the first legislative initiatives was the Human Transplantation Act 2013 which introduced the concept of assumed consent in organ transplantation despite the opposition of some groups in Wales such as the Church in Wales. The Act has since been copied in other countries and it appears that some lives have been saved as a result of this legislation but it has not fully addressed the chronic shortage of organ donations in Wales as well as elsewhere (Antoniw, 2019). There have been other eye-catching and innovative legislation, such as the Food Hygiene Rating (Wales) Act 2013 which tackled the risks of food poisoning by introducing compulsory standards on food outlets and introduced a simply understood rating scale of one to five which all outlets have to display publicly to their customers. Other significant eye-catching legislation has included the Abolition of the Right to Buy and Associated Rights (Wales) Act 2018 to protect the social housing stock from privatisation and contribute to tackling Wales' chronic problem of homelessness (see Chapter 6). The Public Health (Minimum Pricing for Alcohol) (Wales) Act 2018 was introduced to address harmful drinking focussing on low cost and strong alcohol products which contribute to poor health and costs to the economy and the NHS. This act's chief purpose was to address the cheap prices for alcohol in supermarkets. At the time of writing the minimum price for one unit of alcohol in Wales is fifty pence. Other notable successes have been free access for over sixties to free public transport and free parking in hospital car parks. The access to the former has since been narrowed to address increasing costs. Moreover, some testing regimes in schools have been abandoned and the Welsh Baccalaureate has been introduced. However, the Welsh Government remains committed to meeting Pisa education standards and monitoring despite scepticism about their benefits on the education and well-being of the child (Zhao, 2020).

Since the beginning the Welsh Assembly has been concerned with social care reflecting a strong social policy identity for devolution in the early years. Numerous innovations were made in the organisation and regulation of social care culminating in the Regulation and Inspection of Social Care (Wales) Act 2016. Care Wales has taken over the responsibilities of the former Care Council for Wales, the Social Services Improvement Agency and Social Care Wales and has become a powerful institution for regulating social care in Wales building on the provisions of the Social Services and Well-being (Wales) Act 2014. The SSWB has become a key piece of legislation regarding the delivery of social welfare services in Wales with its focus on the concepts of participation, co-production, prevention and agency collaboration (see Chapters 11 and 13).

At the time of writing the Welsh Government has introduced the Social Partnership (Wales) Bill creating a statutory tripartite system between government, business and trades unions in Wales. This is similar to what already successfully exists in other European Union countries. It is a highly significant piece of legislation since it represents a departure from the UK government's approach to the economy and industrial policy where the emphasis in recent times has been on a free market approach and the disempowerment of trades unions. The new Bill creates a framework for key sectors of the economy and industry, namely, government, businesses and unions to work together in a partnership approach. This is very much the model in successful social democratic countries such as Denmark where a tripartite partnership between the three key sectors of the economy has worked harmoniously for a very long time. Such an approach in Wales may well raise the profile of the Assembly far higher than ever before in an area that affects the daily lives of ordinary working people in Wales.

The demography of Wales has changed significantly since 1999 with an overall increased population of about 225,000, currently standing at 3.125 million. Accounted for by internal migration within the UK and international migration from outside the UK. All counties in Wales have seen a population increase except for Ceredigion and Blaenau Gwent which saw a population decrease. The highest population increase was in Cardiff which rose by 17 per cent reflecting the capital city's prosperity and appeal post devolution also symbolised by civic buildings such as the new and iconic Welsh Assembly building designed by the award-winning architect company namely Richard Rogers and Partners. There has been a slight change in the ethnic composition of the Welsh population with those describing themselves as white British falling from 96 per cent to 93 per cent and those describing themselves as non-white increasing from 2.2 per cent to 4 per cent. However, Wales remains the least diverse part of the United Kingdom. The number of Welsh speakers was about one in 5 at the last census in 2011 (Office for National Statistics, 2020). During this time life expectancy in Wales increased to 78.5 for men and 83.2 for women. In 1999 this had been forecast to be higher at 84 and 97 respectively. The age of the population over 65 increased from 17 per cent to 21 per cent while the population of under 16-year-olds decreased to 18 per cent.

Predicting future population trends is hazardous because no one knows exactly what the effects of Brexit will be. However, the challenge in Wales for the next twenty years is undoubtedly going to be an ageing population. The over sixty fives will increase by 30 per cent placing challenges on the health system and social care, both areas already fully stretched. At the same time, the population of under sixteen-year olds will decrease further – a concern since this will mean a reduced work force and reduced production and wealth creation. The working age population of sixteen to sixty-four-year olds is also forecast to decrease by 4.6 per cent which will impact on public finances to pay for health and social care for older people. Less migration from European Union countries following Brexit will also have an impact on the workforce and wealth creation especially in residential and community care work.

The Active Wales Act 2013 sought to increase cycling and walking but has had very limited success because of a lack of funding and ambition. Wales needs to vastly improve cycling opportunities especially in a city like Cardiff which compared to Copenhagen and Amsterdam lags far behind with a city-wide integrated and prioritised cycling routes that take precedence over the car. At the time of writing Cardiff is considering introducing a congestion charge for cars driving into the city centre. This would obviously contribute significantly to reducing pollution and nudging commuters to use public transport and cycling. Since 1999 while rail journeys are up people mostly travel by car (National Assembly for Wales Commission, 2019).

The Welsh budget is dominated by health accounting for 52 per cent of spending and increasing largely because Wales has not successfully addressed the problems of poverty and other social determinants of health (National Assembly for Wales Commission, 2019). Having a larger older population than the rest of the UK the social care budget will have to double by 2030 to meet demand which will be an enormous burden on the Welsh economy and the Welsh Government's budget. No significant differences have been detected in the performance of the Welsh health services compared to that in England. While in 1997 17 per cent of the population was over 65 by 2040 28 per cent of the population will be in this age group which will be especially challenging since over 22 per cent could be experiencing long-term limiting conditions such as stroke, heart disease and dementia. In every society the poor suffer more and in Wales they are likely to have poor life quality because of ill health for a duration of 19 years for men and 18 years for women and die nine and seven years earlier.

While employment in Wales has risen since 1999 so has low pay and zero-hour contracts. Women in work is a particularly positive-growth area. However, overall, the Welsh economy has not improved since 1999 with continued problems of low productivity. Wales' Gross Domestic Household Income has been the third least in the UK nations and regions since 1999 (National Assembly for Wales Commission, 2019). This is in fact a worsening of the position in comparison with the other nations and regions since 1999. Critics point out that devolution was not accompanied by significant powers that could have lifted the Welsh economy to greater heights (Evans, 2018). The Welsh Government's latest approach to economic development is to focus on the foundation economy, such as local businesses providing for large public sector institutions in localities such as hospitals (Business Wales, 2020). This will create more resilient communities with greater security of employment and wealth creation since such large institutions will always be present in poor areas. Of course, it might not be reasonable to expect devolution with very limited powers and no control over the major leavers of the economy, especially in the early days, to achieve much in terms of Wales' overall economic performance. Wales' reduced production rate from the 1970s is part of an international pattern and not necessarily unique to Wales (Streeck, 2017). However, the causes of decline in Wales has been related to the closure of traditional industries and globalisation, often accelerated by UK government policies that have not been tailored and sympathetic to Wales. These have occurred as a change of focus in the UK state from ameliorative regional policies to the free market under Thatcherism in the 1980s. This was further pursued by subsequent UK governments of all colours in what is regularly described as a neo-liberal process (Evans, 2018). Wales' relative absence of large conurbations and poor transport links as well as lack of skills acquisition explains why Wales lags behind the rest of the UK, and these are areas for much needed future improvements.

Education is crucial for future prosperity, but Wales has made no serious progress in this respect and indeed in some areas there are reverses, such as in higher education where English universities receive more money per student than Welsh universities. There is also the question of whether the universities in Wales cater for and address the needs of Wales, such as the expertise of law and business schools for the requirements of Wales. It is sometimes regarded as an error of judgement for the Welsh Government to have abolished the Welsh Development Agency since inward investment in Wales failed to keep up with the rest of the UK following abolition. The Welsh Development Agency's work was incorporated into the civil service which might have led to a loss of focus and drive. The introduction of legislation capability and tax powers in 2019 might facilitate a drive towards prosperity. But there is also pessimism that the nature of Welsh Government is contrary to innovation because of the dominance of the Labour Party in every Welsh government since 1999 (Holtham, 2019).

New goals

Significant developments in the devolution of the justice system is in progress (See Chapter 12). Afterall, other social policy areas related to justice have already been devolved, such as youth justice. Indeed, Wales used to have a more independent judicial system before the abolition of the Courts of Great Sessions in Wales in 1831 (Melding, 2012). Hitherto the Assembly was only concerned with tribunals, but this will soon change in important ways. Strong arguments have been made for justice to be the responsibility of a single ministry of justice in Wales. Such a ministry could take charge of the residualised legal aid system in Wales, provision in legal advice and the role of the Schools of Law in Welsh universities to develop Welsh laws and a Welsh legal system. This is an exciting prospect since with the support of the Law Schools in Welsh universities Welsh legislation as passed by the Welsh Assembly is likely to be more robust and its impact more effectively evaluated. It would also raise the profile of Welsh law amongst the academic community and students of law studying in Wales.

In the Brexit referendum of 2016, 52.5 per cent of the Welsh electorate voted to leave the European Union despite the main political parties in Wales campaigning to remain. Brexit poses many challenges to devolution in the UK. The asymmetrical evolution of devolution and differing stances of the political parties in the UK has meant that intergovernmental institutions and relations have been fraught and poorly developed (Mullen, 2019). Such arrangements are based on a Memorandum of Agreement which for the most part is an informal understanding controlled by central government. The Joint Ministerial Committee established and involving all devolved areas and Westminster has been ineffective and dominated by Westminster. There is no great trust between members of the Joint Ministerial Committee, particularly between the SNP Scottish Government and Westminster, where British politicians suspects the Scottish Government will use membership to further their campaign for complete independence. Fraught relationships have been made worse by the European Union (Withdrawal) Act 2018 which sees the return of some competencies to the Westminster Government in areas which have already been devolved to Wales and the other nations. Although some compromises were made about which powers would be retained by Westminster there remained an atmosphere of mistrust. Thus, tensions and mistrust that exist at the intergovernmental level in the UK have been made much worse by Brexit.

It is not yet fully clear how the UK's exit from the European Union will impact on Wales. But many believe it will impact negatively on regional inequalities and the social divide (Armstrong, 2019). Ironically, these poor areas demonstrated the strongest support for Brexit in the 2016 referendum. Wales was a net benefactor from the EU not least because some parts of Wales experience poverty levels as bad as anywhere in the European Union, such as Rhyl West which consistently tops the Welsh Index of Multi Deprivation (Welsh Government, 2020b). These areas have demonstrated an enormous poverty entrenchment over many years in registering the highest levels of poverty in Wales despite Welsh Government measures to tackle poverty. Since 2010 according to Welsh Government, European Union funding has created 47,000 new jobs and 13,000 new businesses (National Assembly for Wales Commission, 2019). Significantly, the years immediately after Brexit will mean more centralisation in the UK since the EU Withdrawal Act will repatriate powers to Westminster even in some areas of policy that have been devolved. At the time of writing political controversy is raging about the prospect of UK Government holding on to repatriated powers and over-ruling the Welsh Government on the highly controversial £1bn extension of the M4 in Newport. It is of concern whether post-Brexit the poorer areas of Wales will continue to attract the same levels of financial support that they did from the European Union. The effects on the workforce particularly the reliance on migrant workers in health and residential care settings is also a matter of great concern.

If Brexit has adverse economic effects the shift in support for independence might mobilise in Wales and especially so in Scotland which might move closer to independence and in Northern Ireland where a united Ireland might appear more attractive than ever. Although Wales historically has shown little appetite for independence, in post Brexit referendum Wales, well attended rallies have been held in support of independence and support appears to be increasing as reflected in the opinion polls.

The dominant economic ideology of recent times namely neo-liberalism, with its focus on the free market and the huge service industries and banks centred on the City of London, raises future questions about whether these developments have fractured the UK and will lead to a further sense in Wales about the legitimacy of the British State. Evans (2018: 494) argues that devolution in 1997 was created in a period of economic crisis as a response to the Thatcher deindustrialisation of Wales and thus devolution was an 'antidote' to the 'excesses' of Thatcherism. However, the period since the global financial crash of 2008 have been equally as bad for the Welsh economy and society with wages falling back and greater precarity in the work market. The rise of food banks in Wales has been chronicled and demonstrates a huge increase in the use of food banks since the Welfare Reform Act 2012 (Beck and Gwilym, 2020).

Conclusions

Devolution has famously been described as a process and not an event. This chapter has charted that process since the inception of the Welsh Assembly following the 1998 referendum. Many notable achievements have been chronicled as the Assembly has tried to address the social and economic needs of Wales within limited but gradually increasing legislative and economic powers. Gradual constitutional change has always involved an element of mystery with no one able to firmly predict where the process will end. At the time of writing the profile of the Welsh Government has increased as it takes the lead in dealing with the Covid-19 pandemic in Wales. Support for Welsh independence according to opinion polls and large rallies across Wales has increased significantly. While impossible to predict where all these processes will lead it is probably safe to say that Wales will never be the same again.

References:

Armstrong, A (2019) 'Effective Devolution' *National Institute Economic Review* No250 November 2019

Antoniw, M (2019) 'Not a Bad Start: 20 Years of Devolution' *The Law Society Gazette* 20 May 2019

Beck, D and Gwilym, H (2020) 'The Moral Maze of Foodbank Use' *Journal of Poverty and Social Justice* Published online on 15/06/20 at:
www.ingentaconnect.com/content/tpp/jpsj/pre-prints/content-jpsjd1900050

Business Wales (2020) *Foundation Economy*, Welsh Government, Accessed online on 15/10/20 at https://businesswales.gov.wales/foundational-economy?_ga=2.96778783.123020553.1602767198-804171595.1602767198

Coutts P (2019) 'Has devolution produced successful policy innovation and learning?' in Paun A and Macrory S (eds.) *Has Devolution Worked? The First 20 Years* Institute for Government

Evans, J E (2018) 'Welsh Devolution as Passive Revolution' *Capital and Class* 42(3): 489-508

Evans, H (2020) 'New YouGov Poll Shows Highest Ever Support for Welsh Independence', *Daily Post*, 27 August 2020, Accessed online 15-10-20: www.dailypost.co.uk/news/north-wales-news/new-yougov-poll-shows-highest-18832964

Holtham, G (2019) 'Has devolution led to more effective government in Wales? The case of the economy' in Paun A and Macrory S (eds.) *Has Devolution Worked? The First 20 Years* Institute for Government

Law Wales 'How is devolved government in Wales financed?' https://law.gov.wales/constitution-government/government-in-wales/finance/ ?lang=en#/constitution-government/government-in-wales/finance/?tab=overview&lang=en

Melding, D (2012) 'Foreward, Issue on Welsh Devolution' *Statute Law Review* 33(2): 97-102

Minnis, A, Clifton A, Boshier, P, Dauncey, M, Scurlock, L, Corbyn, C, Stokes, B, Thomas A, Wilkes, J, Jones, S, Morgan, L, and Douch, T (2019) 20 Years as a Devolved Nation – How has Wales Changed? Devolution 20. Senedd Research, National Assembly for Wales

Mullen T (2019) 'Brexit and the Territorial Governance of the United Kingdom' Contemporary Social Science 14(2): 276-93

National Assembly for Wales Commission (2019) '20 years as a devolved nation – how has Wales changed? Devolution 20' National Assembly for Wales Commission: Cardiff Accessed online 15/10/20 https://senedd.wales/research%20documents/19-29/20%20years%20as%20a%20devolved%20nation%20-%20how%20has%20wales%20changed.pdf

Office for National Statistics (2020) 2011 Census, Accessed on 15/10/20 www.ons.gov.uk/aboutus/transparencyandgovernance/freedomofinformationfoi/numberofwelshgaelicirishandcornishspeakersfromthe2011census

Shortridge, J (2010) New Development: 'The Evolution of Welsh Devolution' *Public Money and Management* 30(2): 87-90

Streeck, W (2017) *Buying Time, The Delayed Crisis of Democratic Capitalism* London, Verso

Welsh Government (2020a) Welsh Taxes Accessed online on 21/10/20 at: https://gov.wales/welsh-taxes

Welsh Government (2020b) 'Welsh Index of Multiple Deprivation' StatsWales, Accessed on 17/10/2020 at https://statswales.gov.wales/Catalogue/Community-Safety-and-Social-Inclusion/Welsh-Index-of-Multiple-Deprivation

Zhao, Y (2020) 'Two Decades of Havoc: A Synthesis of Criticism Against PISA' *Journal of Educational Change* 21: 245-66

Chapter 2

Social care: research, policy and practice in Wales

Diane Seddon, Gill Toms, Fiona Verity

Introduction

Following devolution Wales has developed a distinct social care policy and practice landscape offering unique opportunities for research that speaks to Wales, other UK regions and an international audience. The features of this dynamic landscape are continuously evolving. Social care research, as it is defined by Health and Care Research Wales (Social Care Wales, 2018), can explore:

- Provision of care, support and personal assistance in the context of interpersonal relationships
- Provision of advice, practical assistance in the home, visiting and befriending services, meals and facilities for occupational, social, cultural and recreational activities
- Provision of protection or social support
- Social needs of people receiving social care
- Organisational systems involved in social care, including related systems such as healthcare, education, housing and the criminal justice system

The multi-faceted nature of social care research can make it difficult to distinguish from other fields of enquiry (Sharland, 2013) and our exploration of the social care research landscape shall have relevance to researchers and practitioners in other welfare and allied health disciplines.

In this chapter we highlight the current direction of travel, including the opportunities for research-informed policy and practice to enhance the well-being of the population in Wales, and we consider some of the challenges that arise. We describe how a bespoke research support landscape has started to develop to supplement the existing infrastructure and strengthen research capacity in social care. For instance, we describe new initiatives, developed in Wales, to promote innovative approaches to research development and knowledge exchange. To set the scene, we consider the Welsh Government's vision for social care, before moving on to explore how research can support the implementation of this vision into practice.

Vision for social care policy, practice and research in Wales

The Government of Wales Act (Welsh Government, 2006) enabled Wales to pass primary legislation and over the last decade a Welsh vision for social care has been enacted in law. The policy direction was signalled in 'Sustainable Social Services for Wales: A Framework for Action' (Welsh Government, 2011), which called for greater collaboration and integration between social care providers, a stronger voice for people engaging with social care organisations and focus on prevention. The Social Services and Well-being (Wales) Act (Welsh Government, 2014) draws together policy and law governing social care into a single overarching piece of legislation. It establishes the legal framework for delivering social care in Wales to improve the well-being of people needing care and support and their carers. The Act commits to developing innovative ways to help individuals achieve personal well-being outcomes and is underpinned by five key principles:

- Voice and control – putting the individual and their needs at the centre of their care
- Prevention and early intervention – providing preventative community services to minimise the escalation of critical needs
- Well-being – supporting people to achieve well-being
- Co-production – encouraging individuals to become involved in the design and delivery of services
- Multi-agency working

Following on from this landmark legislation, the Well-being of Future Generations (Wales) Act (Welsh Government, 2015a) established public service boards in each local authority to assess and promote well-being objectives. Based on their assessments boards set local well-being objectives and publish an achievement plan for implementation. A review in 2018 identified seven area plans in the 2017-2018 period (Noyes and Vinnicombe, 2019), illustrating that this policy is becoming embedded. Going forward, A Healthier Wales plan for health and social care (Welsh Government, 2018a) describes the move towards community-based care close to home and an integrated whole system approach to supporting:

- Improved population health and well-being
- Better quality, more accessible health and social care services
- Improved health and social care provision that is innovative, evidence informed and focused on outcomes
- A motivated, skilled and sustainable workforce
- The involvement of those engaging with social care services

There are unique opportunities for members of the public, researchers, policy makers and practitioners across Wales to co-produce research to support the translation of this policy vision into practice. Research evidence plays a critical role in the development of social care policy (League of European Research Universities and Science Business, 2017). It also informs how best to implement evidence into practice (Rycroft-Malone, 2004) and the ways we commission, deliver and manage social care services. Research offers insights, from a range of stakeholder perspectives, helping us to understand what works well and for whom, and the underlying causes of social issues. For example, research highlights the challenges faced by people with complex support needs and their carers, as well as their interaction and engagement with social care services and social care professionals, including home carers and support workers employed in third sector organisations (Kuluski *et al.*, 2017). These insights are especially pertinent given the policy emphasis in Wales on individualised, outcome-focused support and the mandate in the UK to support people with complex care and support needs to achieve *what matters* (Welsh Government, 2015b:15) to them.

Welsh Government envisions research having a strong, visible role in social care (Welsh Government, In Press). Legislation and policy initiatives acknowledge the contribution that research makes to the well-being of citizens in Wales. The Social Services and Well-being (Wales) Act (Welsh Government, 2014) states that Welsh Government and local authorities can conduct, commission or assist in the conduct of research into the Act's functions and its effectiveness. More recent plans have similarly highlighted the role of research. For instance, the Dementia Action Plan for Wales 2018-2022 (Welsh Government, 2018b) envisages research as a pathway to the delivery of high quality, flexible and responsive provision. It commits to providing opportunities for people affected by dementia across Wales to be involved and engaged in research, recognising the right for them to:

- Know about research
- Decide if they want to participate
- Receive support to participate

It also places a duty on researchers to increase understanding about what matters to people living with dementia and what enables people to live fulfilled lives.

The Welsh Government's social care research agenda is outlined in the Social Care Research and Development Strategy for Wales 2018-2023 (Social Care Wales, 2018). This strategy provides a structure for a nationally co-ordinated approach, led by Social Care Wales, to social care research capacity building. It incorporates five focus areas:

- Involving the public in social care research
- Research priorities encompassing three strategic improvement areas: care and support at home, people with dementia, and children who are looked after
- Use of existing and routinely collected data
- Developing the workforce and organisations
- Communication and use of research

There is a commitment to enhance the research infrastructure, for instance through developing guidance on social care research ethics and creating a national data set for social care in Wales. A support network for research champions in social care organisations is planned and there is a commitment to decide research priorities in consultation with public and practitioner stakeholders.

To summarise, Wales has unique visions for social care policy, practice and research. These visions are integrated and complementary, creating exciting opportunities for innovation. In the next section we consider the challenges to realising this vision for social care research.

Realising the vision

Since the 1990's the importance of evidence-informed social care policy and practice has been acknowledged and the use of evidence is now established as integral to the duty of care that practitioners hold (Sharland, 2013; Ghate and Hood, 2019). However, over the same time period there have been substantial fluctuations in the funding and prominence afforded to social care research by the UK Government (Ghate and Hood, 2019). Similarly, whilst the importance of research minded practice in social care is recognised as a precursor to continuing professional development and enhanced social care provision (McLaughlin, 2012; Hardwick and Worsely, 2016), research and knowledge mobilisation remains emergent. Before exploring how the social care research agenda is being taken forward across Wales, it is important to understand some of the challenges facing social care research.

The first systematic map of social care research in Wales was undertaken in 2015-2016 (Wales School for Social Care Research, 2017) and only 266 projects were identified. This snapshot does not measure up to the vision of a strong and dynamic research landscape and the authors identified that social care research faces significant challenges. Some of these challenges resonate with other sectors, for example, short-term research funding (Huxley, 2009), whilst others relate specifically to the social care sector, including the number of stakeholders involved and the nature of social care research.

Number of stakeholders

Social care is provided by a mixed economy of organisations (Ghate and Hood, 2019) and in Wales, the private and voluntary sectors account for over 80 per cent of provision (Huxley, 2009). This provision is varied across the country (Oung, 2020). In UK social care research there is a similar drive to diversify the organisations involved so that voluntary, social enterprise, industrial, commercial, third sector and academic organisations are represented (Ghate and Hood, 2019). For instance, the Huxley Report (2009) advocates for the involvement of statutory and non-statutory provider organisations and Health Care Research Wales (HCRW: formally the National Institute for Social Care and Health Research and the Wales Office of Research and

Development) encourages collaboration with industry and partners in and beyond Wales (HCRW, 2016). Within academia, there are signs that more sectors are undertaking social care relevant research and social care practice can increasingly draw on a cross-disciplinary evidence base (Ghate and Hood, 2019). Unfortunately, outside of academia there are few indications of diverse stakeholder involvement.

Drivers of the disconnect between vision and implementation probably include the need for various stakeholders to agree shared research priorities (Huxley, 2009). This is challenging when there are numerous, sometimes competing, perspectives and interests. For instance, HCRW wants research to be recognised as a core activity for social care organisations (Welsh Government, In Press). However, it is challenging for organisations to implement this. Organisations need to be able to draw on academic specialisms and skills to conduct research and evaluations. Some of this expertise, for example, economic analysis, is not readily available across Wales (Social Care Wales, 2018). Further, social care practitioners tend to distrust academic research, which they perceive to be disassociated from and therefore not relevant to practice (Orme and Powell, 2007). The time lag between the development of research questions and the finalisation and presentation of research findings can be one of the reasons for this. For organisations to undertake their own, independent research, practitioners in these organisations need appropriate research skills, however, some research skills, for instance quantitative skills, are lacking in the social care workforce (Social Care Wales, 2019a).

The diversity of stakeholder groups also poses a barrier to knowledge mobilisation. The implementation plan for the 'Social Care Research and Development Strategy for Wales' highlights that over the coming years different methods of research communication will be piloted (Social Care Wales, 2019a) with the hope that ways will be found to improve research dissemination across the range of social care stakeholders. However, making social care research visible is only the first step on the pathway to impact.

The nature of social care research

Key aspects of social care research create areas of challenge:

- **Its funding and practice context**
  To be effective in their work, practitioners need to be aware of the empirical evidence about the effectiveness of interventions. There are, however, important considerations about how such evidence is located, understood, contextualised and joined with other forms of knowledge (Webb, 2001). Even though evidence-informed practice is now as much of a mantra in social care as it is in health, in the UK social care research remains a poor relation to health research, which is more generously funded and afforded higher status. This parallels the discrepant funding and status accorded to the social care sector compared to the National Health Service (NHS); the social care sector experiences significant staff shortages and turnover. This turbulence coupled with limited funding seriously impedes research

approaches that are dependent on standardisation and large-scale application (Ghate and Hood, 2019).

There are some national initiatives currently on-going in Wales to track well-being and its determinants and to evaluate policy. The Prosperity for All (Welsh Government, 2017) strategy introduced Health Wise Wales as an initiative to develop a population-based approach to health and care research. Additionally, the University of South Wales has led the recent Measuring the Mountain project to capture approximately 500 personal stories of social care experiences across Wales since the introduction of the Social Services and Well-being (Wales) Act (SCW, 2019b). However, these large-scale endeavours are exceptions to the norm. Instead, most social care research in Wales is small-scale, local and service-based, and rooted in particular contexts. These projects are unlikely to attract substantial funding from research bodies outside of Wales. They will also be limited in achieving impact that leads to scale-up and implementation in wider practice contexts, even though they can have valuable contributions to local contexts and practice. Additionally, due to the often-limited transferability of findings, this research is less likely to inform national social care policy.

■ Its common methodologies

In contrast to the large-scale trial research agenda common in health, distinct research approaches are emerging in social care (Ghate and Hood, 2019). This includes research that:

- Is locally generated, funded and delivered
- Uses diverse types of evidence
- Attempts to translate international research findings to the UK context

In Wales, it is the local generation of evidence that is most apparent. Small scale research is likely to draw upon qualitative methods that maximise data collection from small populations. Participatory methods (for example, practitioner research and participatory action research) are common and resonate with the ethos of social care practice, for instance, having a focus on emancipatory practice in social work (Kramer-Roy, 2015). Similarly, dialogical methods that traverse the boundaries of practice development and research are gaining prominence (for example, the most significant change technique – Dart and Davies, 2003 – and other well-developed methods in community development). Upcoming approaches can be predicted. Systems thinking is more influential in social care practice: social care is a multi-faceted and changing system and many of the issues addressed are complex, as in made up of many parts. Understanding this is fundamental to gathering and using evidence. Systems thinking is not new in fields such as social work and community development, with long standing emphasis on the relationships between people and their environments. Throughout its history, social work has had a focus on dynamic social interactions exemplified by social work theories such as systems theories and ecological social work (Siporin, 1980). Contemporary research and evaluation methods like social network analysis and principles focused evaluation (Patton, 2018) have built on this history and helped to produce research grounded in a perspective of the existence of dynamic, fluid environments. These methods present opportunities for deeper exploration of the systemic contexts of practice and the use of interventions in different and emerging contexts (Ghate and Hood, 2019).

The population of people who engage with social care organisations and the nature of social care interventions and their outcomes create further methodological challenges. Researchers in social care must contend with the dearth of measures that capture the expressed hoped-for outcomes of people engaging with social care services (Huxley, 2009). One of the continuing dilemmas is how to collect such data in ways that are meaningful, mindful of bureaucratic rationality and the multiple perspectives on the question of what constitutes 'meaningful' (Miller and Barrie, 2016). Social care populations are not always easy to engage in research. For instance, meaningful and inclusive research in care homes for older adults requires the involvement of participants some of whom cannot give informed consent (Johnstone and Donaldson, 2019). Further challenges are encountered when researching early intervention and prevention initiatives to support community wellbeing as these are notoriously difficult to evaluate (Ghate and Hood, 2019). Curry (2006 p1) argues there is 'a paucity' of long-term quantitative studies that track the implementation of various levels of preventative programmes in social care. The limited research evidence base can make it harder to understand the conditions under which certain approaches work best and the positive value of certain types of preventative services and approaches, a point made by Miller and Whitehead, 2015.

For the reasons just detailed, social care research is not easily supported by an existing infrastructure primarily designed to support large, multi-centre quantitative and trial-based research.

■ Its chief investigators

Social care research is often undertaken by practitioners (McLaughlin, 2012). This approach has significant advantages. For social care practitioners, undertaking their own research can encourage a continuous reflexive relationship with practice, enabling them to answer critical questions, chiefly, is what I do effective, and how do I combine knowledge from practice with 'research knowledge'? Careful thinking, critical reflection and an ability to understand situations from new perspectives can benefit social care practice and affect positive change. However, there are significant challenges for social care practitioners wishing to engage in their own research or enhance their awareness of existing empirical research.

Practitioner researchers can lack practical support. High caseload commitments and pressure of work can form serious obstacles as engaging in research activity (empirical or desk-based) demands time. Research can also require access to relevant resources, for instance software to assist with data analysis (Orme and Powell, 2007).

A firm commitment from managers to protect practitioner research time is often required. Senior management buy-in is also a pre-requisite for successful knowledge mobilisation (Andrews *et al.*, 2015). Writing about the use of research evidence in social work settings, McLaughlin (2012) suggests that research is not always seen by senior managers as a legitimate social work task given other pressing priorities. There is often a limited research infrastructure within social care organisations.

Practitioner researchers face the additional disadvantage that they tend to be marginalised in mainstream research culture and they have few career pathways (Gazeley *et al.*, 2019). This was one of the challenges that the Continuing Professional Education and Learning (CPEL) programme in Wales hoped to address. This scheme provided opportunities for graduate social workers studying on Senior Practice in Social Work and Consultant Social Work programmes to conduct their own research. The ongoing challenges faced by practitioner researchers are likely to depress the hoped-for growth in the number of practitioners who are engaging in social care research.

As noted previously some social care professionals may lack some of the pre-requisite research skills to become practitioner researchers. Although research use in policy and practice settings is highly complex and multifaceted, social care posts are disproportionately occupied by people with less academic education (Ghate and Hood, 2019) and professional workers in social care, for example social workers may receive little research training as part of their qualification (Orme and Powell, 2007). Social workers may not know where to access the latest research evidence, have capacity to access journals which require subscriptions or they may not have the requisite skills to interpret or assess the quality of research evidence (McLaughlin, 2012). There is an ongoing debate in the social work literature about whether the skills required by practitioner researchers are similar or different to those required by academic researchers (Smith, 2016).

■ Its opportunity to achieve impact

The proceeding discussion raises a question about what impact social care practitioner research can realistically achieve. In theory impact should be high: ensuring that research focuses on recognised local needs so that findings will resonate with organisations, practice and policy priorities in the locality is a key impact pathway (Keane *et al.*, 2003). However, the worldwide evidence is clear: evidence informed pockets of innovation are not sustainably scaled-up (Ghate and Hood, 2019). One reason for this might be the lack of focus on knowledge mobilisation. An audit in South East Wales identified that researcher practitioners made no distinction between dissemination (i.e. sharing findings) and the active utilisation of these findings in social care practice (Keane *et al.*, 2003). Although this evidence is now somewhat dated, the UK has not yet established (at scale) generalist implementation teams whose expertise is in implementation and improvement science. This new cadre of professionals is required as a workforce is needed who have the capacity and skills to take a more active approach to knowledge mobilisation (Ghate and Hood, 2019). Limited utilisation of evaluation findings is associated with disappointed hopes and expectations (Keane *et al.*, 2003) so a greater recognition of the importance of knowledge mobilisation to capitalise on evaluation and research findings will enhance the vitality of the social care research landscape.

In summary, when thinking about strategies to improve and promote the use of research evidence in social work settings, Hutchinson and Dance (2016) suggested that first and foremost there needs to be greater opportunities for engagement between researchers and practitioners to establish trusting relationships based on mutual respect for one another's experience and expertise. The authors highlight the importance of networks and forums to facilitate such opportunities. Cooke, Gardois and Booth's analysis of 'mechanisms of research capacity building in health and social care' concluded these processes are in part enhanced if there are 'triggers' to 'release research energies' and some level of 'observation' to stimulate and reinforce people's engagement in research activities and capacity building (2018, p32). This has been a fundamental feature of how the vision for social care research in Wales has been taken forward.

Taking forward the social care research vision in Wales

The social care research vision for Wales is for a strategic and coordinated programme of work that generates robust evidence to support the realisation of ambitious policy and practice objectives.

An innovative support landscape encourages collaboration between academia, policy and practice. The last two decades have seen an increasing number of research collaborations established between social care professionals (employed in strategic and operational roles) and social care academics in Wales. Successful collaborations have led to the co-creation of impactful research, with real-world application, to inform the development, commissioning and delivery of social care provision. For instance, the CareShare project in North Wales exploring intergenerational care for older people and people living with dementia has excited local and international interest through the television programme 'Hen Blant Bach' (Woods *et al.*, 2019). Harnessing their respective knowledge and expertise, academics and social care professionals have worked closely to agree overall research objectives, jointly shape plans of investigation and agree knowledge exchange activities.

In parallel, across the UK, a specialised UK infrastructure has developed to provide synthesised digests of social care and health knowledge, for example, SCIE and the National Institute for Health and Care Excellence (NICE). This has made social care research more accessible to practitioners at the point of use.

Research support landscape

As the health and social care policy and practice landscape has evolved, Welsh Government has implemented a support landscape and infrastructure to encourage evidence-informed health and social care provision (NISCHR, 2011). HCRW has a long-established mission of "supporting today's research to inform tomorrow's care" (NISCHR, 2011). Its objective is to create a strong, dynamic evidence base in Wales that shall have positive impacts for the health, wellbeing and prosperity of people in Wales (HCRW, 2016). It is underpinned by a commitment to public involvement in research and the implementation of the new National Standards for Public Involvement in Research (NIHR, 2019). These standards reflect the importance of:

- Inclusive opportunities
- Working together
- Support and learning
- Communications
- Impact
- Governance

Funded by the Welsh Government and managed by HCRW, the research support landscape comprises several research centres (for example the Wales Centre for Ageing and Dementia Research (CADR) and the Children's Social Care Research and Development Centre) who support social care research. Another relevant centre established in 2020 is the Gambling research, evaluation and treatment Wales network. From 2016-2020 social care research in Wales has also been supported by the Wales School for Social Care Research (WSSCR). The WSSCR, founded in 2016, emerged from its predecessor the All Wales Academic Social Care Research Collaboration (established in 2012) and was formally launched in 2017. The WSSCR was pan-Wales with bases in three Welsh universities (Cardiff, Swansea and Bangor). The WSSCR was primarily informed by capacity building and evidence in practice models, so unlike the initial iteration of the National Institute for Health Research School for Social Care Research in England, the WSSCR from its inception has focused on social care research capacity building with a remit to bridge the gaps between research and social care services in Wales. The school also sought to improve public engagement in social care research. Additionally Wales has a generic research infrastructure that includes clinical trials units (for example, the North Wales Organisation for Randomised Trials in Health, Clinical Trials Unit), organisations, such as the Health and Care Economics Cymru service, a research grant funding body and the Support and Delivery centre, which provides training and other forms of research support.

With a focus on current and emerging areas of research excellence in Wales, this support landscape enables high-quality scientific research and encourages the better integration of research, policy and practice. In social care, bespoke capacity building initiatives have emerged. We present two of these innovations:

Social Care Innovations Lab

A new initiative co-hosted by the CADR and the WSSCR is the Social Care Innovations Lab (#SCIL). The CADR and the WSSCR have collaborated with Steve Baker, the co-founder, who has worked in the field of adult social care for almost thirty years, currently as a Quality Support Manager at Home Instead Senior Care.

#SCIL provides unique opportunities for people to hone and take forward research ideas. Each #SCIL is a connecting hub that brings together people with a broad range of academic and practice experiences based on their shared interest in developing collaborations and stimulating innovation to make a positive difference to social care.

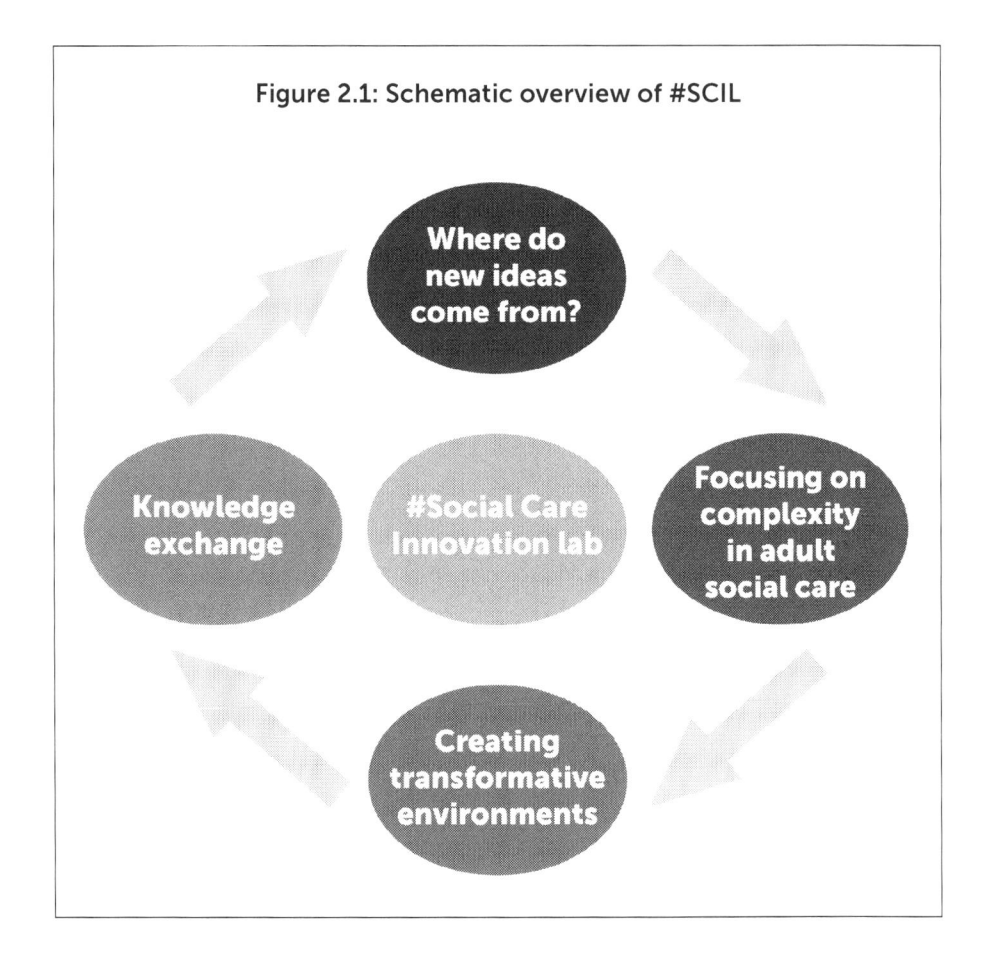

Figure 2.1: Schematic overview of #SCIL

Groups may meet in an actual or virtual space with for example, pop-up labs in community settings. There is no typical #SCIL because each lab is planned to meet the needs of the situation, but every lab offers a safe and comfortable space within which to share ideas, experiences and understandings. Although #SCIL is a simple concept it provides opportunities that are in short supply:

- It is rare to explore social care research ideas with lots of different people who all see and approach a topic from different perspectives
- It is rarer still for all these different people to listen to each other and start thinking together in a supportive environment

#SCIL is underpinned by three key principles:

1. Involving – making meaningful connections and having candid discussions; every person matters
2. Innovating – creating safe and separate spaces for testing out ideas; innovation through experimentation
3. Improving – generating evidence and the confidence to use science in social care to make a positive difference

#SCIL also facilitates knowledge exchange between people, enabling them to share ideas, experience and evidence. Knowledge exchange can contribute towards the achievement of:

- Well-being outcomes
- Continual professional development for social care practitioners
- Quality improvement of services

Developing evidence enriched practice

The Developing Evidence Enriched Practice (DEEP: Andrews *et al.*, 2015) approach to knowledge mobilisation recognises that supporting practitioners to actively engage with research evidence is a process that needs to be conceptually relevant if it is to inform practice. Rarely does research get directly translated into practice. Rather its influence is felt as and when it is transformed through dialogue and reflection and sifting with other forms of knowledge from practice and lived experience. This reflection process is not automatic; practitioners need training and support on how to learn from evidence (Andrews *et al.*, 2015). The DEEP approach resonates with the 'mindlines' model proposed by Gabbay and le May (2011), which suggests that practitioners almost always transform knowledge by melding it, through discussion and reflection, with other new or existing ideas relevant to their practice. Consequently, research evidence is more likely to be used in practice when it has been transformed into 'knowledge-in-practice-in-context' (Gabbay and le May, 2011). DEEP adds to the 'mindlines' model by explicitly acknowledging the value of different types of evidence including research, practitioner knowledge, the voice of people with care and support needs and carers as well as organisational knowledge. This responds to the longstanding call to incorporate the utilisation of tacit, common sense knowledge in social care practice (Keane *et al.*, 2003).

In the DEEP process research evidence is summarised in plain language and presented creatively (and sometimes provocatively) to stimulate learning. There is emphasis on the importance of stories in developing practitioner thinking about evidence. The DEEP approach maintains that how evidence is presented is vital: evidence needs to trigger an emotional, imaginative and intellectual response so that it is engaged with. It is also fundamental that decisions about how to employ evidence are collaborative. Practitioners have reported that they appreciate and see benefits in this mutual approach to knowledge mobilisation, where their knowledge and experience are valued (Andrews *et al.*, 2015; Wales School for Social Care Research, 2019).

Research networks

In addition to capacity building innovations, research networks have evolved in recent years to address some key issues for social care practice. As an example of this evolution, two recently developed networks are highlighted:

- **Enabling Research in Care Homes Cymru**
The Enabling Research in Care Homes (ENRICH) Cymru network was established in 2017, based on the ENRICH Research Ready Care Home network founded in England in 2012. The network positions care home managers and staff as the research experts. Its aims are to increase the amount of research conducted in care homes, mobilise research knowledge in care homes and encourage care homes to be active stakeholders in the research process. Realising these aims has the potential to improve the lives of residents and staff in care homes across Wales. For instance, an increase in care home research could improve care standards, enhance resident quality of life and promote the professional development of staff (Jenkins et al., 2016).

- **The Wales Institute for Social Prescribing**
The Wales Institute for Social Prescribing aims to build a critical evidence base for social prescribing in Wales. Social prescribing often directs citizens to local community and third sector-based sources of support. For example, Men's Sheds is a form of social care intervention that builds friendship between men based on regular opportunities to share in the pursuit of making and mending activities together. There is evidence that Men's Sheds can promote men's physical, mental, social and occupational health (Ormsby *et al.*, 2010). The Wales Institute for Social Prescribing operates a virtual research platform and network with face to face events across Wales. It takes a participatory research approach and the network's priorities were collaboratively developed with practitioners, researchers and other stakeholders. Network members come from all disciplines and sectors. This network is housed within the Wales Centre for Primary and Emergency (including unscheduled) Care Research centre (acronym PRIME).

Summary and conclusions

This chapter has presented the direction of travel in the social care research landscape in Wales and detailed some recent initiatives. Social care research is diverse and touches on many aspects of policy and practice, so understanding this landscape has relevance for professionals working across the spectrum of welfare services. Given its methodological nature and fledgling status, social care research conducted in Wales and beyond will continue to benefit from an emergent, purpose designed research support landscape. Wales has started on this trajectory through its legislation of innovative social care practice policies and its social care research strategy. However, there will continue to be challenges to ensuring that the research landscape thrives due to the numerous vested interests of different stakeholders and the nature of social care research.

In conclusion, we wish to highlight that how best to evaluate the social care research landscape remains undetermined. As Andrews et al. (2015) concluded it is rare to find a simple one-to-one match between proffered evidence and its incorporation into practice. Furthermore, as Orme and Powell (2007) highlighted developing a research culture is not just about undertaking more research. Evaluations of the research landscape effectiveness therefore need to go beyond an investigation of whether research evidence is being generated. Rather there needs to be an exploration that considers whether the newly generated research evidence is being integrated and embedded into the practice culture (Andrews *et al.*, 2015). It is the effective use of research evidence in practice that will achieve the social care policy vision in Wales for improved citizen well-being.

References

Andrews N, Gabbay J, Le May A, Miller E, O'Neill M and Petch A. (2015) *Developing evidence-enriched practice in health and social care with older people.* UK, Joseph Rowntree Foundation

Cooke J, Gardois P and Booth A. (2018) Uncovering the mechanisms of research capacity development in health and social care: a realist synthesis. *Health Research Policy and Systems*, 16(1): 93. Doi: 10.1186/s12961-018-0363-4

Curry, N (2006) *Preventative Social Care: Is it Cost Effective?* King's Fund [online]. Accessed 01/06/2020 www.kingsfund.org.uk/sites/default/files/preventive-social-care-wanless-background-paper-natasha-curry2006.pdf

Dart, J and Davies, N (2003) A dialogical, story-based evaluation tool: the most significant change technique. *American Journal of Evaluation*, 24(2): 137-55. doi: 10.1016/s1098-2140(03)00024-9

Gazeley L, Lofty F, Longman P and Squire R (2019) Under-tapped potential: practitioner research as a vehicle for widening participation. *Journal of Further and Higher Education*, 43(7): 1008-20. doi: 10.1080/0309877X.2018.1441386

Ghate, D and Hood, R (2019) Using evidence in social care in Boaz, A, Davies, H, Fraser, A and Nutley, S (eds.) *What works now? Evidence-informed policy and practice.* Poole, Great Britain, Policy Press, pp89-104

Gabbay, J amd Le May, A (2011) *Practice-based evidence for healthcare: clinical mindlines.* Abingdon, UK: Routledge

Hardwick, L and Worsely, A (2016) Conclusion in Hardwick A, Smith R, Worsley A (eds.) *Innovations in social work research: using methods creatively*. London, UK: Jessica Kingsley, pp345-57

Health Care Research Wales. (2016) *Health Care Research Wales strategic plan 2015-2020*. UK; Welsh Government

Hutchinson, A and Dance, C (2016) Incorporating 'knowledge exchange' into research design and dissemination strategies in Hardwick A, Smith R, Worsley A (eds.) *Innovations in social work research: using methods creatively*. London, UK: Jessica Kingsley, pp314-33

Huxley, P (2009) *Social care research priorities and capacity in Wales. A consultation exercise. Final report*. UK, Centre for Social Work and Social Care Research School of Human Sciences, Swansea University

Jenkins, C, Smythe, A, Galant-Miecznikowska, M, Bentham, P and Oyebode, J (2016) Overcoming challenges of conducting research in nursing homes. *Nursing Older People*, 28(5): 16-23. doi: 10.7748/nop.28.5.16.s24

Johnstone, AM and Donaldson, AIC (2019) Care home research: future challenges and opportunities. *Geriatrics*, 4(2): online. doi: 10.3390/geriatrics4010002

Keane S, Shaw I and Faulkner A. (2003). *Practitioner research in social care: an audit and case study analysis*. UK, Wales Office of Research and Development in Health and Social Care

Kramer-Roy, D (2015) Using participatory and creative methods to facilitate emancipatory research with people facing multiple disadvantage: a role for health and care professionals. *Disability and Society*, 30(8): 1207-24. doi: 10.1080/09687599.2015.1090955

Kuluski, K, Ho, JW, Han,s PK and Nelson, MLA (2017) Community care for people with complex care needs: bridging the gap between health and social care. *International Journal of Integrated Care*, 17(4): 1-11. doi: 10.5334/ijic.2944

League of European Research Universities and Science Business (2017) *How research can inform policy*. Belgium: LERU

McLaughlin, H (2012) *Understanding social work research- second edition*. UK: SAGE Publications

Miller, E and Barrie, K (2016) *Personal outcomes: learning from the meaningful and measurable project. Strengthening links between identity, action and decision-making*. UK: Healthcare Improvement Scotland

Miller, R and Whitehead, C (2015) *Inside out and down. Community based approaches to social care prevention in a time of austerity*. UK: University of Birmingham

National Institute for Health Research (2019) *UK standards for public involvement. Better public involvement for health and social care research*. UK, NIHR

National Institute for Social Care and Health Research (2011) *Today's research – tomorrows care. The NISCHR strategy 2011-2015*. UK: Welsh Government

Noyes, J and Vinnicombe, S (2019) *Local authority area plans- report identifies common pan-Wales priorities and opportunities for future social care research*. UK, National Centre for Population Health and Wellbeing Research. Available from: https://ncphwr.org.uk/portfolio/local-authority-area-plans-report-identifies-common-pan-wales-priorities-and-opportunities-for-future-social-care-research

Orme, J and Powell, J (2007) Building research capacity in social work: process and issues. *British Journal of Social Work*, 38(5): 988-1008. doi: 10.1093/bjsw/bcm122

Ormsby, J, Stanley, M and Jaworski, K (2010). Older men's participant in community-based men's sheds programmes. *Health and Social Care in the Community* 18(6): 607-13. doi: 10.1111/j.1365-2524.2010.00932.x

Oung, C (2020) *Social care across the four countries of the UK: what can we learn?* UK: Nuffield Trust comment

Patton, M (2018) *Principles-focused evaluation: the guide*. USA: Guildford Press

Rycroft-Malone, J (2004) The PARIHS framework – a framework for guiding the implementation of evidence-based practice. *Journal of Nursing Care Quality*, 19(4): 297-304. Doi: 10.1097/00001786-200410000-00002

Sharland, E (2013) 'Where are we now? Strengths and limitations of UK social work and social care research. *Social Work and Social Science Review*, 16(2): 7-19. Doi: 10.1921/300316206

Siporin, M (1980) Ecological systems theory in social work. *The Journal of Sociology and Social Welfare*, 7(4): 507-32

Smith, R (2016). Introduction in Hardwick A, Smith R, Worsley A (eds.) *Innovations in social work research: using methods creatively*. London, UK: Jessica Kingsley, pp11-15

Social Care Wales (2018) *Social care research and development strategy for Wales 2018-2023*. Wales, UK, Welsh Government

Social Care Wales (2019a) *Social care research and development strategy for Wales 2018-2023. Implementation plan*. UK, Welsh Government

Social Care Wales (2019b) *Annual report and accounts 2018-2019* UK, SCW

Wales School for Social Care Research (2017) *From mapping social care research to capacity building: a study in Wales*. UK: Wales School for Social Care Research

Wales School for Social Care Research (2019) Review of the 2017-2019 strategic plan. UK: WSSCR

Webb, S (2001) Some considerations on the validity of evidence-based practice in social work. *British Journal of Social Work*, 31(1): 57-79. Doi: 10.1093/bjsw/31.1.57

Welsh Government (2006) *Government of Wales Act 2006*. UK: The Stationery Office Limited

Welsh Government (2011) *Sustainable Social Services for Wales: A Framework for Action*. UK: The Stationary Office Limited

Welsh Government (2014) *Social Services and Well-being (Wales) Act 2014*. UK: The Stationery Office Limited

Welsh Government (2015a) *Well-being of Future Generations (Wales) Act 2015*. UK: The Stationery Office Limited

Welsh Government (2015b) *Social Services and Well-being (Wales) Act 2014. Part 3 Code of Practice (Assessing the Needs of Individuals)*. UK: The Stationary Office Limited

Welsh Government (2017) *Prosperity for All: The National Strategy*. UK: The Stationery Office Limited

Welsh Government (2018a) *A Healthier Wales: Our Plan for Health and Social Care*. UK: The Stationery Office Limited

Welsh Government (2018b) *Dementia Action Plan for Wales 2018-2022*. UK: The Stationary Office Limited

Welsh Government (In Press) *Code of Practice in Relation to the Performance of Social Services in Wales*. UK: Welsh Government

Woods, R, Hamer, L, Jones, C and Williams, N (2019) CareShare: an intergenerational programme for people with dementia and nursery children. Psychology of Older People: *The FPOP Bulletin*, Vol. 145, 01.2019, pp33-37

Chapter 3
Tackling Poverty and Inequality

David Beck

"It often seems that if you put five academics (or policy makers) in a room you would get at least six different definitions of poverty" (Gordon, 2006).

Introduction

In the account above, David Gordon captures the difficulty of objectively trying to justify what is a highly subjective condition. Poverty, in its simplest sense means to be *poor*; to be *without* something, or to have had something *taken away*. Other emotive words identify poverty as *destitution, penury, hardship and deprivation*. Nevertheless, to examine poverty in any meaningful sense asks us to identify the obvious differences between those who *'have'*, and those who do *'not-have'*. In terms of poverty within Wales (and the rest of the UK), identifying who *has* and who *has-not* is not such a straightforward task. As a developed nation, it may be right to assume existing levels of poverty are not reflective of poverty that exists in countries with a less developed Social Security system. This is because when the foundations of the welfare state were laid by William Beveridge, as a form of Post War Welfare Consensus, it was broadly agreed that support in terms of welfare would be offered to citizens. Envisioned as a need to tackle the Five Giants (want, idleness, ignorance, squalor and disease) that were responsible for poverty, the welfare state ensured a plateau below which no one should be allowed to fall. However, fallen below many since have.

Wales has a population that is just over three-million people, a population similar to that of Greater Manchester (2.8 million) yet has a smaller economy (Marmot, 2020). As the Conservative Government presses ahead with their austerity driven reforms to social security, poverty has risen across Wales, not just poverty for those out of work, but poverty for those in work too. Symptomatic of increasing poverty and social insecurity, the food bank has become a symbol of government neglect, standing-in where a statutory welfare provision once existed. So, what has happened?

Discussions of the rise, cause and issues associated with poverty between the start of the welfare state and the end of New Labour have been examined at length by scholars (see Fraser, 1984; George and Wilding, 1985). The arguments presented here, focus on governmental and societal responses to rising poverty and inequality in the 21st Century in what has been dubbed 'the most radical shake-up for 60 years' for the welfare state (Ramesh, 2011). As discussed elsewhere in this edition, social security is not a devolved issue for the Welsh Government with significant decision making still held in Westminster. This means that any possibility of substantially reducing persistent high levels of poverty across Wales are seriously hampered. The challenge now is how can devolved nations such as Wales work to protect its citizens from the most pernicious reforms to welfare since the 1940s.

What is 'poverty'?

For Wales, as with the whole of the UK, poverty is measured at a national level, indicative of households/individuals who have an income below 60 per cent of the median income. However, understandably, this figure is difficult to pin-down, especially with annual fluctuations in average income and not to mention external factors such as interest rates, the cost of living and a progressing national minimum wage. Significantly, what any objective and analytical figure does not consider is the subjective nature of what it *really* means to be in poverty, as one person's experience may not resonate with another different and altogether individual experience. Why do I aim to take this approach? Well, for example, ask anyone who is on or near the National Living Wage, they will tell you that it doesn't matter that their wage is up-rated annually, because the cost of things they need to pay for usually goes up too, making them no better off. What I mean to argue here is that a numerical position offered as an identifier of poverty is useful, granted, as it plays a significant role defining who can participate within our society, regulating social and financial inclusion or exclusion. It also significantly regulates levels of wellbeing within a capitalist economy, especially one that is becoming increasingly neoliberal. For my approach here however, I reflect upon the lived experience of poverty, reflecting upon the subjective nature of *felt* poverty as a more human approach to identifying 'poverty'.

Poverty inside and outside of Wales

According to the latest statistics produced by the Joseph Rowntree Foundation, fourteen million people across the UK are locked into poverty. Those 14 million people across the UK are representative of; eight million working-age adults, four million UK children and two million UK pensioners (JRF, 2020). This, as the latest 'UK Poverty 2019/20' report continues, represents 22 per-cent of the entire population, or one in every five UK citizens (JRF, 2020). This notion of being 'locked into poverty' points to the endemic issue of being in long-term poverty and as a situation that is not easily remedied. For children, growing-up in poverty means lower levels of healthy development (Marmot, 2020), it also means that there is an increased potential that the same child could be in poverty as an adult.

In Wales, commencing in 2001 the Communities First Programme was an ambitious ten-year poverty reduction policy programme designed to work within the one hundred most deprived electoral regions of Wales (James, 2007); aiming to reduce the intergenerational transmission of poverty. Considered as the Welsh Government's flagship anti-poverty scheme, Communities First also encompassed thirty-two further 'pockets of deprivation' and ten 'communities of interest'. Identifying additional areas of support the programme also included targeted community development within Black and Minority Ethnic communities in Cardiff and Newport, survivors of domestic abuse in Pembrokeshire and several deprived rural communities (Welsh Government, 2011). Over its ten-year duration, Communities First provided support to almost 20 per cent of the Welsh population (Welsh Government, 2011). Importantly however, Williams (2016) identifies that almost half of the people who are deprived live outside Communities First areas.

Critically still, despite the success of the Communities First Programme and several other policy initiatives aimed at challenging structural drivers of poverty, the most recent ten years have seen levels of deprivation in Wales increasing. In 2018 the Joseph Rowntree Foundation Poverty in Wales report highlighted that 710,000 people or nearly a quarter (24 per cent) of the population in 2018 were living in poverty; a figure made up of 185,000 children; 405,000 working-age adults and 120,000 pensioners (Barnard, 2018).

Current structural drivers

The fate of pensioners in Wales has changed significantly. Twenty years ago, the rate of pensioner poverty in Wales was the second *lowest* across the whole of the UK. Today, Welsh pensioner poverty is recorded as being the second *highest* rate of the UK (JRF, 2020). But why has this happened? Effective social policy focuses on the use of policy measures to uphold the wellbeing and welfare of citizens (Alcock, 2016), the examination of wider areas of social policy is necessary to understand why poverty seems to be such a perennial issue across Wales. Poverty is not established in isolation, it is embodied within other associated disadvantages such as; income and employment levels, housing and the cost of living and, geography and the access to services (Fisher, 2017).

In housing, for example, privately renting tenants in Wales are likely to spend over a third of their income (39 per cent) on housing, with social tenants spending similar amounts (33 per cent). This is associated with the multiple structural dimensions known to drive poverty within families; high rents, low income, poor quality housing and inadequate levels of Housing Benefit (JRF, 2020). For an effective social policy that adequately tackles poverty, as we can see from the example, challenging wider social policy issues is crucial. Tackling Wales' high housing costs, in combination with other policy areas, is significant in understanding the structural causes of persistent high levels of poverty. The difficulty of not doing so is that it leaves families with less income to pay for essentials (Barnard, 2018), as disposable levels of income become constrained under increasing fixed costs.

The money that is left to pay for essentials is often spoken of as being a disposable income and this is money that is remaining after statutory taxes have been deducted. However, considerations of *disposable* income may also now include deductions for the essential payment of bills (rent, taxes, and gas and electric etc.), as all these costs are normally fixed too and are almost universally unavoidable costs. The ONS (2019) have calculated that the 10 per cent most deprived households typically spend around 42 per cent of their income on food and housing costs, compared with 26 per cent spent by the wealthiest 10 per cent of households. Proportionate to income, what this means for low-income households, is that there is less disposable income after normal living costs have been deducted. Therefore, increasingly, real *disposable* income starts to resemble the ever-shrinking pot of money that is left to buy other *essential* parts of living; such as costs associated with sending children to school, transport to work, clothing and food. Scott, Southerland and Taylor (2018) estimate that 31.6 per cent of Welsh households need to spend more than a quarter of their disposable income after housing costs have been deducted, simply to buy essentials such as food (a serious point that I will return to later).

Geographical considerations

Geography also contributes to the levels of relative poverty within Wales. Many parts of Wales reflect the beauty of open green spaces that are associated with maintenance of good mental health and general overall wellbeing. The role of green spaces should not be understated in helping to alleviate several vital symptoms of deprivation such as developing good mental and physical health, and also, the social connections associated with being out in the countryside. However, a green and beautiful land doesn't always provide sufficient levels of sustainable income vital for the maintenance of wellbeing within a neoliberal capitalist economy. Therefore, the focus here will be on rural deprivation and implications of rural poverty.

The Office for National Statistics (ONS) (2013) defines rural to be settlements with less than 10,000 residents. Many parts of Wales outside of the large population districts of the South will, therefore, be either rural or semi-rural in nature, as they include smaller village settlements close to large towns and cities. For the most part, areas such as Gwynedd, Ynys Môn, Ceredigion, Carmarthenshire Pembrokeshire, Monmouthshire and Powys, plus Denbighshire and Conwy are classified as rural (WLGA, 2019).

The Welsh Index of Multiple Deprivation (WIMD) is a statistical collection of relative deprivation data collected across local areas of Wales. It works through combining multiple indices of deprivation into geographically representative data, which can be used to see levels of associated deprivation across Wales (StatsWales, 2019a). Significantly, the current Welsh Index of Multiple Deprivation (WIMD, 2019) highlights that the above nine predominantly rural Local Authority counties are also some of the *least* income deprived parts of Wales (WIMD, 2019). Conversely, it is significant to note, however, that one of these counties – Denbighshire is also home to the *most* deprived area of Wales – Rhyl West; emphasising that the average affluence of some hides the relative poverty of others. Although Rhyl is not a rural community, it underlines the significant difficulty of objectively identifying small areas of poverty (rural or otherwise), as pockets of relative deprivation become obscured through official statistics.

StatsWales (2014) calculate that 20 per cent of the Welsh population live in rural areas, highlighting not just the obvious difficulties in accessing paid employment opportunities, but also the inherent impact of not being able to access wider services; necessary health care, appropriate education and affordable housing. Although these are key identifiers of poverty within rural areas, they are correspondingly symptoms of poverty within urban areas too. Many people in towns and cities across Wales will also recognise limited access to appropriate social policy areas of affordable housing, decent schooling and necessary health care provision. Therefore, it is difficult to objectively delineate urban poverty from rural poverty entirely (Jones, 2014). However, what is significant is that the experience of poverty can be magnified when examined with the additional impact of rurality; finding work, travelling to that work; access to services and so on.

It is clear that a geographical discussion of poverty is complex and requires a multidimensional approach to both examining subjective causes and impacts. This shifts the character frame of poverty to consider the wider association of *deprivation*, questioning what it means to be 'deprived'. Williams and Doyle (2016) in their analysis of international literature find that four identifiers of rural poverty are significant:

- Transport and access to services;
- The economy, employment and income;
- Housing; and
- The rural poverty premium.

Indices of multiple deprivation such as these highlight well the issues that face Wales' rural poor. However, significant to note is the more particular area blighting both rural and urban areas alike – the rising incidence of 'in-work' poverty a domain not easily deduced from deprivation data.

Here is where an equalities-based approach may also be considered as a secondary layer identifying poverty. An equalities-based approach focuses on who, defined by identifiable protected characteristics (race, disability, religion, gender, LGBTQ+, age etc.) are either at risk of, or currently living in poverty. Williams (2016) argues that this approach differs from the area-based approach identified through the Welsh Index of Multiple Deprivation, as the WIMD risks overlooking groups which are disadvantaged simply by their characteristics.

Families and in-work poverty

Former PM Teresa May declared in the 2018 Conservative Party conference speech that austerity is over, however, poverty for millions across the UK and Wales still seems to be rising. Evidence from the JRF (2020), highlight that Wales has the highest poverty rate for people in full-time work across the UK – standing at 13 per cent. Not only was this the highest rate across the UK, it was also the fastest rising rate over the last five years (JRF, 2020). This, combined with the multiple factors associated with poverty described above make it very difficult for people to connect with voices of the Welsh political establishment when they claim the best way out of poverty is to "get a job" (Cairns, 2017).

Notwithstanding significant data that conflicts with political rhetoric, it is generally assumed that being in paid work lessens the menace of poverty compared with not being in paid employment. The ONS (2020) have estimated that UK employment figures reached a record high in January 2020 (76.5 per cent), with an unemployment rate of 3.9 per cent. Moreover, these figures are also part of a general trend set in motion since lowest employment rate figures of 2012, showing that more and more people are entering paid employment. Curiously however, if employment is the best route out of poverty and paid employment is increasing, then why is poverty still rising?

There are several reasons why poverty is rising for those who are in-work and what is clear is that being in low-paid work makes it increasingly challenging to effectively escape poverty. In Wales this is particularly true where 26 per cent of employees earn less than the Real Living Wage in 2017/18 (JRF, 2020).

Across the UK, the last five years have seen a substantial increase in child poverty linked with declining living standards, as more than half (56 per cent) of people in poverty are living in working households (JRF, 2020). Welsh children, in particular, have some of the highest rates of relative poverty across the UK, with around a third of all Welsh children identified as living in poverty. What makes this figure more astonishing is that 60 per cent of these children live in waged households (Fawcett and Gunson, 2019).

As noted above, Barnard (2018) evidences that there were approximately 185,000 or 28 per cent of children in Wales living in poverty. By 2019 this figure had risen to 29 per cent highlighting the shocking notion that now almost nine children in every class of thirty in Welsh schools are living in poverty (Evans, 2019; StatsWales, 2019b). Further to this, it is anticipated that by 2021-22 the cumulative result of UK government welfare and tax reforms will advance this figure close to 40 per cent, or 12 children in every classroom in Wales (Holland, 2019).

In schools, poverty can notionally be seen through rudimentary instruments such as Free School Meals (FSM). I say rudimentary because not all children in need actually receive a free school meal provision and, with no automatic enrolment in place, they have to be claimed by the parent/guardian. StatsWales (2019c) using headteacher supplied data show that 59,397 children across Wales claimed a free school meal for the academic year 2018/19. However, figures show that 78,902 children in Wales were in fact eligible (StatsWales, 2019d) meaning that almost 19,500 eligible children went without a free school meal. The problem doesn't end there. Recent academic study has raised important political questions of 'holiday hunger' and what meal provisions are in place for children outside of term time with significant pressure added to low-income parents (Denning, 2019). During school holidays low-income parents not only have the added pressure of their children not receiving a free school meal, they also must negotiate a potential drop in income, as they balance childcare responsibilities and work.

Evans (2019) argues that these families are at a risk of falling into the poverty of holiday hunger; despite the presence of Welsh Government policies. SHEP, the School Holiday Enrichment Programme was set-up in 2016 and works across areas of multiple deprivation, providing *'fun and food'* during the school holidays. Research undertaken by Food Cardiff (2018) finds that 35 per cent of the children who accessed SHEP said that they skipped meals on days that they do not attend the programme. Evans (2019) maintains that, although the work conducted by SHEP is fantastic, the Welsh Governments approach to dealing with the wider issue of school holiday hunger has been unsatisfactory; confirming that in 2018, the programme only served 2,500 children across the whole of Wales.

Food poverty and food banks: An identification of modern poverty

Poverty for children is not just reflected within the classroom. Across Wales, thousands of families, both with and without children, currently face the rising prospect of poverty within the home too. In providing a modern discussion of the persistent high levels of poverty within Wales, it is the presence of food poverty and the subsequent emergence of the 'food bank' that has come to symbolise all that is currently wrong with the present administration of social security.

Food banks are, however, the obvious indication of food poverty, and rising food poverty highlights the failure of social policies more generally. Food poverty, therefore, is the *inadequate access* to food or an *insufficient income* to purchase food. It also includes the feeling of security over future food purchasing ability. Wider than this however, food poverty also means a recognition of the *social acceptability* of the food and how it is consumed, reflecting the *choice* of the consumer (adapted from Radimer, Olsen and Campbell, 1990).

Food banks are a relatively new occurrence in the social structure of the UK, and they have come to dominate social policy discussions as a residual social security welfare safety-net. Food banks offer help through providing emergency food aid provision and are a wonderful representation of localized welfare response and social consciousness. According to the Trussell Trust (the UKs largest single provider of food banks), they are responsible for providing around 113,000 three-day food parcels to families and individuals in poverty across Wales (Trussell Trust, 2019). This figure increases by about an additional third with the inclusion of food aid provided by Welsh food banks outside of the Trussell Trust network (Beck, 2018). This provision raises serious questions for social policy and the current governments position on tackling rising UK poverty, as an increasing use of food aid is indicative of a political handwashing (Beck and Gwilym, 2020).

Having a community response to localised problems is nothing new, as this was very much the case throughout other tough times. Collectivized responses to poverty have seen the establishment of the British and National Kitchens throughout both World Wars. Moreover, Welsh Valleys communities came together throughout the miners strikes of the mid-1980s to form what would resemble modern-day food banks. However, what we know of food banks today in Wales started in 1998 in Newport as a modest approach to helping the homeless community in the South Wales town. Standing alone, it was not until 2005 in Prestatyn that a second food bank was established, again, with the same recognition of the need to help the street homeless (Beck, 2018). By December 2008 aligned to the economic disruption of the Great Recession, a further three food banks had opened across South Wales, this time families were beginning to be the focus of need. As the economic crisis of the Great Recession bit deeper the development of the food bank landscape of Wales reflected the rise in need. Between 2010 and 2015, community groups had risen to meet the dual challenge of a declining social security system and rising poverty (Beck, 2018).

Food bank numbers swelled across the country as secular and church-based community groups responded. However, it was not until 2012/2013 and the introduction of significant draconian policies under the Welfare Reform Act 2012 that food bank numbers across Wales received their biggest surge. During these twelve-months fifty new food bank openings were documented across Wales as both Trussell Trust and independent food banks expanded their reach across communities. Over the next two-years, new food bank openings continued, with twenty-four opening in 2014 and an additional nine in 2015; bringing the total number of food banks across Wales by December 2015 to 160 (Beck, 2018).

More recent figures have shown that food bank numbers have continued to grow unabated with rising demand pushing for new food banks in both new and existing areas. Most surprising, and expressive of austerity times that continue to blight deprived regions, Rhyl, the most deprived region of Wales, towards the end of 2019 launched its fourth food bank, meaning that the town now has more food banks than supermarkets (Williams, 2019).

Recognised as spaces of care and support (Lambie-Mumford, 2017), food banks have come to symbolise a normalised and familiar presence in society, as they develop more and more as accepted facilitators of emergency food aid. However, as the UK Government turns its back on its poor and food poverty becomes unavoidable food banks are filling the void. This should not be the case for a country with a sophisticated welfare infrastructure.

We have arrived at this situation through the reshaping of the Post War Welfare Consensus and the unravelling of Beveridge's great vision. As argued below, welfare reform policies that centred around 'conditionality', such as the 'Bedroom Tax, imposed cutting measures to peoples' sense of security, both financial and in terms of food provision. However, as a social policy approach to welfare provision, the Welfare Reform Act 2012 seems to have misplaced its requirement to promote the welfare of citizens.

The radical shake-up: Conditionality and eligibility

Following the financial crisis of 2008, the incoming Conservative led Coalition Government forced changes to the way welfare is distributed, emphasizing the need to challenge 'welfare dependency and making work pay' (Shildrick *et al.*, 2012). The intention was to cut welfare expenditure by £15 billion in the aftermath of the Great

Recession, restructuring entirely the social security system of the UK. Alterations were proposed not just to the amount of welfare that is paid-out but, also forcing fundamental transformations to the way in which it is paid. This change is seen as the government at Westminsters' hardening approach to welfare policy, as it aimed to tackle welfare dependency through heightened conditionality and less eligibility. Exploring the conditional approach adopted by the Coalition Government's Welfare Reform Act 2012, various policy transformations encouraged an increase in poverty, as already struggling people suddenly found themselves significantly worse off. For example, one significant reform within the Welfare Reform Act 2012 saw the introduction of the Under-Occupancy Penalty; imposing conditionality in the form of a reduction in housing benefit payments to social housing tenants living in houses with additional bedrooms. However, this under-occupancy penalty became more widely known as a 'bedroom tax' due to the scarcity of social housing and a lack of availability for social tenants to move into. Other significant policies that were key to heightening people's feelings of social insecurity brought about by the Welfare Reform Act 2012: The Work Programme and the devolution of the Social Fund over to Local Authorities worked to substantially increase all forms of poverty for low-income and vulnerable individuals and families.

This is no more evident than in the new approach to providing social security through the new Universal Credit system. In short, 'Universal Credit' (UC) combines six former social security provisions now termed 'legacy benefits', into one welfare benefit payment. This means that entitlements to: Working Tax Credits, Income Support, Housing Benefit, Income-based Jobseekers Allowance (JSA), Income-related Employment and Support Allowance (ESA), and Child Tax Credits are now one combined payment.

However, Universal Credit seems to be neither *'universal'* or to be of much *'credit'* to claimants. *'Universal'* in this sense does not indicate a universal availability for claimants, as it is a highly conditional system. Nor does it mean that the *'credit'* available is delivered in a helpful way either. First, there is an in-built waiting period of five weeks before the first payment is made. This means, that the receipt of any payment is made in arrears and forces the claimant to secure further credit; usually in the form of an advanced UC payment loan, or to borrow from a family member. Dangling the *carrot* of an advance payment loan has also highlighted the implication of the repayment *stick* that is to follow in terms of reduced future UC payments. The BBC (2020) recently aired a three-part documentary following the UC system, which highlighted the devastating affect that advance payments are having on vulnerable people facing financial destitution. Second, following the initial wait, Universal Credit continues to be paid monthly in arrears, as further payments also reflect the repayment of any advance payment loan taken-out. This is a situation that Beck, Closs-Davies and Gwilym (2019) highlight as causing significant financial distress and plunges many already vulnerable people further into poverty. Adding to this, Guy Standing (2020) has identified Universal Credit to be the most vindictive form of social policy for a century.

What gets measured gets mended

As the discussion above highlights, Welfare is not a devolved policy area for the Welsh Government, Wales therefore, is beholden to decisions that are made by the UK Government at Westminster. However, the Welsh Government does have powers to augment the impact of non-devolved decisions. In terms of welfare, several poverty alleviation initiatives have been launched across Wales providing a softening of some of the harshest impacts of UK Government welfare reforms. As an example, this chapter has already highlighted the work of the Communities First Programme as one such policy response.

Noteworthy here is the Welsh Governments Child Poverty Strategy (2011) a commitment to eradicating child poverty by 2020 as a fundamental priority (Welsh Government, 2014). Admirable as this may have been, the six-year period between the release of the Welsh Child Poverty Strategy evaluation report (2014) and present day has been dogged by stubbornly high figures of child poverty, Universal Credit and food banks. Persistent low-income seems to be, sadly, something of an unshakable issue for Wales as the latest Income Dynamics Report highlights out of the four regions of the UK Wales has the highest levels of children living in persistent low-income households (14 per cent); followed by England and Northern Ireland (12 per cent) and Scotland (10 per cent) (Gov.UK, 2020).

Further to this, 2015 saw the launch of the Well-being of Future Generations (Wales) Act, identifying seven well-being goals that safeguard the wellbeing of future generations. The Act requires that all public bodies across Wales consider the longer-term impact of their decisions conditional upon several key areas. What this means is that decisions made should reflect a sustainable development approach and in doing so should preserve the seven well-being goals of: a prosperous Wales; a resilient Wales; a more equal Wales; a healthier Wales; a Wales of cohesive communities; a Wales of vibrant culture and thriving Welsh language; and, a globally responsible Wales (Well-being of Future Generations (Wales) Act 2015).

The Well-being of Future Generations Act therefore, creates a statutory responsibility for public bodies to protect the well-being of Wales' future generations, thus presenting it as an ideal place for the Welsh Government to measure and mend rising levels of poverty. As the Children's Commissioner for Wales, Sally Holland (2019) highlights, the Well-being of Future Generation Act provides several key areas that stop the intergenerational transmission of poverty within Wales, for example by increasing the life expectancy between the most and least deprived; reducing the educational attainment gap between children who are, and children who are not, eligible for Free School Meals; increasing disposable household income levels; encouraging civic engagement of people; and increasing mental well-being for people.

Here, it is important to state that the intergenerational transmission of poverty is not due to personal failure, argued by political rhetoric such as through the 'Troubled Families Programme'. Persistent poverty that occurs across generations is more readily associated with a multiplicity of underlying structural causes, typically driven by structural intergenerational deprivation (Marmot, 2020). This is evident in places such as rural ex-mining villages of South Wales, whereby the closure of traditional industry created an imposed structural decline for subsequent generations.

The future well-being of Wales

The above discussions tend to paint a rather gloomy representation of the struggles faced across Wales and across all life stages in both rural and urban locations. However, new policies and ways of working highlight that the future should be bright for Wales, especially so if collective approaches are adopted towards tackling persistent levels of poverty. Understanding the nature of poverty, however, is key, as this chapter has so far argued. In taking measurable steps we can better understand poverty, both in terms of causes and of remedies. The work of the Well-being of Future Generations Commission presents itself as the best possible political way forward, especially considering the cutting austerity measures imposed from beyond the Welsh boarder. However, as the emphasis of the Well-being of Future Generations Act makes clear, this is a sustainable development approach that involves more than policy makers.

One new approach, which compliments policy development that is future orientated is Deep Place Thinking. In challenging both rising poverty levels and acknowledging the impact of environmental responsibility, the Deep Place approach challenges both issues head-on as 'twin-wicked' problems, exacerbated by neoliberalism (Adamson, 2017). Furthermore, Deep Place also recognizes poverty and environmental sustainability as being intrinsically linked and policy areas that need to be challenged together. In terms of approach, a Deep Place methodology identifies significant *structural* causes as drivers of environmental issues and poverty, i.e. long-term economic inactivity at the community level (Lang, 2017). Identified as 'causes of causes', these structural drivers also breed other long-term issues associated with poverty. Lang (2017) identifies that reconnecting individuals and their communities with good employment prospects would help in the fight against long-term issues such as poverty and social exclusion, many of which centre on young people's experiences and disengagement with learning.

In such locations, long-term economic inactivity may increase the potential for the transmission of intergenerational poverty, potentially normalizing the situation and encouraging entrenchment (Adamson and Lang, 2017). Again, as a 'cause of causes', in terms of the well-being of future generations; young peoples' academic disengagement encourages a knock-on effect to the sustainability of the local labour market, resulting in an increase in localized poverty, a decline in health outcomes and challenges to local service provision. However, through continued and sustained approach, the potential for community regeneration that is reflective of a Deep Place examination seems to be a perfect fit in maintaining a focus on the well-being of future generations.

Future challenges

At the time of writing the UK and the rest of the World is gripped by the 2020 Coronavirus pandemic. With a state of national emergency called by the Prime Minister Boris Johnson, schools and businesses closed and large swathes of the population currently in forced isolation, it is not clear what the impact will be on the economy. Yet what is clear is that it will likely have a profound impact on any advancements made in reducing the amount of poverty, especially within communities already suffering with deprivation. Based on the Department for Work and Pensions (DWP) data it is currently understood that 500,000 people on one single day applied for UC and totally swamped the system. Online applications per-day are typically 9,751, however, at the start of the lockdown, the DWP saw an 832 per cent increase as people began their UC application due to a sudden loss of employment (Lewis, 2020). Although this is an unprecedented time for social policy in the UK (and Wales) it is clear that having a strong social security, health and welfare safety-net is vital in challenging rising poverty, especially in the face of adversity such as is being caused by the Coronavirus.

Conclusions

As this chapter has shown, the impact of poverty is both a long-term and an intergenerational issue that both the Welsh Government and the UK Government must deal with. Poverty is damaging to people across all life-stages in both urban and rural settings. This, in turn, has a damaging effect on the economy and individual resilience. As this chapter has shown, on a political front, the Welsh Government is restricted through a limited devolution of policy making powers, as Welfare decisions remain with the UK Government. It is this which has been argued to be the structural driver of poverty, currently seen through the Welfare Reform Act 2012 and its associated policies of conditionality.

Child poverty and food poverty are indicative of austere times, as the growth of the emergency food aid landscape exemplify the severity of the current situation. However, the persistent levels of poverty in Wales can be challenged, especially through constructive future-orientated policy approaches. The work of significant Welsh focused poverty alleviation polices, aimed at providing relief, should be commended; chief amongst these is the Well-being of Future Generations Act 2015. This provides a future-orientated approach to challenging inequality in a sustainable development way so as not to hinder future generations.

References

Adamson, D (2017) 'The Deep Place Method' Available: www.deepplace.org/single-post/2017/11/24/The-Deep-Place-Method

Adamson, D and Lang, M (2017) 'Lansbury Park A Deep Place Plan' Available: https://f12f767f-5e18-448a-bb4f-86ccefa3d352.filesusr.com/ugd/920757_6fd4b3d6406e49738168b7fd044fae09.pdf

Alcock, P (2016) 'What is Social Policy' in Alcock, P, Haux, T, May, M and Wright, S (eds.) *The Students Companion to Social Policy*, Chichester, Wiley Blackwell, pp7-14

Barnard, H (2018) 'Poverty in Wales' Available: www.jrf.org.uk/report/poverty-wales-2018

BBC (2020) 'Universal Credit. Inside the Welfare State' Available: www.bbc.co.uk/iplayer/episodes/m000f1xj/universal-credit-inside-the-welfare-state

Beck, D (2018) 'The Changing Face of Food Poverty With Special Reference to Wales' A PhD Thesis Submitted to Bangor University Available: https://rescarch.bangor.ac.uk/portal/files/22198649/2018_Beck_D_PhD.pdf

Beck, D, Closs-Davies, S and Gwilym, H (2019) 'The Equality, Local Government and Communities Committee: Welsh Government' Available: https://research.bangor.ac.uk/portal/files/23156734/BW_14_Dr_David_Beck_Dr_Sara_Closs_Davies_Dr_Hefin_Gwilym_Bangor_University.pdf

Beck, D. and Gwilym, H (2020) 'The Moral Maze of Foodbank Use', *Journal of Poverty and Social Justice*, 28(3): 1-17, DOI: 10.1332/175982720X15905998909942

Cairns, A (2017) 'General Election: Tory Alun Cairns says job is best route out of poverty' Available: www.bbc.co.uk/news/uk-wales-politics-39974811

Denning, S. (2019) 'Voluntary sector responses to food poverty: responding in the short term and working for longer-term change' *Voluntary Sector Review* 10(3): 361-69.

Evans, S (2019) 'How can devolution loosen the hold of child poverty in Wales?' Available: www.jrf.org.uk/blog/how-can-devolution-loosen-hold-child-poverty-wales

Fawcett, J and Gunson, R (2019) 'A 21st Century Skills System for Wales: Challenges and Opportunities' Available: www.ippr.org/files/2019-07/a-21st-century-skills-system-for-wales-july2019.pdf

Fisher, A (2017) *Big Hunger: The Unholy Alliance Between Corporate America and Anti-Hunger Groups* London: MIT Press

Food Cardiff (2018) 'Building Resilience Food Cardiff's Five Year Food Security Plan 2018-2023' Available: www.cardiffandvaleuhb.wales.nhs.uk/sitesplus/documents/1143/Building%20Resilience%20Food%20Security%20Plan.pdf

Fraser, D (1984) *The Evolution of the British Welfare State* London: Macmillan

George, V and Wilding, P (1985) *Ideology and Social Welfare* London: Routledge

Gordon, D (2006) 'The Concept and Measurement of Poverty' in Pantazis, C, Gordon, D and Levitas, R (eds.) *Poverty and Social Exclusion in Britain* Bristol: The Policy Press, pp29-70

Gov.UK (2020) 'Income Dynamics: Income movements and the persistence of low incomes, 2010 to 2018' Available: https://assets.publishing.service.gov.uk/government/uploads/system/uploads/attachment_data/file/875641/income-dynamics-income-movements-and-persistence-of-low-incomes-2010-18.pdf

Holland, S (2019) 'A Charter for Change: Protecting Welsh Children from the impact of poverty' Available: www.childcomwales.org.uk/wp-content/uploads/2019/04/A-Charter-for-Change-Protecting-Welsh-Children-from-the-Impact-of-Poverty.pdf

James, R (2007) 'Communities First: National Assembly for Wales' Available: www.assembly.wales/NAfW%20Documents/tb-07-008.pdf%20-%2028072009/tb-07-008-English.pdf

Jones, L (2014) 'Welsh Index of Multiple Deprivation 2014: A guide to analysing deprivation in rural areas' Available: https://gov.wales/sites/default/files/statistics-and-research/2019-05/welsh-index-of-multiple-deprivation-2014-a-guide-to-analysing-deprivation-in-rural-areas.pdf

Joseph Rowntree Foundation (JRF) (2020) 'UK Poverty 2019/20' Available: www.jrf.org.uk/report/uk-poverty-2019-20 York: JRF

Lambie-Mumford, H (2017) *Hungry Britain. The Rise of Food Charity* Bristol: Policy Press

Lang, M (2017) 'The Deep Place Approach' Available: www.deepplace.org/single-post/2017/10/06/The-Deep-Place-Approach

Lewis, M (2020) 'Don't dismiss universal credit (and other benefits)...' Available: www.moneysavingexpert.com/news/2020/03/coronavirus-self-employed-and-employment-help/?utm_source=MSE_Newsletter&utm_medium=email&utm_term=31-Mar-20-50599902-2903&utm_campaign=nt-hiya&utm_content=2

Marmot, M (2020) Health Equity in England: The Marmot Review 10 Years On. BMJ 2020;368:m693

Office for National Statistics (ONS) (2013) '2011 Census Analysis – Comparing Rural and Urban Areas of England and Wales' Available: www.basw.co.uk/system/files/resources/basw_41648-6_0.pdf

ONS (2019) 'Family spending in the UK: April 2018 to March 2019' Available: www.ons.gov.uk/peoplepopulationandcommunity/personalandhouseholdfinances/expenditure/bulletins/familyspendingintheuk/april2018tomarch2019

ONS (2020) 'Labour market overview, UK: March 2020' Available: www.ons.gov.uk/releases/uklabourmarketmarch2020

Radimer, K L, Olsen, C M, and Campbell, CC (1990) 'Development of Indicators to Assess Hunger' *The Journal of Nutrition* 120(11): 1544-48

Ramesh, R (2011) 'Welfare reform: most radical shake-up for 60 years' Available: www.theguardian.com/politics/2011/feb/17/radical-welfare-reform-analysis

Scott, C, Sutherland, J and Taylor, A (2018) 'Affordability of the UK's Eatwell Guide' Available: https://foodfoundation.org.uk/wp-content/uploads/2018/10/Affordability-of-the-Eatwell-Guide_Final_Web-Version.pdf

Shildrick, T, MacDonald, R, Webster, C and Garthwaite, K (2012) *'Poverty and Insecurity: Life in Low-pay, No-pay Britain'* Bristol: Policy Press

Standing, G (2020) 'Basic Income Now! Blogpost'. Available: www.idler.co.uk/article/why-coronavirus-must-lead-to-a-basic-income-for-all

StatsWales (2014) 'National Survey for Wales Data' Available: https://statswales.wales.gov.uk/Catalogue/National-Survey-for-Wales/2012-13

StatsWales (2019a) 'Welsh Index of Multiple Deprivation' Available: https://statswales.gov.wales/Catalogue/Community-Safety-and-Social-Inclusion/Welsh-Index-of-Multiple-Deprivation

StatsWales (2019b) 'Percentage of all individuals, children, working-age adults and pensioners living in relative income poverty for the UK, UK countries and regions of England between 1994-95 to 1996-97 and 2015-16 to 2017-18 (3-year averages of financial years)' Available: https://statswales.gov.wales/Catalogue/Community-Safety-and-Social-Inclusion/Poverty/householdbelowaverageincome-by-year

StatsWales (2019c) 'Number of pupils taking free school meals on census day by local authority, region and year' Available: https://statswales.gov.wales/Catalogue/Education-and-Skills/Schools-and-Teachers/Schools-Census/Pupil-Level-Annual-School-Census/Provision-of-Meals-and-Milk/pupilstakingfreeschoolmealsoncensusday-by-localauthorityregion-year

StatsWales (2019d) 'Pupils eligible for free school meals by local authority, region and year' Available: https://statswales.gov.wales/Catalogue/Education-and-Skills/Schools-and-Teachers/Schools-Census/Pupil-Level-Annual-School-Census/Provision-of-Meals-and-Milk/pupilseligibleforfreeschoolmeals-by-localauthorityregion-year

Trussell Trust (2019) 'End of Year Stats' Available: www.trusselltrust.org/news-and-blog/latest-stats/end-year-stats

Well-being of Future Generations (Wales) Act (2015) Available: www.legislation.gov.uk/anaw/2015/2/contents/enacted

Welsh Government (2011) 'The Evaluation of Communities First' Available: http://gov.wales/docs/caecd/research/110913-evaluation-communities-first-en.pdf

Welsh Government (2014) 'Evaluation of the Welsh Child Poverty Strategy: Summary of main report' Available: https://gov.wales/sites/default/files/statistics-and-research/2019-07/140709-child-poverty-strategy-wales-final-summary-en.pdf

Welsh Index of Multiple Deprivation (2019) Available: https://gov.wales/sites/default/files/statistics-and-research/2020-02/welsh-index-multiple-deprivation-2019-results-report.pdf

Williams, E (2016) 'Alternatives Approaches to Reducing Poverty and Inequality: Existing Evidence and Evidence Needs' Available: www.wcpp.org.uk/wp-content/uploads/2019/06/Alternative-approaches-to-poverty-reduction.pdf

Williams, E and Doyle, R (2016) 'Rural Poverty in Wales: Existing Research and Evidence Gaps' Available: http://ppiw.org.uk/files/2016/06/An-introduction-to-Rural-Poverty.pdf

Williams, K (2019) 'Welsh Town with more food banks than supermarkets' Available: www.walesonline.co.uk/news/wales-news/welsh-town-more-food-banks-16872815

WLGA (2019) 'Future funding clarity "crucial" for rural communities' future, says WLGA Rural Forum' Available: www.wlga.wales/future-funding-clarity-crucial-for-rural-communities-future-says-wlga-rural-forum

Chapter 4
Ending child poverty in 2020 in Wales?
Martin Elliott

Introduction

The year is 2020 and we should be celebrating the demise of child poverty in the United Kingdom (UK). Sadly, this is clearly not the case and the adverse impact of poverty on many children's lives is still with us. The failure to eradicate child poverty in Wales is not just about statistics and a failure to get the number of children living in poverty below five per cent, but the continuing real-life impact on the lives of children and young people of living in poverty. As reported by the Children's Commissioner for Wales (2019) the day-to-day experiences of poverty of children, young people and their families in Wales still include: going to school hungry; parents struggling to provide food during school holidays; and not being able to afford basic clothing and hygiene products.

This chapter will begin by outlining some of the key social policy milestones, both in Wales and the UK, relating to attempts to eradicate child poverty in the last 15 years. It will then go on to briefly describe the nature and extent of poverty in all its forms. Welsh Government attempts to eradicate child poverty, since devolution, have latterly focused on increasing employment and addressing inequalities. The implications of these approaches, including for social work practice in respect of child welfare inequalities, will be described.

The target of ending child poverty was and remains an ambitious one, perhaps too ambitious. However, it should be placed in the context of the UK being the world's fifth richest economy and that the numbers of children living in poverty has been reduced in recent history to lower than current levels. And yet in Wales approximately 185,000 children currently still live in poverty, representing around 28 per cent of the child population. Whilst child poverty has become stubbornly stuck around this level in recent years, it is estimated that it will increase to closer to 40 per cent of children in Wales by 2021-22.

The ambition to end child poverty in the UK was first articulated by the New Labour Government of Tony Blair in the late 1990s. Blair set out the aim that:

> 'ours is the first generation to end child poverty forever, and it will take a generation. It is a 20-year mission, but I believe that it can be done' (Blair, 1999, p7)

The intention of the Labour Government was to reduce child poverty in the UK by a quarter by 2005 and by half by 2010. In the period between 1998 and 2010 significant inroads were made in the battle to eradicate child poverty in the UK, but despite this both milestones were missed. However, during this period the number of children living in poverty fell by over one million, levels of debt and deprivation fell, and child wellbeing improved (Bradshaw, 2012). Had this progress been maintained the target of ending child poverty would still be achieved by 2027 (Child Poverty Action Group, 2012). The years that subsequently followed these 'good times' (Crowley, 2011: 71) have been characterised by the impact of the global recession and the austerity years in the UK with their devastating impact on children and their families. Child poverty has been rising since 2011-2012, almost entirely in working families (Joseph Rowntree Foundation, 2018). The hope that despite setbacks the target would still be met by 2027 is ebbing away. Progress towards reducing the numbers of families in poverty have become stuck and predictions now paint a gloomy picture of it increasing across the UK and likely to hit 4 million children in the near future.

The Child Poverty Act 2010, introduced by the UK Government, established a set of binding child poverty reduction targets and a duty for the government to have, and report on progress against, a child poverty strategy. The Act also created the Child Poverty Commission, later renamed the Social Mobility and Child Poverty Commission by the Coalition Government. This period saw the coalition government introduce two child poverty strategies which:

> *"did not sufficiently address families' material resources and the high costs they faced, which allowed child poverty to rise as support for families – both financial and in terms of services – was cut as part of the austerity programme"* (Flew, 2020, p11).

By 2016, legislative changes at a UK level had removed the requirement for a child poverty strategy, got rid of income targets and the Commission was renamed, dropping child poverty from its remit. Arguably from 2016, with a UK Government less focused at a policy level on reducing child poverty and introducing benefit changes and other austerity measures that had significant negative impacts on families, a Welsh Government response to child poverty was called for which had a sharpened focus on what a devolved Welsh Government could do to address child poverty. As this chapter will go on to discuss, whilst there is much that has been done by the devolved administration, there is also an argument that the lack of a minister with specific responsibility for co-ordinating action to tackle child poverty and a lack of clear and ambitious action plans has meant insufficient progress has been made towards the target of eradicating child poverty in Wales.

One of the drivers for this increase are welfare and tax reforms driven by the austerity policies of successive UK governments post 2010, but Plaid Cymru and other have argued some of the responsibility for not reducing child poverty in Wales lies with the Welsh Government. In later sections of the chapter this tension between UK and Welsh policies and calls from within Wales for more action will be discussed.

In 2002, Peter Clarke, Wales' first children's commissioner branded the levels of child poverty in Wales 'a national disgrace' (Children's Commissioner for Wales, 2002: 15). Subsequently, a commitment was also made by the Welsh Government to eradicate child poverty in Wales by 2020. How this would be achieved was outlined in the first Child Poverty in Wales Strategy (Welsh Government, 2005) published in 2005. However, 17 years later, as the deadline for achieving this aim approached, Professor Sally Holland, the current children's commissioner for Wales, stated that the Welsh Government's plans to tackle child poverty require a major overhaul. Having considered what has happened in the intervening years and what has been achieved in Wales, the chapter will conclude with discussion of the need for a reinvigorated vision for the eradication of child poverty in Wales – what the Children's Commissioner describes as 'A Charter for Change' (Children's Commissioner for Wales, 2019).

Timeline and key events

In order to understand how we have arrived at the position we find ourselves in, in 2020, it is perhaps useful to briefly summarise some of the key legislation and publications in the past 15 years related to child poverty by both the Welsh and UK Governments.

February 2005 first Welsh child poverty strategy, A Fair Future for our Children, published

February 2010 The Children and Families (Wales) Measure received Royal assent. It placed a duty on Welsh ministers to develop a Child Poverty Strategy for Wales.

March 2010 The UK Child Poverty Act is passed with all-party support. The Act committed successive governments to prioritising the eradication of child poverty by 2020. The act, in conjunction with the Children and Families Wales Measure, provided "a framework of statutory duty stretching from the UK Government, the Welsh Government, through to Local Authorities and named Welsh Government Sponsored Bodies with a view to driving action to eradicate child poverty" (Save the Children, 2012:31).

February 2011 Welsh Government publish its first statutory Child Poverty Strategy, fulfilling the duty placed on ministers by the Children and Families Measure. The strategy covered the period from 2011 to 2014 and set out the strategic objectives for improving the outcomes of low-income households. The strategy reaffirmed the commitment to eradicate child poverty by 2020. Shortly afterwards guidance and regulation were published setting out the duties placed on Welsh authorities to tackle child poverty between 2011 and 2014.

March 2011 the UK Government published its Child Poverty Strategy 'A New Approach to Child Poverty: Tackling the Causes of Disadvantage and Transforming Families' Lives'

July 2012 publication of the Welsh Government Tackling Poverty Action Plan 2012-2016 which outlined the key objectives of their commitment to prevent poverty, help people out of poverty and mitigate the impact of poverty. The Action Plan was praised by the Economic and Social Research Council (ESRC) as an example of the type of broad strategy required to address child poverty in the United Kingdom (ESRC, 2011).

March 2015 following consultation on the strategic aims of the Child Poverty Strategy, a revised strategy is published.

December 2016 publication of the Welsh Government Child Poverty Progress Report, in which the target to eradicate child poverty in Wales was dropped (Welsh Government, 2016)

December 2019 a further child poverty progress report is published by Welsh Government (2019a) outlining progress against the strategic aims of the 2015 Child Poverty Strategy

Definitions, measures, and the scale of child poverty

Wales has the highest relative poverty rate in the United Kingdom, with one in four people living in relative income poverty. Despite the ambition to end child poverty, in 2020, 28 per cent of children in Wales still live in poverty (StatsWales, 2020). That is equivalent to 8 children in a classroom of 30. The definition of poverty used within the Welsh Government's Child Poverty Strategy is:

> "*A long-term state of not having sufficient resources to afford food, reasonable living conditions or amenities or to participate in activities (such as access to attractive neighbourhoods and open spaces) that are taken for granted by others in their society*
> (Welsh Government, 2016, p3)

This definition is one which draws on the work of Townsend (1979) in *Poverty in the United Kingdom: A survey of household resources and standards of living.*
    The most often used measure of child poverty is the relative income measure of child poverty. This measure is based on the number of children living in households below 60 per cent of UK median income. This can be calculated based on either household income before housing costs (BHC) or after housing costs (AHC). It is the measure most often used as it is employed by a range of international institutions such as the Organisation for Economic Co-operation and Development (OECD) and the European Union (EU) and as such enables both national and international comparison over time.

Within the Welsh context 'eradication' was defined as no more than five per cent of children living in a low-income household on the Before Housing Costs (BHC) basis.

Living in poverty as a child can not only blight childhood but can have a significant impact into adulthood too. At birth, a male born in the most deprived local authority in Wales will have a life expectancy on average 4.5 years shorter than their peers born in the least deprived local authority. Those babies are also more likely to have been born with a low birth weight (Public Health Wales Observatory, 2016).

Poverty has a major impact upon levels of educational achievement in Wales. Research undertaken for Save the Children Cymru found that "By age five around a third of children living in poverty (30-35 per cent) were already falling behind across a range of cognitive outcomes (i.e. vocabulary, problem solving, dexterity and coordination) compared with a fifth of those from better-off families (20-21 per cent)" (Save the Children Cymru, 2018, pvii). There is evidence of the effect of poverty on the educational attainment of children from across all stages of their educational journey.

At the UK level, Child Poverty Action Group (CPAG) highlighted that in March 2019: 47 per cent of children living in lone parent households were in poverty; 72 per cent of children growing up in poverty were living in a household where at least one person works; 43 per cent of children living in families with three or more children live in poverty; Children from Black, Asian and Minority Ethnic (BAME) groups are also more likely to be in poverty with 45 per cent living in poverty, compared with 26 per cent of children in White British families (CPAG, 2019).

Not just about the money: understanding poverty in all its forms

Whilst the main indicator used to capture the extent of poverty measures levels of household income, poverty is more than the absence of sufficient money, the experience of living in poverty is multi-dimensional. This is perhaps best captured by the findings of ATD Fourth World research project undertaken in collaboration with Oxford University, 'Understanding poverty in all its forms: A participatory research study into poverty in the UK' (2019). The research is noteworthy not least because it was a collaboration that brought together those with direct experience of living in poverty and those with expertise in research. The research identifies and describes six dimensions that summarise poverty in the UK.

Stigma, blame and judgement – the ways in which poverty "gets under the skin" of individuals resulting in feelings of inferiority and of being undervalued. "Shame and it's opposite, pride, are rooted in the processes through which we imagine others see us" (Wilkinson and Pickett, 2009:41). The shame associated with living in poverty therefore has an impact on personal identity and feelings of being de-valued (Featherstone, White and Morris, 2014). It is also the ways in which being in poverty is misrepresented, which leads to people in poverty being negatively blamed and judged.

Lack of control over choices – the ability for poverty to undermine people's choices, characterised by a lack of good options, which reduces people's control over their lives and traps them in repetitive cycles of hardship, disappointment, and powerlessness.

Unrecognised struggles, skills, and contributions – characterised by a public discourse which too often "undervalues the contribution that people in poverty make to society and to their communities while facing the daily impact of poverty" (ATD Fourth World, 2019, p10).

Damaged health and well-being – the negative impact of poverty on health and well-being, covering everything from an increased likelihood of being born with a low birth weight to shorter average life expectancy (Public Health Wales Observatory, 2016).

Financial insecurity, financial exclusion, and debt – Money and its absence is a key part of what it is to live in poverty, but financial insecurity is also the constant daily stress of worrying about money and making ends meet.

Disempowering systems, structures and policies – poverty caused or made worse by economic, political and social structures as a result of them: disempowering people; not working in the ways people need or want; or exacerbating inequalities as a consequence of systemic cuts to the funding of support.

The six dimensions outlined provide a useful lens through which to consider the impact of social policy at both the Wales and UK levels in relation to child poverty and the extent to which it addresses the issues highlighted by those with lived experience.

From worklessness to in work poverty

The Welsh Government in their 2019 progress report (Welsh Government, 2019a) highlight the reduction in economic inactivity in Wales since devolution. During this period, the number of workless households in Wales fell from 223,000 to 182,000, representing a decline of 18.3 per cent. However, during the same period there has also been a move from children living in poverty being in workless to working households.

The UK Governments overall approach to poverty in the last decade is perhaps best articulated in the 'Five Pathways to Poverty', first put forward in the *Breakthrough Britain* report (Centre for Social Justice, 2006). The five pathways: family breakdown; educational failure; worklessness and dependency; addiction; and serious personal debt have arguably fed a narrative that labels people as being responsible for their poverty by being feckless and lazy. Such narratives have been used as a way of focusing on personal choice and individual agency rather than placing these issues in their structural context. To uncritically promote the idea that just by getting a job people will leave behind poverty is to fail to acknowledge that "working families… in Wales are at greater risk of poverty now than they were a decade ago" (Joseph Rowntree Foundation, 2015).

Whilst employment levels in the UK are currently relatively high, the last decade has seen an increasingly unstable labour market, leading to increased risk of households moving in and out of in-work poverty. In 2018 the Child Poverty Action Group highlighted that in work poverty had been rising at a faster rate than employment (Child Poverty Action Group, 2018). These risks are driven by the rise of zero hours contracts, temporary work, and the rise of the 'gig economy' with its lack of employment law protections including no minimum wage, no sick pay, and no pensions. Arguably, work of itself is not therefore the route out of poverty, but rather stable, decently paid employment and this as we will see later has implications for the Welsh Government approach. Poverty in Wales is driven by employment that is too often poorly paid and insecure, a benefit system that is punitive and which pays insufficient benefits and in where the essentials such as a home and heating are expensive relative to the average income (Bevan Foundation, 2019). Between 2018 and 2019 there was a 35 per cent increase in the number of employees on zero hours contracts in Wales with the figure rising to 50,000, accounting for 3.4 per cent of those employed (Trades Union Congress (TUC) Cymru, 2019). The TUC in Wales must however predominantly direct their calls for improved conditions for workers to the UK rather than Welsh Government.

A focus on inequalities

The Child Poverty Strategy for Wales (Welsh Government, 2015a) included five key priorities. The third of these objectives is focused on reducing the inequalities which exist in the health, education and economic outcomes of children and families living in poverty, by improving the outcomes of the poorest. But such inequalities also manifest themselves in other ways in the lives of children living in poverty. Recent research undertaken in the UK has also highlighted inequalities in child welfare outcomes. The two studies identified a stark connection between social deprivation and child welfare interventions. Children living in the 10 per cent most deprived neighbourhoods in Wales are almost 12 times more likely to be subject to child welfare interventions by the state, such as being subject to child protection procedures or placed in the care of the state, than their peers living in the least deprived neighbourhoods (Elliott, 2020). This 'social gradient' in child welfare interventions is present in all the nations of the UK, but it is steepest in Wales with the largest disparity in intervention rates between the most and least deprived neighbourhoods (Bywaters *et al.*, 2020). Over and above the often-cited impacts of poverty on children and their families, this provides a further example of the wider implications of poverty for families. It has become rather taken for granted that the work of children's social services takes place largely in the poorest communities (Elliott and Scourfield, 2017). What these findings suggests is not only that poverty reduction needs to be at the heart of social work interventions, but that tackling such inequalities should sit alongside health, education and economic inequalities within the framework of social policies designed to tackle child poverty.

The UN rapporteur report

The United Nations Special Rapporteur, Philip Alston, undertook fieldwork during November 2018 for his report on extreme poverty and human rights in the United Kingdom of Great Britain and Northern Ireland (United Nations, 2019). The report highlights the impact of benefit changes introduced by the UK Government on families, identifying the disparate impact of these social support changes on children. The introduction of the so called 'bedroom tax', the imposition of the two-child policy and benefit caps are identified. The impact is also felt in terms of benefits failing to keep pace with the costs that families must meet, because of sub inflationary increases and the current benefits freeze. For example, the report highlights the Child Poverty Action Group finding that in real terms Child Benefit has lost 23 per cent of its value in the last 10 years (CPAG, 2018). The Welsh Government approach in recent years has been to focus on increasing economic prosperity and employment as the gateway to poverty reduction development, but as discussed in the earlier section on in work poverty, the UN rapporteurs report highlighted that work does not guarantee a route out of poverty. 70 per cent of children growing up in poverty in the UK live in households where at least one person works (CPAG, 2019).

The report highlights that in Wales the post of Minister for Communities and Tackling Poverty was scrapped in 2017 and tackling poverty now comes under the portfolio of the Minister with responsibilities for Housing and Local Government. Coming on the heels of the dropping of the target to eradicate child poverty in 2016 this is perhaps indicative of a decline in priority. Also highlighted is that the Welsh Government's Prosperity for All Strategy (Welsh Government, 2017), has no strategic focus or ministerial responsibility for poverty reduction, and lacks clear performance targets and progress indicators.

A family in which both parents are working in jobs that pay the minimum wages, their household income will still fall 11 per cent short of what would be adequate to raise a child (Joseph Rowntree Foundation, 2018). The report further argues that benefit reductions in the last decade have undermined the capacity of recipients "to escape from the grip of poverty (p9)". The UK Government's response to the UN report was to repeat the claim that "there are more people in employment than ever before overlooks inconvenient facts: largely as a result of slashed government spending on services, close to 40 per cent of children are predicted to be living in poverty two years from now… and millions of those who are in-work are dependent upon various forms of charity to cope." (OHCHR, 2019).

The tensions between UK and Welsh Government policies

There is a tension between the actions of the UK Government and their impact on Welsh families and the policies and initiatives brought forward by the Welsh Government. The long-term aim of Welsh Government to loosen the grip of child poverty in Wales was to an extent only ever a realistic ambition if there was also an equal commitment by the UK Government (Joseph Rowntree Foundation, 2019). The UN special rapporteur called upon the UK Government to reverse regressive measures such as the cap on benefits and the two-child limit. Such decisions are currently beyond the scope of devolved powers and therefore to an extent the Welsh Government are hostage to decisions made in Westminster. In the Ministerial Forward to the Child Poverty Progress Report 2019 the Minister rightly highlights the "pressures coming from beyond our borders (Welsh Government, 2019a:5)", such as UK government welfare reforms, which impact on poverty in Wales. There is recognition that actions such as the benefit changes brought about by UK government austerity policies are one of the structural causes behind the increase in poverty in Wales (National Assembly for Wales, 2018).

However, whilst it is right to highlight the impact of UK government policies on the children of Wales that is not to say that more cannot be done by the Welsh Government. It has been argued that whilst Welsh Government may have been overly ambitious in its target of eradicating child poverty in Wales, in other respects its responses to tackling child poverty has lacked such ambition (Joseph Rowntree Foundation, 2019).

The response to child poverty in Wales

Whilst acknowledging the challenges and tensions between what happens at a UK Government level and what can be done here in Wales to address child poverty, it is right to identify the initiatives and positive examples of action that have been taken to support children living in poverty and their families. What is presented here is not exhaustive but is instead intended to give a flavour of initiatives aimed at both helping people out of poverty and to mitigate the impact of poverty for children and their families. It also highlights some of the issues that are behind calls for a more ambitious approach here in Wales.

Flying Start. Whilst support for families with young children, such as Sure Start, has been decimated in England as a consequence of austerity cuts, the Welsh Government has continued to invest in programs of early support and early intervention such as the Flying Start program. However, there is clearly a view that more can be done. Plaid Cymru called for further action to "ensure equal access to high quality early childhood education and care for all children, with a specific focus on providing additional support to all children living in poverty, as recommended by Save the Children Cymru" (Save the Children Cymru, 2018).

Free School Meals. A free school lunch is a lifeline for many children living in poverty. For those on low incomes receipt of a free school meal is worth around £400 a year per child. There are 76,500 children eligible for free school meals, but it is argued there are a further 55,000 children living in poverty who are not eligible (Children's Society, 2018). In April 2019, the Welsh Government introduced a £7,400 income threshold for those claiming Universal Credit, following the introduction of the same threshold in England (Welsh Government, 2019b). This was a consequence of Universal Credit replacing benefits that would not have previously made families eligible for free school meals. Had the cap not been introduced, by the time that Universal Credit has been rolled out fully, Welsh Government predicted that half of all children in Wales would have been eligible for free school meals (Welsh Government, 2019b). Arguably, this was "a missed opportunity, meaning those children who could have benefited in the future will instead continue to miss out". The Welsh Government could, for example, have chosen a more generous threshold as they have in Northern Ireland, where a threshold of £14,000 has been introduced (Children's Society, 2018). The Children's Commissioner has called for a review of the eligibility criteria for Free School Meals and a widening of the threshold to make them accessible to more families. Under the present system, who is identified as being eligible for free school meals is important not only in its own right, but also because of the impact of that decision on accessing further support such as the Food and Fun programme and Pupil Deprivation Grant that we will go on to discuss.

The School Holiday Enrichment Programme (SHEP). In order to address holiday hunger for those children who receive free school meals in term-time, Welsh Government funds a school-based programme that provides healthy meals, food and nutrition education, physical activity and enrichment sessions to children in areas of social deprivation during the summer holidays. The 'Food and Fun' programme is coordinated through the Welsh Local Government Association (WLGA). The scheme, however, is not available across the whole of Wales and the way it is administered can sometimes mean that it is not always accessible to all the families who need it most (Children's Commissioner for Wales, 2019). Whilst the programme received additional funding during 2019/20 to expand its reach, it still only provides support to a fraction of 76,200 families that are eligible for free school meals. This is before the additional 55,000 school age children living in poverty in Wales who are currently not eligible for free school meals are factored in. Whilst programmes such as Free School Meals, 'Food And Fun' and Free Breakfast in Primary Schools (Welsh Government, 2015b), go some way towards the Children's Commissioners vision of ensuring that making 'sure that all children are well fed' (Children's Commissioner for Wales, 2018), arguably there is still more that could and should be done.

Pupil Development Grant (PDG) – Access, is a Welsh Government scheme which provides £125 to children in receipt of Free School Meals (or looked after children) at the point at which they enter year 3 or reception in primary school; or entering year 7 or 10 at secondary school (Welsh Government, 2020). The grant can be put towards the costs of school uniform and sport kits. Again, the research conducted by the Children's Commissioners office highlighted the process for families accessing the grant could be streamlined through automatic enrolment of all children entitled to Free School Meals.

Pupil Deprivation Grant. Introduced in 2011, the grant provides additional funding to schools to plan interventions that focus on improving the attainment of children from deprived backgrounds, specifically those who are eligible for free school meals (Welsh Government, 2015c). The grant focuses on reducing the impact of poverty on educational attainment through two main strategies. Firstly, learning and teaching focused interventions, and secondly, student, family, and community focused interventions (Joseph Rowntree Foundation, 2013).

Council Tax Reduction Scheme. With in-work benefits such as Universal Credit insufficient to overcome the challenges of the labour market for many and keep them out of poverty, Welsh Government schemes such as the Council Tax Reduction Scheme enable families on low income, or claiming certain benefits, to pay some or all of their Council Tax bill. However, benefit changes imposed at the UK level, such as the two-child limit and the removal of the family premium, have had implications for how this is administered in Wales and on the level of support some households receive.

Period Poverty. In April 2019, the Welsh Government announced funding to address period poverty. They allocated a £3.3 million fund available to every school, college, and nursery across Wales to allow them to make sanitary products freely available to any learner who may need them. In addition, a further £220,000 was made available to community spaces such as libraries and hubs. Returning to the ideas of stigma and shame associated with poverty, this initiative addresses period poverty by ensuring the free products are available to women and girls in a practical and dignified way (Children in Wales, 2019). However, period poverty schemes are being developed locally and there is a need for Welsh Government to monitor how these are rolled out (Children's Commissioner for Wales, 2019). Again, a child poverty delivery plan with clear monitoring and targets would enable this to happen systematically.

Conclusions: A charter for change?

So, with the likelihood of ending child poverty in Wales ebbing away, where next? In 2019 the Children's Commissioner for Wales, produced a report: *A Charter for Change: Protecting Welsh Children from the impact of poverty*. The report had the stated aim of stimulating a discussion about the Child Poverty Strategy in Wales, which has not been reviewed since the last iteration published in 2015. The report was also a call for Welsh Government "to publish a Child Poverty Delivery Plan, which sets out short to medium-term actions which will drive tangible changes to the lives of children and young people living in poverty" (Children's Commissioner for Wales, 2019:4). The Children's Commissioner is not the only one to make this call. During the Plaid Cymru debate on child poverty in the Senedd in 2018 there were also calls for "a new plan for eliminating child poverty that includes SMART targets rather than vague statements" (Senedd Cymru/Welsh Parliament, 2018). In developing a new Child Poverty Delivery Plan it has also been suggested milestones could also be mapped across by Welsh

Government to the national indicators towards achieving the seven well-being goals as laid out in the Well-being of Future Generations (Wales) Act 2015 leading to a stronger approach across the life course. These calls for a renewed focus suggest a national policy that has lost its way and needs reinvigorating. With the national target for eradicating child poverty in Wales dropped in 2016; the UN rapporteur highlighting a lack of strategic focus or ministerial responsibility; a lack of a delivery plan with identified actions; and a strategy that has not been revised for five years; a policy that once was trumpeted has sadly in recent years become increasingly side-lined.

As well as a focused delivery plan of actions for Wales, the recommendations of the Children's Commissioner's report also calls for that plan to form the basis of a revised Child Poverty Strategy. Whilst acknowledging the lack of control of some of the key drivers for poverty reduction including power over aspects of work and the social security system, which have been discussed earlier within the chapter, the report highlights much that can be done by Welsh Government, local authorities and schools to reduce the effects of poverty on children in Wales.

The Child Poverty Progress Report 2019 published by Welsh Government includes a commitment to undertake a cross-government review of Welsh Government programmes and services to ensure they have maximum impact on the lives of children, young people and families living in poverty. At the time of writing that review of existing funding programs is underway with a report due to be published in March 2020. The report it states, will include proposals for a future programme of activity and a timetable for delivery based on the recommendations of the review. This will potentially meet the calls from both the Children's Commissioner and Plaid Cymru for a concrete action plan, but there is a question as to why it has been five years since the last published strategy, which has only been reviewed publicly twice during that period. During a period of economic recession and austerity policies (including benefit changes with far reaching implications for families) should there have been more focus on the issue of child poverty in Wales and more done by Welsh Government to support children and their families?

Much of the social policy focus in the last 20 years in Wales has been on preventing people living in poverty or lifting them out of poverty through employment. Whilst an important strand of any social policy approach, with 67 per cent of children living in poverty in Wales in working households perhaps there has been too much focus "on boosting employment without sufficient focus on the type and quality of work or on other issues that contribute to pulling people into poverty" (Joseph Rowntree Foundation, 2019).

The Welsh Government have identified a lack of control over some of the drivers of poverty including control of social benefits. There is exploration of the opportunities for the devolved administration of some benefits with Welsh Government commissioning a study by the Wales Centre for Public Policy (WCPP). The opportunities presented by such devolved administration of aspects of the benefits system is potentially a system that is more compassionate and fairer, and where people are treated with more dignity and understanding (Welsh Government, 2019a). Such a system would not only increase household income but have the potential to work in ways that acknowledge, and address lived experience of poverty and the six dimensions of poverty described earlier (ATD Fourth World, 2019). The vision would be one in which social security is strengthened "so that it fulfils its purpose as a public service anchoring people who are struggling to get by" (Joseph Rowntree Foundation, 2019) and one in which support for low income families includes coordinated and consistent access to income maximisation services that ensure families access all that they are entitled to, whether those benefits are administered in Wales or from Westminster.

References

ATD Fourth World (2019) Understanding Poverty in All its Forms: A participatory research study into poverty in the UK. Accessed online at https://atd-uk.org/projects-campaigns/understanding-poverty

Bevan Foundation (2019) Solving poverty: pipe dream or policy goal? Accessed online at www.bevanfoundation.org/commentary/solving-poverty-pipe-dream-or-policy-goal

Blair, A (1999) Beveridge Lecture, Toynbee Hall, 18th March reproduced in Walker, R (ed.) *Ending Child Poverty: Popular welfare for the 21st century?* Bristol: Policy Press

Bradshaw, J (2012) Chapter two, Child wellbeing in the 2000s in Ending child poverty by 2020: progress made and lessons learned. London: CPAG

Bywaters, P, Scourfield, J, Jones, C, Sparks, T, Elliott, M, Hooper, J, McCartan, C, Shapira, M, Bunting, L, Daniel, B (2020) Child welfare inequalities in the four nations of the UK. *Journal of Social Work* 20(2): 193-215

Centre for Social Justice (2006) Breakthrough Britain. London: Centre for Social Justice. Accessed online at www.centreforsocialjustice.org.uk/policy/pathways-to-poverty

Child Poverty Action Group (2019) Child poverty facts and figures. Accessed online at https://cpag.org.uk/child-poverty/child-poverty-facts-and-figures

Child Poverty Action Group (2018) The cost of a child in 2018. Accessed online at https://cpag.org.uk/sites/default/files/files/CostofaChild2018_web_0.pdf

Child Poverty Action Group (2012) Ending child poverty by 2020: Progress made and lessons learned. Accessed online at www.cpag.org.uk/sites/default/files/CPAG-Ending-child-poverty-by2020-progress-made-lessons-learned-0612.pdf

Children in Wales (2019) Period Poverty. Accessed online at www.childreninwales.org.uk/news/news-archive/period-poverty

Children's Commissioner for Wales (2002) Report and Accounts 2001-2002. Accessed online at www.childcomwales.org.uk/wp-content/uploads/2016/04/Report-and-Accounts-01-02.pdf

Children's Commissioner for Wales (2018) A Wales fit for Children. Accessed online at www.wlga.wales/SharedFiles/Download.aspx?pageid=62&mid=665&fileid=730

Children's Commissioner for Wales (2019) A Charter for Change: Protecting Welsh Children from the Impact of Poverty. Accessed online at www.childcomwales.org.uk/wp-content/uploads/2019/04/A-Charter-for-Change-Protecting-Welsh-Children-from-the-Impact-of-Poverty.pdf

Children's Society (2018) Free school meals in Wales. Accessed online at www.childrenssociety.org.uk/news-and-blogs/our-blog/free-school-meals-in-wales

Crowley, A (2011) Child Poverty in Wales – A Failed Promise? Williams. C. (ed). In *Social Policy for Social Welfare Practice in a Devolved Wales (second edition)*. Birmingham. BASW/Venture Press, pp71-92

Economic and Social Research Council (ESRC) (2011) Child poverty casts a long shadow over social mobility. Evidence Briefing. Accessed on-line at https://esrc.ukri.org/news-events-and-publications/evidence-briefings/child-poverty-casts-a-long-shadow-over-social mobility/#:~:text=Research%20identifies%20a%20range%20of,to%20meet%20child%20poverty%20target.

Elliott, M (2020) Child welfare inequalities in a time of rising numbers of children entering out of home care. *British Journal of Social Work* 50(2): 581-97

Elliott, M and Scourfield J (2017) Identifying and understanding inequalities in child welfare intervention rates. Project Report. [Online]. Child Welfare Inequalities Project. Available at: www.coventry.ac.uk/research/research-directories/current-projects/2014/child-welfare-inequality-uk/cwip-project-outputs

Featherstone, B, White, S and Morris, K (2014) *Re-imagining Child Protection*. Bristol: Policy Press

Flew, L (2020) Why we need a child poverty strategy pp10-18 in Unison. 2020. *Ending child poverty: 20 years on*. London: Unison

Joseph Rowntree Foundation (JRF) (2015) In-work poverty is keeping poverty rates in Wales high. York: JRF. Accessed online at www.jrf.org.uk/blog/work-poverty-keeping-poverty-rates-wales-high

JRF (2013) Poverty and low educational achievement in Wales: Student, family, and community interventions. York: JRF. Accessed online at www.jrf.org.uk/sites/default/files/jrf/ migrated/files/wales-education-poverty-summary.pdf

JRF (2018) UK Poverty 2018. York: JRF. Accessed online at www.jrf.org.uk/report/uk-poverty-2018

JRF (2019) How can devolution loosen the hold of child poverty in Wales. York: JRF: Accessed online at www.jrf.org.uk/blog/how-can-devolution-loosen-hold-child-poverty-wales

National Assembly for Wales (2018) Life on the Streets: Preventing and Tackling Rough Sleeping in Wales. Accessed online at https://senedd.wales/laid%20documents/cr-ld11517/cr-ld11517-e.pdf

Office of the High Commissioner for Human Rights (OHCHR) (2019) UN expert laments UK's 'doubling down on failed anti-poor policies.' Accessed online at www.ohchr.org/EN/NewsEvents/Pages/DisplayNews.aspx?NewsID=24636&LangID=E

Public Health Wales Observatory (2016) Measure Inequalities 2016: Trends in mortality and life expectancy in Wales. Accessed online at www.publichealthwalesobservatory.wales.nhs.uk/measuring-inequalities-2016-files

Save the Children (2012) Child Poverty Snapshots: the local picture in Wales. Accessed online at https://resourcecentre.savethechildren.net/library/child-poverty-snapshots-local-picture-wales

Save the Children Cymru (2018) Little Pieces. Big Picture: Harnessing Early Childhood Education and Care to Make Sure No Child in Wales is Left Behind. Accessed online at www.savethechildren.org.uk/content/dam/global/reports/education-and-child-protection/stc-wales-childcare-report-2017.pdf

Senedd Cymru/Welsh Parliament (2018) NDM6723 – Plaid Cymru debate – Child poverty. Accessed online at https://business.senedd.wales/mgIssueHistoryHome.aspx?IId=22011&Opt=0

StatsWales (2020) Percentage of all individuals, children, working-age adults and pensioners living in relative income poverty for the UK. Accessed online at https://statswales.gov.wales/Catalogue/Community-Safety-and-Social Inclusion/Poverty/householdbelowaverageincome-by-year

Townsend, P (1979) *Poverty in the United Kingdom: A survey of household resources and standards of living* London: Penguin

Trades Union Congress (TUC) Cymru (2019) 35% annual jump in zero hours contracts in Wales: Wales TUC calls for ban. Accessed online at www.tuc.org.uk/news/35-annual-jump-zero-hours-contracts-wales-wales-tuc-calls-ban

United Nations (2019) Report of the Special Rapporteur on extreme poverty and human rights on his visit to the United Kingdom of Great Britain and Northern Ireland. Accessed online at www.bristol.ac.uk/poverty-institute/news/2019/un-rapporteur-final-report.html

Welsh Government (2005) A fair future for our children: The Strategy of the Welsh Assembly Government for Tackling Child Poverty. Accessed online at www.bris.ac.uk/poverty/downloads/keyofficialdocuments/Fair%20Future%20Wales.pdf

Welsh Government (2012) Tackling Poverty Action Plan 2012-2016. Accessed online at https://business.senedd.wales/documents/s500001880/CELG4-20-14%20Paper%205.pdf

Welsh Government (2015a) Child Poverty Strategy for Wales. Accessed online at https://gov.wales/sites/default/files/publications/2019-06/child-poverty-strategy-for-wales-report.pdf

Welsh Government (2015b) Free Breakfast in Primary Schools. Accessed online at https://gov.wales/sites/default/files/publications/2018-03/free-breakfast-in-primary-schools.pdf

Welsh Government (2015b) Pupil Deprivation Grant: Essential guidance. Accessed online at https://gov.wales/sites/default/files/publications/2018-03/pupil-deprivation-grant-essential-guidance.pdf

Welsh Government (2016) Child Poverty Strategy: Assessment of Progress 2016. Accessed online at www.assembly.wales/laid%20documents/gen-ld10867/gen-ld10867-e.pdf

Welsh Government (2017) Prosperity for All: the national strategy Accessed online https://gov.walcs/sites/default/files/publications/2017-10/prosperity-for-all-the-national-strategy.pdf

Welsh Government (2019a) Child Poverty Progress Report 2019. Accessed online at https://gov.wales/child-poverty-strategy-2019-progress-report

Welsh Government. (2019b) Changes to free school meal eligibility criteria – contextual information. Accessed online at https://gov.wales/sites/default/files/publications/2019-03/changes-to-free-school-meal-eligibility-criteria-contextual-information.pdf

Welsh Government (2020) Pupil Development Grant – Access: Guidance. Accessed online at https://gov.wales/pupil-development-grant-access

Wilkinson, R and Pickett, K (2009) *The Spirit Level* London: Penguin Books

Chapter 5

Health Policy in Wales: Two Decades of Devolution

David Matthews

Introduction

As a consequence of the devolution of political power to Wales, Scotland, and Northern Ireland, while all three devolved institutions have limits to their legal and political authority, they have near full control of health and social care provision, with health arguably being the policy sphere from which some of the most significant expressions of difference have emerged throughout Britain during the era of devolution. The result has been the growth of a variegated health agenda, with the decentralisation of decision making allowing for the pursuance of alternative policy programmes.

Prior to devolution healthcare in Wales largely reflected that of England, and on the eve of the establishment of the devolved institutions, as Greer (2016) argues, there was little expectation Wales, Scotland, and Northern Ireland would deviate greatly from the broad health policy agenda reflected throughout Britain. However, by the time of the second round of devolved elections in 2003, clear distinctions were emerging (Greer, 2016). With regards to Wales, Sullivan and Drakeford (2011) argued that by the start of the second decade of the millennium, a sharp divergence of policy characterised health provision in Wales, epitomizing a distinctive 'Welsh way.'

In this chapter the purpose is to provide an overview of the healthcare agenda in Wales throughout the two decades of devolution. Rather than focus on specific policy detail, as is befitting an evaluation of two decades, an illustration will be made of some of the distinctive organisational characteristics, themes, key policy developments, and the central values which have underpinned the organisation of healthcare, in an effort to construct a picture of the Welsh healthcare system during the era of devolution.

The policy context

After a decade of devolution, it was clear, Greer (2009) contended, that among the nations of the UK, Wales had been 'the most radical innovator of health policy.' (Greer, 2009:79). Assertions of the radical nature of Welsh health policy have largely been made in terms of it having developed as part of a wider 'Welsh socialist project' (Davies and Williams, 2009).

Arguably more explicit during the first decade of devolution, largely as a result of efforts at nation building whereby all devolved regions attempted to cultivate their own sense of national identity to inform the political process (Mooney and Williams, 2006), a narrative of 'Welsh socialism' infused political discourse among Welsh governments, all of whom have been dominated by the Labour Party since 1999, either governing on its own or in coalition with other left-orientated parties. A decade after the referendum victory, Drakeford (2008) defined the agenda of all Welsh governments as one of 'progressive universalism.' Moreover, Drakeford and Sullivan (2011) characterised the political platform of Welsh governments as being a commitment to the promotion of equality, social justice and social inclusion.

It is within this ideological context that claims of a radical health agenda in Wales have been made. Sullivan (2004) explicitly identified Welsh health policy as influenced by traditional social democratic values of state intervention and redistribution of wealth. Additionally, Greer (2005:509) argued the era of devolution began in Wales by inheriting a tradition of 'socialist health thinking.' For Davies and Williams (2009:73), health provision in Wales was one that could be considered 'recognisably socialist in aspiration.' In concurrence, Sullivan and Drakeford (2011) asserted the organisation of healthcare in Wales had been established upon a platform of Welsh democratic socialism. This agenda is in stark contrast to England, where, as Greer (2016:20) argues, market values have been more fundamental to influencing the structural organisation of the English NHS over the last two decades.

Aspirations to achieve a society underpinned by a progressive left-wing agenda, has, to varying degrees of influence and success, framed the discourse surrounding the organisation and delivery of healthcare in Wales during the era of devolution. Emerging from this political agenda, it can be argued five core values have acted as the foundations upon which the organisation of healthcare has been established. Being the focus of attention to a greater or lesser extent during the last twenty years, these values have been collaboration, localism, democratic participation, public health and well-being, and public provision.

Collaboration, localism, and participation

Made explicit during the early years of devolution in *Making the Connections: Delivering Better Public Services for Wales* (Welsh Assembly Government, 2004), a clear rejection was made in Wales of a competitive approach to the provision of public services, as is characteristic of the influence of market values on provision, as was already a feature of England at the time (Greer, 2005:507). In Wales, collaboration was favoured, with the creation of more cohesive and integrated provision. Identified as a central partner in the delivery of collaborative public services was the service user, with it being strenuously argued that enhanced democratic accountability must be at the heart of delivery. Rejecting the notion that service users are customers, as they are often constructed as being within market-orientated services, instead they were firmly understood as citizens, which conferred ownership of public services upon them. Consequently service users were to have the opportunity to participate in their delivery. To encourage this, there emerged the notion that services should be centred within local communities.

Applied to health, collaboration and localism, Greer (2005) argued, had significantly influenced the organisation of healthcare provision in Wales during the early years of devolution, with efforts to devolve the centre of decision-making regionally, enhancing the role of local authorities (LAs), and integrating, to a greater degree, healthcare with social services. From the beginning, Sullivan and Drakeford (2011) argue, a 'Welsh way' to health was grounded in a localist impulse, which, for Davies and Williams (2009:63), was a 'resolutely progressive' approach.

A significant initial effort to embed the values of collaboration and localism within the provision of health was the replacement of Primary Care Trusts in 2003 with Local Health Boards (LHBs). Originally numbering 22, having originally been coterminous with each LA, reorganisation in 2009 reduced their number to seven. Consisting of representatives of GPs, children's services, social services, and the voluntary sector, among other stakeholders, it was argued they would better reflect local needs (Greer, 2005:509-10) by supporting collaboration between professionals grounded upon an enhanced awareness of local priorities (Sullivan and Drakeford, 2011). Central to the introduction of LHBs were efforts to enhance the relationship between LAs and health providers. By pooling resources between them, it was expected local health and social care needs would be met through a process of joint planning to support the promotion of local, regional, and national health and social care objectives.

Additionally, collaboration can be exemplified further with the establishment under the Social Services and Well-being (Wales) Act 2014 of Regional Partnership Boards (RPBs). With the onus on social care, seven RPBs, reflecting the boundaries of all seven LHBs, have been tasked with solidifying the integration of social services with healthcare provision through the development of co-ordinated partnership arrangements between providers based upon regional population needs. It is expected that RPBs prioritise the integration of services for older people with long-term and complex needs, learning disabilities, children with complex needs due to learning disabilities, and provision for carers. Members must include representatives of LAs, LHBs, social services, the voluntary sector, care providers, and service users. RPBs have the authority to commission, manage and develop services at the regional level.

The principles of localism and collaboration have also emerged as the foundations upon which the notion of integrated care in Wales has been pursued. Although, as Lewis (2015) argues, the establishment of LHBs were intended to act as the mechanism by which local health services were brought into alignment, for much of the era of devolution there has been little sole focus on integrated care. Instead, it has been made reference to while pursuing other healthcare priorities (Lewis, 2015). However, in *A Healthier Wales: Our Plan for Health and Social Care*, integrated care was explicitly identified as integral to the Welsh Government's health priorities (Welsh Government, 2018a:3).

As part of a 'whole system' approach to the provision of healthcare, influenced by an extensive Parliamentary Review in 2018, the health agenda of the Welsh Government moving forward into the third decade of the twenty first century was to solidify further the focus on the co-ordinated delivery of health and social care services at the community level. A co-ordinated partnership approach would be epitomised, it was argued, by professionals, community volunteers, family and friends, collaborating to deliver the health and social care needs of service users at the local level (Welsh Government, 2018a:9). In organisational terms, RPBs have been identified as central to the integration of care. They have been given the responsibility of co-ordinating and encouraging local level partnerships and models of service delivery. In particular facilitating the operation of over sixty primary care clusters located throughout Wales. Working together, RPBs and primary care clusters are expected to interpret national policy agendas in a manner relevant for communities.

Despite the emphasis placed upon collaboration in Wales, it is by no means uniquely associated with Wales. For instance, RPBs are broadly akin to Scottish Integration Joint Boards (IJBs), whereby the Scottish NHS and LAs delegate the responsibility for planning and resource allocation to IJBs for adult health and social care services, in an effort to integrate services. Similarly, in England, while competition and a fragmentation of services have been common characteristics of health and social care during the last two decades, Health and Wellbeing Boards (HWBs) were established as part of the Health and Social Care Act 2012. Found in all English LAs, they are charged with the task of producing a joint health and social care assessment of needs for the locality, upon which methods of integrating health and social care services are proposed. Unlike RPBs in Wales and IJBs in Scotland, however, HWBs do not have the authority to commission services.

While not unique to Wales, a collaborative approach to service provision has indeed characterised Welsh health and social care delivery. Furthermore, 'localism,' and a devolution of delivery to more regional and local levels, has infused this approach Yet, an element of caution is required in suggesting that this has enhanced greater democratic engagement. For Hughes, *et al.* (2009) efforts to stimulate public involvement in the provision of healthcare in Wales was, to some extent, reflected in organisational reform of services, as exemplified by LHBs, under the guise that local collaborative services would be more representative. However, as Wallace (2019:93) argues, there exists the risk of confusing the integration of local state services, and notions of partnership practices, with enhanced public participation, with there being no guarantee the devolution of state services and their collaboration will include the service user.

That there exists a weakness regarding service user participation was evidenced by the 2018 *Parliamentary Review of Health and Social Care in Wales* (Welsh Government 2018b:18), which stated 'there needs to be much stronger effort to find out what users think of the care they have received…and that this information is regularly incorporated into the management of care at local and national level.' There should exist a greater effort, it was proclaimed, to encourage members of the public to be actively involved in the creation of new models of service provision, especially at the local level. In response, the Welsh Government (2018) accepted there existed a need to construct an infrastructure which allowed for the comprehensive engagement of the public in the management, delivery and construction of services.

Public health and well-being

As the era of devolution began, it soon emerged that central to a devolved healthcare programme in Wales would be public health. For Davies and Williams (2009:74), Greer (2009:338), and Sullivan and Drakeford (2011), the first decade of devolution illustrated that the attention given to public health by Welsh governments was greater than that by their English and Scottish counterparts. For Davies and Williams (2009:74) the focus given to public health was illustrative of a wider acknowledgement that health was not to be considered just a biological phenomenon, but greatly influenced by societal determinants. Health policy in Wales, they argued, adopted a holistic position, with health recognised as determined by a 'full range of social, economic and environmental factors, not simply as a universal, undifferentiated attribute that can be maintained or restored by various discrete treatments.' (Davies and Williams, 2009:74). Within this context, health services were understood as one among many methods to promote good health. As Drakeford (2006a:548) argued, the NHS in Wales was viewed as 'but one powerful tool in a far wider set of measures needed to address the determinants of health.'

Inextricably related to the notion that societal determinants shape the distribution and experience of health has been that Wales, like many nations, is characterised by health inequalities. With little controversy it has been accepted in Wales that health inequalities have their origins in wider social and economic inequalities, operating at the macro level and influencing micro level lifestyles. That health inequalities blight Wales can be illustrated with recourse to various phenomena, with the impact of the COVID-19 pandemic in 2020 one such example, being without doubt the greatest public health challenge experienced during the era of devolution. Its impact in Wales, as within other regions of Britain, was most acute in regions of high deprivation. Using the Welsh Index of Multiple Deprivation, it can be illustrated that between the 1st March and 31st May 2020, the fifth most deprived localities in Wales had a death rate per 100,000 of the population nearly double that of the least fifth deprived (ONS, 2020). Moreover, susceptibility to contracting COVID-19 was influenced by various existing conditions, such as respiratory, dietary, and cardiovascular conditions, which themselves are related to socio-economic inequalities. Thus illustrating the extent to which the experience and consequence of wider social and economic inequalities influenced the spread of COVID-19 and its regional severity throughout Wales.

By emphasising macro determinants of health, and inequalities related to them, an argument can be made this explicitly illustrates an attempt to pursue a more radical health agenda in Wales. As Richmond and Germov (2012:477) argue, focusing on individual lifestyles tends to be a more conservative approach, adopting a victim-blaming position, in comparison to the potentially more radical agenda of improving health with attempts to correct the structural causes of ill-health. Acknowledgement of the need to focus on the macro determinants of health in Wales, Davies and Williams, (2009:73) argue, was another example of the Welsh healthcare agenda reflecting socialist health ideals, as it accepted the detrimental role social inequalities have for individuals.

This has been in contrast to England, where more individualistic approaches to health prevention have prevailed. For much of the period from the late 1990s to the early years of the Coalition Government, Longley (2012:49-50) argued, rather than the state attempting to intervene in society and rectify structural determinants of ill-health, in England the dominant health prevention paradigm was characterised by attempts to balance support offered by government to help people live healthier lives and make healthier informed choices on the one hand, but limiting intervention so as to protect personal freedoms on the other.

With wider social and economic inequalities acknowledged as significantly determining health inequalities in Wales, greater equality within society was recognised as essential to promoting positive health. As Drakeford (2006b:51) argued, the Welsh health agenda was to be seen as imbued with a 'radical shift from the politics of equality of opportunity, to the far more fundamental politics of equality of outcome.'

On a micro scale, legislatively, the Public Health (Wales) Act 2017 has gone some way to demonstrating the prevention agenda. Among other initiatives, the legislation required the implementation of a national strategy preventing and reducing obesity levels, as well as restricting further those public spaces where it is acceptable to smoke in an effort to reduce its visibility. It is, arguably, however, with the Well-being of Future Generations (Wales) Act 2015, that more radical intentions for the promotion of good health have been exhibited, focusing upon wider structural conditions in an effort to promote the more holistic ideal of well-being.

Well-being, as Longley (2012:55) argues, has been a dominant concern for the devolved nations, and thus its is not unique to Wales. As Wallace (2019:46) claims, Scotland was the first nation within the UK to implement a well-being framework, doing so in 2007, influencing policy development across government. With Northern Ireland, incidentally, being the last to implement any significant well-being strategy (Wallace, 2019:104). Wales, however, Wallace (2019:74) contends, has in recent years surged to the global forefront on issues of well-being as a result of the Well-being of Future Generations legislation.

Anticipating the agenda of a devolved healthcare system, in 1998 the enhancement of well-being was emphatically emphasised as a core principle upon which a Welsh healthcare programme would be established. In *Better Health Better Wales* (Welsh Office, 1998), a clear conceptualisation of health was adopted of it being not just a biomedical phenomenon, but equated with well-being. Positive well-being was predicated upon the creation of favourable social, cultural, and economic conditions, with it accepted there exists certain societal determinants conducive to the promotion of positive well-being. Subsequently, permeating all Welsh government's understanding of well-being has been a societal definition, one which views individual well-being as related to the wider social context.

Four years later the relationship between health and well-being was strengthened. In *Well Being in Wales* (Welsh Assembly Government, 2002), it was made explicit that well-being was determined by a mixture of social, economic, and cultural factors, with economic and social policy subsequently having a vital role to play. While biomedical circumstances were recognised as important, it was clearly identified as only one aspect of what constituted greater well-being.

The centrality of well-being to the promotion of positive health arguably culminated in the Well-being of Future Generations (Wales) Act 2015. Being infused by a societal definition of well-being, the legislation has compelled all public bodies in Wales to promote the social, environmental, economic, and cultural well-being of both current and future generations, to maximise national well-being goals. In the process, the desire to promote collaboration and partnership working has continued, with the establishment of Public Service Boards (PSBs). With each LA having a representative PSB, their primary purpose is the enhancement of the social, cultural, economic, and environmental well-being of the locality, being mandated to achieve this through co-ordinated action in those areas of public service delivery where collaboration is thought to be most needed. For Wallace (2019:86) this is indicative of the Welsh Government acknowledging that the promotion of well-being can only be tackled through joined-up methods.

While collaboration is embedded within the legislation, criticism has emerged regarding a potential democratic deficit. The national well-being goals, Wallace (2019:93) argues, do not emphasise participation in efforts to realise them, nor do any of them explicitly relate to democratic concerns. As a consequence, as Wallace (2019:94) proclaims, there risks a disconnect between the well-being goals and indicators of measurement on the one hand, and the well-being needs of citizens on the other.

The attention given to public health has not been without its critics. In the first decade of devolution, this focus was argued to have occurred at the expense of concentrating upon the provision of secondary care, in particular hospital waiting times (Greer, 2005), as finances were perceived to be directed towards public health measures rather than the day-to-day delivery of services and investment in resources. Related to this was the very public rebuking by Welsh Ministers in the period between 2000-05 of a target-driven performance agenda, with Wales initially rejecting such an approach in relation to waiting times, with Scotland also demonstrating antipathy, in comparison to England who embraced it, as did, to a lesser extent, Northern Ireland. However, what was dubbed 'targets and terror' (Bevan and Hood, 2006) proved successful, with waiting times in England, relative to other devolved nations, notably declining (Timmins, 2013:13).

In response to criticism, a renewed focus in Wales was directed towards cutting waiting lists, mirroring the prevailing ethic of the English NHS. The result, Sullivan and Drakeford (2011) argued, was a success, with a notable reduction in the length of waiting times the numbers of service users waiting. Nonetheless, at the start of the third decade of the millennium, waiting times remain higher in Wales, with the absolute number of service users in Wales waiting twelve hours or more in A&E having progressively increased since 2013.

Additional criticisms of the public health agenda in Wales are reflected in questions concerning to what extent Welsh governments, given their authority, are in a position to mitigate against the wider impact of negative societal determinants of health and well-being. In particular, whether the legislative intentions of the Well-being of Future Generations (Wales) Act 2015 are obtainable. Moreover, with budgetary constraints on public bodies, and the funding arrangements of Welsh governments being determined on an annual basis by central government, this, Wallace (2019:98) asserts, constitutes a challenge to sustained long-term efforts to enhance well-being as defined by the legislation.

While public health has been central to the Welsh healthcare agenda, with the significance of social and economic inequalities acknowledged, not having the authority to intervene quantitatively and qualitatively as required calls into question the very effectiveness of a core health policy principle in Wales. As one of the most significant public health threats experienced for a century, the unequal impact of COVID-19 on Wales, for example, illustrates that for all the discursive rhetoric and policy intentions over the last twenty years, the available resources to Welsh governments, as well as their lack of authority over fiscal policy and social security, has meant that efforts in Wales to combat those social and economic inequalities contributing to the unequal experience of public health issues, such as COVID-19, have largely been limited in their impact at best.

Public provision and ownership

The dominant paradigm for the last three decades in Britain has been to organise healthcare within a context of competitive market relations (Humber, 2019:27). However, as has already been stated, a key characteristic in Wales during the era of devolution, has been to limit the incursion of free market values within the organisation of healthcare.

For much of the last three decades, public healthcare systems of many Western European countries have increasingly succumbed to free market reforms (Gaffney and Muntaner, 2018; Humber, 2019; Schrecker and Bambra, 2015). Such developments have included expanding the use of private finance, increasing out-of-pocket payments, encouraging service users to opt for private insurance for some treatments, and implementing internal market restructuring. In Wales, however, a decisive attempt has been made to combat the incursion of market values and competition within the organisation of healthcare, as illustrated by the restructuring of LHBs in 2009.

Following Scotland in 2004 which implemented similar arrangements, the reorganisation of LHBs in 2009 encouraged the abolition in Wales of the market-driven split between purchaser and provider. Prior to this the NHS in Wales, similar to England, was characterised by an internal market, with a separation between LHBs which planned and commissioned healthcare and its provision delivered by NHS Trusts. Since 2009, however, Welsh governments have dismissed the notion of an organisational distinction between institutions who finance and purchase healthcare, and those who deliver it. This has resulted in a rejection of the principles underpinning this model, in particular the argument that competition between providers encourages efficiency and cost effectiveness, and is more responsive to service user needs. Here, as elsewhere, the principles of collaboration have dominated.

This repudiation of free market values was recognised by the Organisation for Economic Co-operation and Development (OECD) who acknowledged 'Wales has chosen to abolish the purchaser-provider split and does not accept that competition is the best driver for quality improvement' (OECD, 2016). Abandoning this model, Wales has firmly grasped a 'top-down' unified approach, one where there exists a coherent organisational chain emerging from the Welsh Government down to LHBs.

Each LHB plans, designs, and delivers primary and secondary healthcare regionally, collaborating with local government. Originating from the Welsh Government, an initial strategic health plan for the whole of Wales is devised based largely upon policy goals and targets set at the national level. From this, LHBs implement the strategy in accordance with the health needs of their regions. On this basis, in Wales the state remains the central coordinator, with LHBs being regional administrative state providers of the NHS, implementing a nationally organised health plan and being answerable to the Welsh Government. The extent to which the government in Wales plans healthcare was, again, recognised by the OECD (2016) who argued the Welsh NHS is 'a "planned" system, based upon unified decision making and integration of service delivery, and a systematic planning cycle.'

The organisational structure of the Welsh NHS contrasts with England, which, since the enactment of the Health and Social Care Act 2012, has been witness to a further solidification of the internal market. Under the Health and Social Care act the purpose of the state has evolved to primarily funding the provision of healthcare, with it increasingly relinquishing its role as provider, entrusting this to NHS England, a semi-autonomous public body. The transformative role of the government in England was also recognised by the OECD, who argued that with many of the government's responsibilities for commissioning care and ensuring increased quality have now been transferred, the government had become more of a strategic body.

Being responsible for much of the health budget, NHS England reallocates much of this to approximately two hundred local Clinical Commissioning Groups (CCGs), independent of government, and accountable to NHS England, who commission services. Being cloaked in the language of consumer choice and anti-competitive practice, CCGs have competition rules imposed upon them. These measures enshrine into law the requirement that the private sector must have an opportunity to deliver health services.

Coterminous with rejecting the internal market has been to subsequently limit the use of private capital and services. In 2013, the then Welsh First Minister, Carwyn Jones, made explicit his opinion of the English NHS, being 'a health service…that is being wrecked and privatised' (Moon, 2013). Rejecting market interventions within healthcare, this sentiment built upon similar assertions made by his predecessor. In 2007, after the establishment of the coalition Government between Labour and Plaid Cymru, firm opposition to the use of the private sector within the Welsh NHS was made explicit. In a joint statement it was argued 'We firmly reject the privatisation of NHS services or the organisation of such services on market models. We will guarantee public ownership, public funding and public control of this vital public service' (Welsh Assembly Government, 2007). In 2016 Welsh Labour's opposition to privatisation continued, arguing in its manifesto 'we have stood firm against privatization and will keep the profit motive out of our Welsh NHS' (Welsh Labour Party, 2016).

The extent to which the private sector is involved in the NHS throughout Britain is hotly contested given the limited data that is made available. Nevertheless, in 2017-18, NHS expenditure in Wales directed towards private and voluntary sector organisations amounted to 1.4 per cent of the total Welsh NHS budget invested directly in the delivery of services. During the last decade, similar figures have existed for Scotland. In comparison, in England, the combined expenditure of all CCGs directed towards non-NHS bodies in 2017-18 amounted to 11.8 per cent of total operating expenditure.

Despite this there has not been a wholesale rejection of the private sector within the Welsh NHS. In 2017, the Welsh Government proposed tentatively to make use of its own public-private partnership in the form of the mutual investment model (MIM) for limited services. However, arguably the concious effort to limit the extent to which market principles underpin the provision of healthcare, and to ensure organisation is modelled on a centrally administered state service, has meant the Welsh NHS has evolved in a manner over the last two decades which defies the trajectory of many healthcare systems, not just England, but throughout Western Europe (Matthews, 2017).

Conclusions

Surveying the broad evolution of healthcare in Wales during the first two decades of devolution, while caution must exist in overstating the case, it is nonetheless reasonable to contend that a distinct political vision, based upon social democratic values, has broadly shaped its organisation. In doing so, as Sullivan and Drakeford (2011) argued, contributing to a 'Welsh way.' Commonly, assertions of a 'Welsh way' are made as a means of suggesting Wales is unique among the nations of the UK in terms of its policy agenda. And while diversity does characterise health and social care across the UK, claims Wales is distinctly unique, barring clear individual policy differences, can only be made with varying degrees of accuracy.

In comparison to England, it is undoubtedly the case that diverging policy paths have been pursued, primarily as a result of distinctly different political values underpinning the health agenda of both Wales and England. As such devolution has made but a distant memory the era prior to devolution when, as remarked at the start of the chapter, the health systems of both nations largely mirrored each other. Moreover, similarities exist between the Northern Irish health service and that of England, largely as a result of the influence of a market agenda within the wider provision of social policy in Northern Ireland (Horgan and Gray, 2012). It is with Scotland, however, where greater similarity exists. With all devolved governments adopting a broad centre-left position since the inception of devolution, a similar policy trajectory has been pursued, and in some cases to a greater degree given the authority of the Scottish Parliament. Scotland and Wales have followed broadly similar paths in relation to abolishing the internal market, having regional collaboration as central to the delivery of services, having well-being at the centre of a health agenda, and limiting the use of the private sector relative to England.

While the validity of claims to Wales being unique are mixed at best, a 'Welsh way,' rather than focusing on differences between Wales and the rest of the UK, should instead be predicated on the values and principles which have shaped the Welsh health agenda. As illustrated here, the principle values shaping this agenda over the last twenty years include collaboration replacing competition, the state retaining a commanding role in the ownership of facilities and delivery of services, the intellectual and policy acceptance to focus attention on macro social and economic inequalities with greater social equality paramount to good health, and infusing this whole agenda has been acknowledgement of the need to enhance democratic accountability.

Certainly, in practice, the success of this agenda can be questioned. With some justification, it can be argued the Wales' public health agenda can be considered ambitious for any Welsh Government who does not have full control over fiscal policy as well as specific social security measures. Moreover, democratic participation has been limited. Furthermore, while waiting times in Wales remain higher than in England, as long as a market-orientated agenda remains a dominant political and economic paradigm elsewhere, Welsh governments who continue to limit the role for the private sector will always be susceptible to the criticism that they are obstructing the expansion of capacity and the introduction of more efficient organisational practices.

These limitations in practice are real, and can have potentially real consequences, pressing upon service users day-to-day experience of healthcare and wider efforts to enhance citizen well-being. However, the broader picture of healthcare in Wales during the first two decades of devolution, this 'Welsh way,' is one of an attempt, relative to other healthcare systems of similar countries, to construct a progressive alternative to the market-inspired reforms of other health systems, and promote a healthy society, not just through challenging behaviour, but through recognising that society itself must change through the pursuance of greater equity.

References

Bevan, G and Hood, C (2006) 'Targets and gaming in the English public health system' *Public Administration* 84(3): 517-38

Davies, N and Williams, D (2009) *Clear Red Water: Welsh devolution and socialist politics*. London: Francis Boutle Publishers

Drakeford, M (2006a) 'Health Policy in Wales: Making a difference in conditions of difficulty' *Critical Social Policy* 26(3): 543-61

Drakeford, M (2006b) 'To those that Have' *Agenda* (spring 2006), pp50-51

Drakeford, M (2008) 'Progressive Universalism' in Osmond, J (ed) *Unpacking the Progressive Consensus* Cardiff: Institute of Welsh Affairs, pp48-55

Gaffney, A and Muntaner, C (2018) 'Austerity and Healthcare' in Waitzkin, H (ed) *Healthcare under the Knife: Moving beyond capitalism for our health*. New York: Monthly Review Press, pp119-36

Greer, S L (2005) 'The Territorial Bases of Health policymaking in the UK after Devolution' *Regional and Federal Studies* 15(4): 501-18

Greer, S L (2009) 'Devolution and Divergence in UK Health Policies' *British Medical Journal* 338, pp78-80

Greer, S L (2016) 'Devolution and health in the UK: policy and its lessons since 1998' *British Medical Bulletin* 118, pp17-25

Horgan, G and Gray, A M (2012) 'Devolution in Northern Ireland: A lost opportunity?' *Critical Social Policy* 32(3): 467-78

Hughes, D, Mullen, C, Vincent-Jones, P (2009) 'Choice vs Voice? PPI policies and the repositioning of the state in England and Wales' *Health Expectations* 12, pp237-50

Humber, L (2019) *Vital Signs: The deadly costs of health inequalities* London: Pluto Press

Lewis, M (2015) 'Integrated Care in Wales: A summary position' *London Journal of Primary Care* 7(3): 49-54

Longley, M (2012) 'Wellbeing: A Guiding Concept for Health Policy?' in Walker, P and John, M (eds.) *From Public Health to Wellbeing: The new driver for policy and action.* Basingstoke: Palgrave Macmillan, pp47-57

Matthews, D (2017) 'The Battle for the NHS: England, Wales and the socialist vision' *Monthly Review* 68(10): 25-35

Moon, D S (2013) 'Welsh Labour in Power? 'One Wales' vs 'One Nation'?' *Renewal: a journal of social democracy*, 21(1): 77-86

Mooney, G and Williams, C (2006) 'Forging 'New Ways of Life'? Social Policy and Nation Building in Devolved Scotland and Wales' *Critical Social Policy*, 26(3): 608-29.

Office for National Statistics (ONS) (2020) Deaths involving COVID-19 by local area and socioeconomic deprivation: deaths occurring between 1 March and 31 May 2020. Accessed online: www.ons.gov.uk/peoplepopulationandcommunity/birthsdeathsandmarriages/deaths/bulletins/deathsinvolvingcovid19bylocalareasanddeprivation/deathsoccurringbetween1marchand31may2020#welsh-index-of-multiple-deprivation

Organisation for Economic Co-operation and Development (2016) *OECD Review of Health Care Quality: United Kingdom 2016 rising standards.* Paris: OECD

Richmond, K and Germov, J (2012) 'A Sociology of Health Promotion' in Germov, J *Second Opinion: An introduction to health sociology.* Oxford: Oxford University Press, pp 476-98

Schrecker, T and Bambra (2015) *How Politics Makes Us Sick: Neoliberal Epidemics.* Basingstoke: Palgrave Macmillan

Sullivan, M (2004) 'Wales, devolution and health policy: Policy differentiation and experimentation to improve health' *Contemporary Wales* 17(1): 44-65

Sullivan, M and Drakeford, M (2011) in *Social Policy for Social Welfare Practice in a Devolved Wales* 2nd Edition (ed. Williams, C). Birmingham: BASW/Venture Press

Timmins, N (2013) *The four UK health systems: Learning from each other.* London: The Kings Fund

Wallace, J (2019) *Wellbeing and Devolution: Reframing the role of government in Scotland, Wales and Northern Ireland.* Basingstoke: Palgrave Macmillan

Welsh Assembly Government (2002) *Well Being in Wales.* Cardiff: Welsh Assembly Government

Welsh Assembly Government (2004) *Making the Connections: Delivering better public services for Wales.* Cardiff, Welsh Assembly Government

Welsh Assembly Government (2007) *One Wales. A progressive agenda for the Government of Wales: An agreement between the Labour and Plaid Cymru groups in the National Assembly.* Cardiff: Welsh Assembly Government

Welsh Government (2018a) *A Healthier Wales: Our Plan for Health and Social Care*. Cardiff: Welsh Government
Welsh Government (2018b) *Parliamentary Review of Health and Social Care in Wales – A Revolution from Within: Transforming health and care in Wales*. Cardiff: Welsh Government https://gov.wales/sites/default/files/publications/2018-01/Review-health-social-care-report-final.pdf
Welsh Labour (2016) *Together for Wales*. Cardiff: Welsh Labour Party
Welsh Office (1998) *Better Health Better Wales*. Cardiff: Welsh Office

Chapter 6
Housing as a Social Issue
Edith England & Helen Taylor

Introduction

It is easy to consider 'housing' as a physical structure, in a specific place, that either does or does not meet individuals' or households' particular physiological needs. Indeed, it is often the inability of housing to meet needs, or the lack of access to housing in the first place, that demonstrates its importance to wellbeing in both a physiological and emotional sense. As King (2015) outlines, if housing is working well there should be a sense of contentedness and complacency; we should enjoy the 'banality of the ordinary' (p37). Kemeny (1995, p174) asserts that 'the ability of housing to structure the lives of ordinary people is profound'. There are a variety of interconnections to consider here. Housing in a material sense impacts on our physical and mental health. Where our housing is situated within the broader physical and social environment also impacts on our wellbeing. These connections have been starkly highlighted in the context of the COVID-19 crisis, where individuals' activities have been confined to and defined by where they call home. When considering housing as a social issue in the context of this chapter, it is important to note both the physical and emotive impact of housing on the lives of individuals and communities. Moreover, the spaces that individuals call home and the lack of access to somewhere to call home can both be harmful (Gurney, 2020). This chapter looks at the different ways in which these spaces called home are provided for by the state in a Welsh context. Issues relating to housing, home, and homelessness are often generic, spanning both national and international borders. These issues as experienced by individuals, however, are impacted by a variety of factors such as socio-economic status, health status, household size and type. The focus of this chapter is the response to these issues from the Welsh Government in the form of policy and legislation; how a 'made in Wales' approach to housing as a social issue has been developed, and how this relates to issues of equality and social justice.

When discussing housing as a social issue we are in fact discussing a broad set of ways that the state can meet the needs of those who cannot meet their own needs through the market. This can be described in terms of political obligation – that the state (Welsh Government) recognises that it has a role in providing housing for those who are unable to meet this need for themselves. How this obligation is met can occur through a variety of mechanisms. In the first instance, individuals might find themselves homeless – the state has a set of duties to these individuals based on a variety of legislative tests. The legislation relating to this, and the process by which needs are met in this context is the focus of section one. Second, once there has been a recognition that individuals qualify for the provision of housing of some form, this can be delivered either through the Private Rented Sector (PRS) or through the social sector which includes local authority and housing association housing. The social sector is the subject of section two and the PRS, the subject of section three. In these sections we will be outlining the 'made in Wales' approach to policy and legislation in these areas, with a focus on understanding how the needs of individuals and households are met through social housing in the broadest sense. The final two sections critically evaluate where this 'made in Wales' approach diverges from housing policy in the other UK nations and argues that there are areas where this undermines, rather than contributes to, social justice.

When looking at housing policy in Wales, it is important to note that this context is necessarily defined by the devolution settlement. Housing was one of the key powers to be transferred at the beginning of devolution, and since 2011 the Welsh Government have had primary law-making powers in this area. A swathe of 'made in Wales' legislation has been created relating to housing such as the Housing (Wales) Act 2014, the Renting Homes (Wales) Act 2016, the Abolition of the Right to Buy and Associated Rights (Wales) Act 2018 and the Regulation of Registered Social Landlords (Wales) Act 2018. There has also being cross-cutting legislation developed that impacts on the development of social housing policy such as the Wellbeing of Future Generations (Wales) Act 2015 (Smith, 2018). This legislation clearly shows a divergence in policy between Wales and England, with a recognition by the Welsh Government to regard housing as a human right (Heath, 2019). Wales also has a strong network of housing organisations which act as both critical friend and delivery mechanism for Welsh Government priorities. For instance, Shelter Cymru, Llamau, and Crisis Wales both deliver services for individuals facing homelessness and lobby the government for policy change. There are also a number of membership organisations that support the social housing sector, such as Cymorth Cymru, the Chartered Institute of Housing Cymru, Tai Pawb, and Community Housing Cymru.

The levers that the Welsh Government can use to shape its own approach to ensuring that there is adequate affordable housing available for its population, however, are constrained by the powers relating to welfare that still sit at a UK Government level. The current lack of control over the fiscal welfare system by the Welsh Government fundamentally impacts on their approach to housing in two ways. First, the lack of devolution of housing-related benefits impacts on the finances Welsh Government can use to fund social housing. Secondly, how the welfare system is arranged structures the lives of individuals claiming benefits in Wales in terms of their financial capability, which subsequently impacts on individuals' and communities' health and wellbeing. Housing policy in Wales, although taking a divergent approach to England, cannot therefore be considered in a vacuum. 'Made in Wales' housing policy occurs in the context of a welfare system which is non-devolved, and sits with a government that has been ideologically removed from the Welsh Government since primary law-making powers were made available in 2011.

Homelessness in Wales

Homelessness is an extreme inequality which affects all parts of an individual's wellbeing, compromising education and employment opportunities, and contributing to social exclusion and disadvantage. Homelessness puts individuals and families at very high risk of both physical and mental ill health, compounded by a lack of access to preventative healthcare (Dai and Zhou, 2018; Rogers *et al.*, 2020). Homelessness, including periods of time in temporary accommodation, has a significant effect on childhood wellbeing, elevating the likelihood of longer term health and social difficulties and affecting psychological stability and education (Cutuli *et al.*, 2017; Baptista *et al.*, 2017). Lack of housing stability disrupts relationships and hinders obtaining and maintaining employment (Thomas *et al.*, 2017; Bretherton and Pleace 2019). In Wales work has particularly focused on the needs of rough sleepers, who are widely recognised to be at particular, specific risk of physical, psychological and emotional harm (Mackie, Johnsen and Wood, 2017; Wales Audit Office, 2018; Rowlands and Williams, 2019).

In Wales as with the rest of the UK, homelessness has risen consistently year on year. In 2018/19, local authorities assessed a fifth more households as being 'threatened with homelessness', meaning that they were at serious risk of losing their accommodation within the next 56 days. It is also clear that the numbers of those actually becoming homeless are increasing. In addition to year-on-year rises in those deemed statutorily homeless by the local authority, the numbers of rough sleepers have increased considerably. It should also be noted that measuring homelessness is notoriously complicated. Not all homeless individuals or households are known to local authorities, with women and LGBTQ+ people among the groups who may either not make a formal application, or may disengage from services due to issues with provision (Reeve *et al.*, 2007; England, 2019). UK ethnic minority groups are overall at especial risk of homelessness as a result of complex factors, including both housing discrimination and higher rates of poverty (Beider and Netto, 2012). There is also some evidence that they may be less likely to make homelessness applications, meaning that recorded rates of homelessness for these groups are higher than suggested by official figures (Netto, 2006). The Guidance to the Housing (Wales) Act 2014 does include some specific recommendations to local authorities to make services more accessible to those from certain minority groups, and additionally recent migrants, who are at elevated risk of homelessness (Fitzpatrick *et al.*, 2012).

In 2014, partly in response to rising homeless rates, the Welsh Government passed the Housing (Wales) Act 2014, a 'pioneering' (Mackie, Thomas and Bibbings, 2017) piece of legislation which sought to approach homelessness in line with the Welsh Government's commitment to 'universal, rights-based' (Drakeford, quoted in (Mackie, 2014)) remedies to inequalities. The Act combines the previous approach of a justiciable, rights-based 'safety-net' of secure, affordable state housing for the most vulnerable citizens with a broader commitment to help all those experiencing homelessness through provision of 'assistance'. This represented two shifts in how homelessness was addressed in Wales. First, emphasis was placed on working with individuals to prevent and relieve homelessness. While homelessness legislation prior to 2014 offered help only to those who met a certain criteria of vulnerability, the new Act offered assistance to all households, both in the form of financial help and access to advocacy and advice, to enable them to retain or find new accommodation. The Act places a duty on local authorities to take steps to help people avoid losing their housing – for instance through negotiation with landlords, payment of rent arrears and mediation services, with the aim of reducing both the financial and social cost of homelessness. The Act further requires local authorities to offer assistance to those who are already homeless, for instance, through the payment of deposits, building relationships with private landlords, and access to income maximisation and budgeting advice. Prevention and relief duties are owed to almost all households who are either threatened with homelessness within 56 days (increased from 28 under previous legislation) or currently with nowhere reasonable to occupy, irrespective of why their housing has been lost or threatened, and whether they are at risk of particular harm from homelessness. It is difficult to assess the success of the Act simply through administrative data, since it was introduced at a time of rising homelessness. However, it is clear that a majority of households approaching the council before becoming homeless did have their homelessness prevented, primarily through negotiation and legal advocacy, and assistance with rent arrears (Mackie, Thomas and Bibbings, 2017). Further, outcomes for single people, who were particularly unlikely to receive meaningful help under the pre-2014 legislation, are substantially improved (*ibid*).

Second, the private rented sector became considerably more important in terms of addressing homelessness, with local authorities encouraged to work with both applicants and landlords to house homeless households this way. This is especially significant for the minority of applicants to whom the council owed a duty to provide (rather than help to provide) housing (s75 duty). This group are subject to three eligibility checks: they must be in 'priority need' – at particular risk of harm as a result of homelessness, non-culpable in their homelessness, and, except in certain exceptional circumstances (e.g. domestic abuse), to have a connection to the local area. Whereas under the prior legislation, those who met these criteria became eligible for social housing, and consequently access to long term, secure and affordable housing, this duty can now be discharged into the private rented sector. As will be explored below, this potentially translates into a much lower level of security for those considered at particular risk, since the private rented sector is associated with insecure, low-quality accommodation, and unlike social housing, seldom gives access to tenancy support. It thus represents a particularly risky form of accommodation which elevates the risk of repeated and cyclical homelessness, particularly for vulnerable groups.

This 'priority need' group have experienced a second change under the Act. Unlike the previous Act, they are required to co-operate with the local authority in addressing their own homelessness, for a period of up to 56 days before the local authority must determine whether they are owed a housing provision duty, as well as following this period. Failure to look for private rented accommodation and loss or refusal of temporary accommodation can all justify, in theory, withdrawal of the duty. While it is clear that a very small number of applicants in fact have their applications terminated on the grounds of failing to co-operate, the rewording of the law does create a shift in the balance of responsibilities toward a conditionality-based approach similar to that of other social welfare provision (Watts *et al.*, 2014).

A final criticism of the new Act is its failure to expand the duty to help to all applicants. The Welsh Homelessness Action Group has particularly called for rough sleepers, in light of the extreme health and social impacts faced by this group, to be automatically considered 'priority need' (Homelessness Action Group, 2019). Indeed, several charities, including Crisis and Shelter Cymru, have called for Wales to follow Scotland's example in ending priority need altogether (Abolition of Priority Need Act (Scotland) 2012).

Social rental sector in Wales

The size and purpose of the social rented sector has changed significantly over the past 50 years. In the 1970s this form of tenure housed around a third of the population of the UK, with a focus on providing housing for more affluent households than those in most need. It was characterised by the concept of a social mix within communities and was available to those in need at the time of application. There has been a significant shift in terms of the residualisation of social rented housing following de-regulation and a focus on owner occupation in the late 1970s and 1980s (Malpass, 2008). This combined with a diminution of the building of this type of housing means that this tenure is now often considered solely for those with most pressing need.

In their 2018 research into attitudes towards 'social housing', the Chartered Institute of Housing (CIH) outlined three different roles that social housing might play in society:

1) Social housing as an ambulance service – providing for those in acute need for a short period of time
2) Social housing as a safety net – providing a broader, longer term, form of support for people on lower incomes who cannot afford market housing
3) Social housing as having a wider affordability role – catering for a range of income groups, and competes with private housing through encouraging higher standards and curbing excessive prices.

The CIH argue that social housing should have a wider affordability role, returning to the focus on standards and socially mixed communities which dominated the approach to social housing in the 1960s. The report states (CIH, 2018: 5) 'it's time to reclaim the role of social housing as a pillar of the society we want to become along with free health care and education'. On this approach, the provision of social housing is broader than just 'bricks and mortar'. It impacts on individuals' physical and mental health, as noted in the introduction, but also has a role to play in the socio-economic opportunities that are available to individuals and households. CIH assert that housing does 'more than just providing a roof over people's heads. It extends to healthy, balanced communities and vibrant neighbourhoods.' (CIH, 2018:17).

In Wales, there are just over 1.4 million dwellings, with 16 per cent of these being social stock – dwellings provided by either housing associations or local authorities (Welsh Government, 2020a). The amount of social housing stock differs across Wales, with a higher prevalence in urban areas than rural areas. There has been an increase in the availability of social stock in Wales over the past ten years and this reflects the Welsh Government's commitment to social housing. The Welsh Government recognise the role that good housing plays in communities, and this is demonstrated in the 'made in Wales' approach to social housing that has occurred since (at least in legislative terms) 2011. The white paper for the Housing (Wales) Act recognised housing as a matter of social justice, and the 2016-2021 programme for government outlines housing as a priority area, stating that 'the bedrock of living well is a good quality, affordable home which brings a wide range of benefits to health, learning and prosperity' (Welsh Government 2017a:4).

The majority of social housing is provided by housing associations; organisations that are regulated by the Welsh Government but which operate as social enterprises (in Wales). It is here where the growth in the provision of social housing can largely be seen. Housing associations were established in the 1950s but emerged as a significant delivery mechanism for housing in the 1980s. In Wales, there are 35-40 active housing associations with 11 of these being Large Scale Stock Transfer organisations (where tenants voted to transfer stock from the local authority to a housing association). It is important to note here the particularities of this form of hybrid organisation. Housing associations operate as businesses, but ones with a 'social heart' (Richardson *et al.*, 2014). Organisations focus on the social purpose of their operations – to provide housing for those in need and to shape places where people can thrive – to a different extent, and this defines the type of services that might be provided to their residents. For instance, there has been a growth in the provision of digital and financial inclusion activities within housing associations as a response to the impact of the welfare reforms from 2014. Housing associations also run programmes related to employment support or educational opportunities in order to support the socio-economic development of individuals and communities (Richardson *et al.*, 2014).

This focus on the social purpose of housing associations can be seen as a core element of the 'made in Wales' approach to social housing. This is reflected in the regulatory requirements placed on housing associations through the Regulatory Board for Wales. In comparison to England, the Welsh regulatory framework requires housing associations to not be profit-making and to function as social enterprises. The approach also puts the tenant at the centre of regulatory judgements. The focus here is that housing associations are operating in a way that is designed to meet tenants' needs, with a requirement that tenants are engaged with around the provision of services and/or the strategic direction of the organisation. The framework states that 'tenants remain at the heart of regulation with improved accountability and transparency to tenants and other stakeholders' and outlines the core values underpinning the approach as 'proportionality, transparency and openness, consistency and promotion of learning and development' (Welsh Government 2017b:3).

This regulatory approach, however, is not replicated for those tenants who are living in local authority housing. Local authorities in general are subject to scrutiny from the Wales Audit Office and this extends to their housing function. Regulatory judgements for this provision of social housing only relates to value for money and continuous improvement elements. The Regulatory Board for Wales is currently looking at the concept of domain regulation, and whether local authorities should be subject to the same focus on tenant engagement. The critical element here is that the tenants do not choose which type of mechanism they receive social housing through, yet the experience can be vastly different. Tenants in housing associations are more likely to have the opportunity to be involved in tenant engagement activities, where they are able to shape the services that they can receive.

Although there is a key commitment to social housing from the Welsh Government, and housing organisations in Wales are focussed on the social purpose behind their business, there are still issues that face tenants. The first is highlighted above in terms of the disparity between engagement activities for housing association and local authority tenants. The second relates to affordability. Wales is one of the poorest regions within Europe which causes general issues for housing affordability within the country (Smith, 2018), but this is more acute in some geographical areas than others.

Private rental sector

Nearly a fifth of Welsh households live in the private rented sector. This is a slightly lower figure than for the UK overall, reflecting lower property prices and consequently higher rates of home-ownership (Christiansen and Lewis, 2019). Between 2007 and 2017 the number of households in the private sector in the UK nearly doubled (Christiansen and Lewis, 2019). Welsh private rented tenants are especially likely to be in receipt of rental subsidies, and more likely to have incomes under £15,000 than in England (Christiansen and Lewis, 2019; Walsh, 2019; Whitehead and Scanlon, 2015). In common with other parts of the UK, it is a relatively young tenure, with most occupants aged between 16-24; however, there is also evidence that people are remaining in the private rented sector for longer, with it becoming an increasingly important tenure for older people and families (McKee, Soaita and Hoolachan, 2019; Walsh, 2019; Christiansen and Lewis, 2019; Rugg and Rhodes, 2018; Udagawa *et al.*, 2018; McKee, Soaita and Munro, 2019).

The Welsh private rented sector, in common with the British private rented sector as a whole, is highly financialised. Landlords operate as business owners, with relatively few protections for tenants (Kemp, 2015). Welsh private tenants have very little security of tenure: after an initial four month fixed term period they can be evicted with two months' notice. In contrast, in mainland Europe, much longer tenures and notice periods are standard (Kemp and Kofner, 2010). Another key difference is in the landlord's power to evict. While in Wales, as England, a landlord may evict for any reason after the initial fixed term, in many mainland European countries, and Scotland, landlords can only evict for specified reasons, such as a need to sell, or rent arrears above a certain threshold. This does not only mean that private rented tenants experience considerably more housing precarity than those in either owner-occupation or the social rented sector, but that landlords have considerable negotiating power. There is evidence, for instance, that tenants may be reluctant to complain about maintenance issues for fear of triggering eviction (Rogers, Isaksen, and Brindle 2019). Affordability is another serious issue in the Welsh PRS. Landlords are free to set rents according to the market, with rents rising at or above inflation in recent years. Austerity-based freezing and downgrading of rent subsidies, has also made private accommodation very difficult for low-income tenants to afford in many parts of the UK (Beatty, 2014; Beatty et al., 2014; Cole et al., 2016; Powell, 2015).

There is very little regulation of the quality and adequacy of private rented accommodation. The limited legal protections described above mean that tenants who complain about the quality of their private accommodation can lawfully be evicted. Condition of private rented stock in Wales is particularly poor, with nearly a quarter having serious health hazards (Christiansen and Lewis, 2019). To some extent, issues of quality were considered in the Housing (Wales) Act 2014, which introduced several measures to improve the quality of the private rented sector. Most significantly, it created a compulsory registration and licensing system for private landlords (Rent Smart Wales). This required all those managing a property in Wales (landlords or their agents) to complete training and background checks. Rent Smart Wales has some limited powers to enforce compliance, primarily through relatively low-value penalties and restricting or withdrawing a landlord's licence. In addition to protecting deposits, it issued a set of accommodation standards: these are not legally enforceable but are instead encouraged through a set of 'best practice' guidelines, with no penalties for non-compliance.

A particular issue in the Welsh rental system (in common with the English system), is the lack of a clear route to administrative justice. For tenants to assert their rights, for instance in cases where a landlord refuses to carry out repairs or enters a property unlawfully, the tenant's primary redress is through court action, which is costly and confrontational. Although Rent Smart Wales might penalise the landlord, the tenant will have no redress or protection against losing their property. This offers tenants, particularly those on low incomes, very little protection, especially since landlords who are taken to court are particularly likely to then evict their tenants (Rogers, Isaksen, and Brindle 2019). As the system currently stands, then, there is a strong disincentive for tenants to challenge landlords.

More than any other sector, the Welsh private rented sector is a matter of concern in terms of the quality, affordability and security of the housing it offers. This is of importance following the Housing (Wales) Act 2014 which, as explained above, allows local authorities to discharge their duties to especially vulnerable applicants with a private rented sector tenancy. However, two forthcoming legal changes may improve the situation for Welsh private renters. First, the long-awaited Renting Homes Act, which is expected to be brought into force in 2021, offers several improvements, notably protection from eviction where this appears to be an attempt by the landlord to avoid carrying out repairs. Second, in April 2020 the First Minister announced a plan to extend the notice period which tenants must be given to terminate a tenancy from two to six months. Together, these measures somewhat strengthen the rights of tenants in the private rented sector. However, this falls far short of ending 'no-fault evictions', which would bring the UK into line with Scotland and much of mainland Europe, and which would offer private tenants not only improved security of tenure but with it shift the balance of power to enable landlords to be challenged over disrepair and other breaches of contract.

The impact of home on health

A safe, secure home is of critical importance to wellbeing, offering privacy, control and autonomy. Yet poor quality, insecure housing is also a significant driver of inequality, amplifying existing socio-economic disadvantages (Gurney, 2020; Soaita and McKee, 2019; Marmot *et al*., 2010; Baker *et al*., 2017). Inadequate housing poses specific physical, psychological or emotional health risks to occupants through exposure to environmental risks and hazards. The private nature of the home, while important for ontological wellbeing, is also well-recognised as a risk factor, since it allows behaviours considered unacceptable in broader society (such as abuse) to occur. The housing insecurity which characterises certain tenures also affects health and wellbeing: a lack of housing security causes stress and mental ill-health, as well as disrupted life chances. When we discuss housing policy and legislation, therefore, the impact of poor quality housing is substantial. Housing policy cannot be considered an academic or administrative topic, it shapes individuals' lives in a fundamental way.

Poor quality housing directly affects health. Damp, mould, excess cold, condensation and poor air quality are all particularly associated with respiratory diseases and those living in housing with these hazards are at especial risk of asthma, tuberculosis and pneumonia. Early exposure to these hazards affects children's later health (Howden-Chapman and Chapman, 2012; Howden-Chapman *et al*., 2008; Howden-Chapman *et al*., 2005; Ingham *et al*., 2019; Abrahamsen *et al*., 2016; Cable *et al*., 2014). Fall and trip hazards, as well as accidents within the home caused by faulty wiring and other electrical risks, are especially associated with hospital admissions for children and older people (Giebel *et al*., 2019). The Welsh housing sector overall has an above-average percentage of older, inadequate housing stock, which is disproportionately likely to contain hazards. There is considerable tenure variation in this, with private renters the most likely to be living in sub-standard homes (National Assembly for Wales, 2018). Nearly a fifth of Welsh homes have serious issues with damp while one in ten place occupants at risk of falls. Risk of fire is also a serious issue, affecting nearly a fifth of properties (StatsWales, 2018-19). The cost to the Welsh health service arising from hazards within the home has been estimated at £1,031 million yearly (Nicol *et al*., 2019).

Homes are particularly likely to cause health problems where they do not match the needs of those living within them. Overcrowding is an issue strongly linked to both exposures to other hazards and poor mental health (Pierse *et al*., 2016), and there is some evidence that it may particularly be a problem for some ethnic minority groups

(Jones, 2010). It is associated with a heightened risk of accidents, particularly in children, and is strongly associated with, and compounds, other socio-economic disadvantages (Barratt *et al.*, 2012). Children are particularly likely to live in overcrowded accommodation, with consequent effects upon mental health and educational attainment (Quilgars, 2011). Disabled people often have specific housing needs, yet are also particularly likely to have lower incomes, and so be unable to afford suitable housing (Mitra *et al.*, 2017; Sapey, 1995; Dunn, 1990; Ryan, 2019; ECHR, 2018). While some funding exists for adapting properties better to meet the needs of disabled and chronically ill residents, this is often difficult and complex to access, particularly for tenants in the private rented sector (Wales Audit Office, 2018).

The private nature of the home means it is frequently a place in which people are exposed to danger from the actions of others. Around 2.4 million adults in England and Wales experienced abuse within the home in the last year: this figure includes nearly one in ten women (Elkin, 2019). Home-based adverse child experiences, such as witnessing parental addiction, domestic abuse or mental ill-health, or physical, sexual or emotional abuse or neglect, are all associated with a heightened risk of ill-health and homelessness in later life (Grey *et al.*, 2019). Exposure to environmental hazards caused by other residents, such as second-hand tobacco smoke, is also a particular risk factor for short and long term health, with children from low-income families especially likely to be affected (Pugmire *et al.*, 2017).

Finally, the insecurity associated with private renting and homelessness (see above) has a significant impact on health. Housing precarity is directly related to mental ill-health, particularly stress and anxiety (Preece and Bimpson, 2019). It also complicates access to ongoing healthcare (Martin *et al.*, 2019). More broadly, housing insecurity and frequent moving disrupts social networks, employment, and education, with impacts upon both physical and mental health and wellbeing (Barnes *et al.*, 2013; Desmond and Gershenson, 2016; Bentley *et al.*, 2019). The implications for social welfare practice are clear, not simply in terms of reacting to need but proactive work based on greater inter-professional collaboration and strategic advocacy for individuals and communities.

Conclusions

We can see in the above discussion a clear policy divergence relating to housing and homelessness in Wales. The ideological rhetoric behind discussions of housing and the role of the state in Wales is, and has been for some time, different to that in England for example. The Welsh Government asserts a commitment to progressive universalism, and a strong role for the state in individuals' and communities' lives. This is apparent in the policy and legislative context we have outlined; the Housing (Wales) Act 2014 created a new duty of prevention for all individuals threatened with homelessness, the social housing sector is still very much focussed on its social function as a consequence of regulatory requirements, there is some regulation of the private rented sector. These elements of divergence seem positive in the face of growing inequalities. There are some areas, however, where more work can (and we argue should) be done to match the reality of the impact of policy and legislative on individuals with the ideological rhetoric that underpins it. The issue of affordability of both the social and private sectors remain, and this is particularly pertinent within the socio-economic context of Welsh communities. There are also issues with inequalities within homelessness legislation around the current retention of priority need and access to justice.

It is important to consider these issues in the context of the fundamental role of housing in individuals' lives. As outlined, housing has a substantial impact on physical and mental health, as well as exposure to risk and harm. However, issues of health can also be a driver for housing and homelessness policy and legislation. For instance, there has been a substantial shift in the approach to homelessness in the context of coronavirus. Local authorities have worked with third sector and private sector organisations to provide housing for individuals who are rough sleeping, with a significant reduction of individuals who are sleeping on the streets. There have also been policy changes in terms of implementation of legislation. In effect, the Welsh Government has abolished or at least paused the use of priority need testing (Welsh Government, 2020b). Many of the changes that have occurred as a response to this crisis are ones that stakeholders have been calling for a number of years. The test, here then, is whether these shifts towards an even more progressive approach to housing and homelessness are retained post-coronavirus or are just considered an emergency response to a health crisis.

References

Abrahamsen, R, Veel Svendsen, M, Henneberger, P K, Torén, K, Kongerud, J, Møller Fell, A K (2016) 'Exposure to damp or mould at home in relation to respiratory symptoms and asthma in the Telemark study, Norway' *European Respiratory Journal* Sep 2016, 48 (suppl 60) PA4289; DOI: 10.1183/13993003.congress-2016.PA4289

Baker, E, Beer, A, Lester, L, Pevalin, D, Whitehead, C, Bentley, R (2017) 'Is Housing a Health Insult?' *International journal of environmental research and public health* 14(6): 567

Baptista, I, Benjaminsen, L & Pleace, N & Busch-Geertsema, V (2017) 'Family Homelessness in Europe: 7 EOH Comparative Studies in Homeless'

Barnes, M, Cullinane, C, Scott, S and Silvester, S (2013). People living in bad housing: Numbers and health impacts. UK: Shelter

Barratt, C, Kitcher C and Stewart, J (2012) Beyond safety to wellbeing: How local authorities can mitigate the mental health risks of living in houses in multiple occupation. *Journal of Environmental Health Research* 12(1): 39-51

Beatty, C (2014) *The impact of recent reforms to Local Housing Allowances: Summary of key findings* Department for Work and Pensions

Beatty, C, Cole, I, Crisp, R, Powell, R (2014) *Monitoring the impact of changes to the Local Housing Allowance system of Housing Benefit: final reports* Department for Work and Pensions

Beider, H and Netto, G (2012) Minority Ethnic Communities and Housing: Access, Experiences and Participation. *Understanding 'race' and Ethnicity: Theory, History, Policy, Practice* Bristol: Bristol University Press

Bentley, R, Baker, E and Aitken, Z (2019) The 'double precarity' of employment insecurity and unaffordable housing and its impact on mental health. *Social Science & Medicine* 225 (March 2019): 9-16

Bretherton, J and Pleace, N (2019) 'Is Work an Answer to Homelessness?: Evaluating an Employment Programme for Homeless Adults' *European Journal of Homelessness* pp59-83

Cable, N, Kelly, Y, Bartley, M, Sato, Y and Sacker, A (2014) 'Critical role of smoking and household dampness during childhood for adult phlegm and cough: a research example from a prospective cohort study in Great Britain' *BMJ open* 4: e004807.

Chartered Institute of Housing (2018) *Rethinking Social Housing.* Coventry: Chartered Institute of Housing

Christiansen and Lewis (2019) UK Private Rented Sector 2018. Office for National Statistics. Retrieved from: www.ons.gov.uk/economy/inflationandpriceindices/articles/ukprivaterentedsector/2018#:~:text=In%202017%2C%20the%20private%20rented,for%20the%20UK%20(17%25).&text=The%20proportion%20of%20households%20in,in%202017%20(Figure%206).

Cole, I, Powell, R and Sanderson, E (2016). "Putting the Squeeze on 'Generation Rent': Housing Benefit Claimants in the Private Rented Sector-Transitions, Marginality and Stigmatisation." *Sociological Research Online* 21(2): 1-14

Cutuli JJ, Ahumada SM, Herbers JE, Lafavor TL, Masten AS, Oberg CN (2017) 'Adversity and children experiencing family homelessness: Implications for health' *Journal of Children and Poverty* 2(1): 41-55.

Dai, L and Zhou, P (2018) 'The health issues of the homeless and the homeless issues of the ill-health' *Socio-Economic Planning Sciences*: 100677

Desmond, M and Gershenson, C (2016) 'Housing and employment insecurity among the working poor' *Social Problems* 63(1): 46-67

Dunn PA (1990) The Impact of the Housing Environment upon the Ability of Disabled People to Live Independently. *Disability, Handicap & Society* 5: 37-52

ECHR (2018) 'Housing and disabled people: Britain's hidden crisis' *Equality and Human Rights Commission* London. www.equalityhumanrights.com

Elkin, M (2019) Domestic abuse in England and Wales overview: November 2019: Office for National Statistics. Retrieved from www.ons.gov.uk/peoplepopulationandcommunity/crimeandjustice/bulletins/domesticabuseinenglandandwalesoverview/november2019

England, EA (2019) *Homelessness among trans people in Wales* Shelter Cymru: Cardiff. Retrieved from https://sheltercymru.org.uk/what-we-do/policy-and-research/homelessness-among-trans-people-in-wales_website

Fitzpatrick S, Johnsen S and Bramley G (2012) Multiple exclusion homelessness amongst migrants in the UK. *European Journal of Homelessness* 6(1)

Giebel C, McIntyre JC, Daras K, *et al.* (2019) What are the social predictors of accident and emergency attendance in disadvantaged neighbourhoods? Results from a cross-sectional household health survey in the north west of England. *BMJ open* 9

Grey CN, Woodfine L, Davies AR, *et al.* (2019) Childhood adversity in those with lived experiences of homelessness in Wales: a cross-sectional study. *The Lancet* 394: S45

Gurney C (2020) *Out of harm's way?* Glasgow: CaCHE, University of Glasgow

Heath, L (2019) 'Welsh Government considers incorporating 'due regard' to right to adequate housing into new law'. Available at: www.insidehousing.co.uk/news/news/welsh-government-considers-incorporating-due-regard-to-adequate-housing-into-new-laws-63861

Homelessness Action Group, (2019) *The framework of policies, approaches and plans needed to end homelessness in Wales (What ending homelessness in Wales looks like).* Cardiff: Cymorth Cymru. Retrieved from: https://gov.wales/sites/default/files/publications/2020-03/homelessness-action-group-report-march-2020_0.pdf

Howden-Chapman P, Crane, J, Matheson, A, *et al.* (2005) Retrofitting houses with insulation to reduce health inequalities: aims and methods of a clustered, randomised community-based trial. *Social Science & Medicine* 61(12): 2600-610

Howden-Chapman, P, Pierse, N, Nicholls, S, Gillespie-Bennett, J, Viggers, H, Cunningham, M, ... & Chapman, R. (2008). 'Effects of improved home heating on asthma in community dwelling children: randomised controlled trial'. *Bmj* 337, a1411

Howden-Chapman, P and Chapman, R.(2012) 'Health co-benefits from housing-related policies'. *Current Opinion in Environmental Sustainability* 4(4): 414-19

Ingham T, Keall M, Jones B, *et al.* (2019) 'Damp mouldy housing and early childhood hospital admissions for acute respiratory infection: a case control study'. *Thorax* 74(9): 849-57

Jones A (2010) *Black and minority ethnic communities experience of overcrowding.* London: Race Equality Foundation

Kemeny, J (1995) *From Public Housing to the Social Market.* London: Routledge

Kemp, P and Kofner, S (2010) 'Contrasting varieties of private renting: England and Germany' *International Journal of Housing Policy* 10(4): 379-98

Kemp, P (2015) 'Private Renting After the Global Financial Crisis' *Housing Studies* 30(4):601-20. doi: 10.1080/02673037.2015.1027671.

King, P (2015) *Keeping things close. Essays on the conservative disposition.* London: Arkto

Mackie, P (2014) '1. The Welsh Homelessness Legislation Review: Delivering Universal Access to Appropriate Assistance?' *Contemporary Wales* 27(1): 1-20

Mackie, P, Johnsen, S and Wood, J (2017) 'Ending rough sleeping: what works?' *An international evidence review.* London: Crisis

Mackie, P, Thomas, I and Bibbings, J (2017) 'Homelessness prevention: Reflecting on a year of pioneering Welsh legislation in practice' *European Journal of Homelessness* 11(1): 81-107

Malpass, P (2008) 'Housing and the New Welfare State: Wobbly Pillar or Cornerstone?' *Housing Studies,* 23(1): 1-19

Marmot, M, Allen, J, Goldblatt, P, *et al.* (2010) *The Marmot review: Fair society, healthy lives.* London: UCL

Martin, P, Liaw, W, Bazemore, A, *et al.* (2019) Adults with housing insecurity have worse access to primary and preventive care. *The Journal of the American Board of Family Medicine* 32(4): 521-530

McKee, K, Soaita, A and Munro, M (2019) 'Beyond Generation rent: Understanding the aspirations of private renters aged 35-54.' Available at https://housingevidence.ac.uk/publications/beyond-generation-rent

McKee, K, Soaita, A and Hoolachan, J (2019) '"Generation rent' and the emotions of private renting: self-worth, status and insecurity amongst low-income renters." *Housing Studies* 1-20

Mitra S, Palmer M, Kim H, Mont D, Groce N (2017) Extra costs of living with a disability: A review and agenda for research *Disabil Health Journal.* 10(4): 475-84

#Netto G (2006) Vulnerability to homelessness, use of services and homelessness prevention in black and minority ethnic communities. *Housing Studies* 21(4): 581-601

Nicol S, Garrett H, Woodfine L, Watkins G, Woodham A (2019) *The full cost of poor housing in Wales* Building Research Establishment Ltd, Public Health Wales, Welsh Government

Pierse N, Carter K, Bierre,S, Law L, Howden-Chapman P (2016) 'Examining the role of tenure, household crowding and housing affordability on psychological distress, using longitudinal data' *Journal of Epidemiol Community Health* 70(10): 961-66

Powell, R (2015) 'Housing benefit reform and the private rented sector in the UK: On the deleterious effects of short-term, ideological "Knowledge"' *Housing, Theory and Society* 32(3): 320-45

Preece, J and Bimpson, E (2019) *Housing and Insecurity and Mental Health in Wales* Glasgow: CaCHE, University of Glasgow

Pugmire, J, Sweeting, H and Moore, L (2017) *Environmental tobacco smoke exposure among infants, children and young people: now is no time to relax.* BMJ Publishing Group Ltd

Quilgars D (2011) Housing and the environment for children in Bradshaw, J (ed) *The wellbeing of children in the UK* Bristol: Policy Press. pp 135-55

Reeve, K, Goudie, R and Casey, R (2007) *Homeless women: Homelessness careers, homelessness landscapes* Crisis: London

Richardson J, Barker L, Furness J, Simpson M (2014) *Frontline Futures: new era, changing role for housing officers* Coventry: Chartered Institute of Housing

Rogers, C, Isaksen M and Brindle B (2018) *Touch and Go: How to protect private renters from retaliatory eviction in England* London: Citizens Advice

Rugg, J and Rhodes, D (2018) *The Evolving Private Rented Sector: Its Contribution and Potential* York: University of York

Rogers, M, Ahmed, A, Madoc-Jones, I, Gibbons, A, Jones, K and Wilding, M (2020) 'Interrogating the prevention approach of the Housing (Wales) Act 2014 for people with mental health needs who are homeless' *Social Policy and Society* 19(1): 109-20

Rowlands, B and Williams, J (2019) *Analysis of 2 week National Rough Sleeper Count Questionnaires November 2018.* WLGA: Cardiff

Ryan F (2019) *Crippled: Austerity and the Demonization of Disabled People,* London: VERSO Books

Sapey, B (1995) Disabling Homes: a study of the housing needs of disabled people in Cornwall. *Disability & Society* 10(1): 71-86

Smith, R. 2018 *Social Housing in Wales. Centre for Housing Evidence.* Glasgow: CaCHE, University of Glasgow

Soaita, A and McKee, K (2019) Assembling a 'kind of' home in the UK private renting sector. *Geoforum* 103: 148-157

StatsWales (2018-19) Category 1 and 2 hazards identified by hazard type, dwelling and category. Cardiff: Welsh Government

Thomas, Y, Gray, M and McGinty, S (2017) 'The occupational wellbeing of people experiencing homelessness' *Journal of Occupational Science* 24(2): 181-92

Udagawa, C, Scanlon, K and Whitehead, C (2018) 'The Future Size and Composition of the Private Rented Sector, an LSE London project for Shelter' London: LSE London

Wales Audit Office (2018) 'Housing Adaptations'. Available at www.audit.wales/publication/housing-adaptations

Walsh, E (2019) '"Family-friendly" tenancies in the private rented sector' *Journal of Property, Planning and Environmental Law.* 11(3)

Watts, B, Fitzpatrick, S, Bramley, G, and Watkins, D.(2014) *Welfare Sanctions and Conditionality in the UK.* York: Joseph Rowntree Foundation

Welsh Government (2017a *Prosperity for All: The national strategy* Cardiff: Welsh Government. Available at: https://gov.wales/sites/default/files/publications/2017-10/prosperity-for-all-the-national-strategy.pdf

Welsh Government (2017b) *The Regulatory Framework for Housing Associations Registered in Wales.* Cardiff: Welsh Government

Welsh Government (2020a) *Dwelling Stock Estimates for Wales*, as at 31 March 2020. Cardiff: Welsh Government. Retrieved from: https://gov.wales/dwelling-stock-estimates-31-march-2020

Welsh Government (2020b) *Review of priority need in Wales: summary*. Retrieved from https://gov.wales/review-priority-need-wales-summary-html

Whitehead, C and Scanlon, K (2015) *The potential role of the private rented sector in Wales.* Cardiff: Public Policy Institute for Wales

Chapter 7

The Role of Language Policy, Planning and Legislation in Social Welfare in Wales

Rhian Hodges

Introduction

Minoritized languages worldwide face the constant threat of possible language death (Crystal, 2014). There are an estimated 7,000 languages in the world, and many are predicted to become extinct during the next decade (Eberhard *et al.*, 2020). Minoritized languages and their speakers are often faced with numerous challenges to survive and to compete with more powerful, dominant languages or 'lingua francas' (Crystal, 2014). Indeed, language ecology and the Darwinian notion of 'survival of the fittest' can be applied to languages, such as, Fishman's battle of the jungle (Fishman, 2001). Languages compete against each other; the weaker ones simply die off. Issues pertaining to power, dominance, authority and ideology are at the core of the struggles experienced by minoritized languages within contemporary societies (Fishman, 2001; May, 2011; Skutnabb-Kangas, 2018).

Social welfare and its many reforms usually deal with the most vulnerable members of society (Beatty and Fothergill, 2013). Social welfare provides a range of social services to citizens to ensure well-being and quality of life, especially in times of hardship (social welfare and health and social care will be the terms used within this chapter). Services are largely delivered through the public sector, but key services are also delivered by private and third sector agencies, which often highlight the complex nature of social welfare delivery (Alcock and Powell, 2011). The language choice of service delivery is an important area of the diversity agenda. Language should be afforded equal status to other areas of the agenda; such as gender, race, ethnicity, age and sexuality. Interestingly, however, many have argued that language rights are often on the periphery of human rights discussions. May referred to language rights as 'the Cinderella of human rights' (May 2011:265) outshone by other diversity issues and, 'peculiarly underrepresented and/or problematized as a key human right' (May 2011:265). This marginality of language seems to exist, despite there being over 60 years since the United Nations Universal Declaration of Human Rights:

> *'Everyone is entitled to all the rights and freedoms set forth in this Declaration, without distinction of any kind, such as race, colour, sex, language, religion, political or other opinion, national or social origin, property, birth or other status.'* (United Nations, 1948)

The contestation of language rights as equal human rights, leads many academics, such as Skutnabb-Kangas (2000, 2007, 2018), to fight for linguistic human rights. A key facet of this discussion is the distinction between the private and public spheres of life. Kloss (1977) differentiated between 'tolerance-orientated' and 'promotion-orientated' language rights. He maintained that the use of languages (such as minoritized languages) within a private sphere, such as the family, are not questioned and are 'tolerance-orientated rights'. However, there is much debate regarding the use of languages within more formal administrative, educational, and legal contexts; these he termed, 'promotion-orientated rights'. This juxtaposition between the informal and formal spheres available for language use will play out within this chapter when discussing the use of the Welsh language within the field social welfare in Wales. For example, service users do not always have their language needs met within the delivery of social welfare (Madoc-Jones and Dubberley, 2005; Davies, 2011).

This paper will explore the legislative and language policy context of the Welsh language in Wales, and how these impact on bilingual social welfare delivery. Furthermore, this paper will aim to highlight the paradox between regulations and reality and strategies and practicalities in the field of bilingual social welfare delivery.

Background – the Welsh language

The Welsh language is one of the oldest literary languages of Europe and is the oldest spoken language in Britain (Jenkins and Williams, 2000). Similar to other minoritized languages, Welsh has experienced a history of decline and resurgence, almost in equal measures (Davies, 2014). Indeed, 2011 Census figures state that the Welsh Language is spoken by 562,000 people, 19 per cent of the population. Forecasting data produced by the Welsh Government maps the projection and trajectory of Welsh speakers. This report notes that by the 2021 Census, there will be 580,000 Welsh speakers, this figure remains at 19 per cent of the population (Welsh Government, 2017b:5). Language use is beyond the remit of the Census, but recent research highlights that 13 per cent of Welsh speakers use the language on a daily basis (Welsh Government and Welsh Language Commissioner, 2015). Despite UNESCO categorising the Welsh language as a 'vulnerable' language (Moseley, 2011), the Welsh language has been pioneering in terms of language revitalisation. This has been spearheaded, by and large, by Welsh-medium immersion education (Wyn Williams 2003; Hodges, 2009, 2012; Thomas and Williams 2013). The greatest numbers of Welsh speakers are within the 10-14 age category and account for 75,093 or 13.36 per cent of all Welsh speakers (ONS, 2012).

The linguistic map of Wales is consistently changing, and this is an important consideration when discussing the role of language policy and planning and the need for bilingual social welfare provision across Wales. Differences in the numbers and percentages of Welsh speakers in different localities is evident, but what is clear is there are Welsh speakers in every county in Wales who require social welfare services to be delivered bilingually. The highest percentage of Welsh speakers can be located in rural localities of Wales such as Gwynedd (65 per cent) and Ynys Mon (57 per cent) in North-

West Wales. However, the urbanised localities of south Wales (despite having lower percentages of Welsh speakers, e.g. 7.8 per cent of the population of Blaenau Gwent are Welsh speakers) have higher absolute numbers of Welsh speakers due to densely populated urban localities (ONS, 2012). The Welsh Government's ambitious Welsh language strategy aims to create a million Welsh speakers by 2050 (Welsh Government, 2017a). Forecasting data highlights that by 2050 there will be 666,000 Welsh speakers (Welsh Government, 2017b:5), 21 per cent of the population. This charts a growth of 100,000 speakers since the 2001 Census, but highlights there will be a shortfall of approximately 334,000 speakers by 2050 (Welsh Government, 2017b:5). These figures maintain that bilingual service provision should be an essential consideration when planning and delivering social welfare services across Wales.

Key Welsh language legislative developments

There are many notable historic milestones that have impacted upon the Welsh language and provide a useful backstory to current Welsh language policies that form part of the current language revitalisation agenda. The Act of Union 1535-1542 prevented the use of the Welsh language in any official, administrative and legislative capacity (Morgan, 1991), thus confining the Welsh language to the family and the chapel. Furthermore, the 1847 Report of the Commissioners referred to as, 'The Treason of the Bluebooks', further exiled the Welsh Language from the education system in Wales, thus impacting upon its status and prestige (Morgan, 1991; Davies, 2014).

It was not until the Welsh Court Act of 1942 that the Welsh language could be used within the court system (around four hundred years or so since the Act of Union, which highlights the peripheral nature of the Welsh language within the juridical system). Even then, there were specific conditions to the use of the Welsh language use (for example, when using English would be disadvantageous to the individual (Parry, 2012)). Parry (2012), among others, also notes the weakness of the act as he states that this is an act framed by tolerance rather than providing equality between Welsh and English. This could be reminiscent of Kloss' (1977) 'tolerance-orientated rights' and did not provide enough of a platform for language use in a public sphere.

The 1967 Welsh Language Act called for the validity of both Welsh and English in Wales as it provided the right to use Welsh within the court system and built upon the Welsh Court Act of 1942. However, this act was seen as a weak act as this validity of equality was not reflected in other administrative spheres, simply within the court system (Parry, 2012; Lewis, 2008; Williams and Morris 2000). It wasn't until the 1993 Welsh Language Act that the principle of language equality was fully established (Williams and Morris 2000; Davies, 2011; Lewis, 2008; Parry, 2012). Welsh and English should be treated equally within the public sector in Wales by placing a duty upon them (HMSO, 1993) (an important step in terms of delivering social welfare provision bilingually in Wales). The Welsh Language Act called for the creation of Welsh Language Schemes, overseen by the Welsh Language Board tasked with implementing these schemes and promoting the Welsh language and language use. In terms of delivering social welfare, this act clearly noted the need to provide language choice and language parity to service users. Moreover, it highlighted the needs of vulnerable users, who could be disadvantaged at not being able to communicate in their first (and often preferred) language (Welsh Language Board, 1996).

However, the Welsh Language Act of 1993 was criticised for not placing similar duties upon the private sector, (as exists in Catalonia), (Williams and Morris, 2000; Lewis, 2008; Dunbar, 2009) and this is particularly pertinent as a number of social welfare users receive services from private care-giving companies and agencies, which can make it more difficult to demand language equality. Furthermore, just as other acts before it, the Welsh Language Act (HMSO, 1993:3) contained several caveats that only provided language equality if circumstances were 'practical' and 'reasonable', which further undermined service users and their particular language needs of service users (Vacca, 2013; Dunbar, 2009; Williams and Morris, 2000; Prys, Hodges and Roberts, forthcoming).

It took almost another quarter of a century for the next Welsh language legislative milestone in Wales. The Welsh Language (Wales) Measure 2011 secures the official status of the Welsh language in Wales. Indeed, the two official languages of Wales (Welsh and English) place specific requirements on public bodies, such as social welfare services. As part of this Measure, Language Schemes have been replaced by Welsh Language Standards and placed upon on all public bodies offering services to the public. Welsh should not be treated less favourably than English (Welsh Government, 2011). Welsh Language Standards are categorised according to standards relating to supplying services, standards relating to designing policies, implementation standards and standards relating to keeping records (Welsh Statutory Instruments, 2018).

The Welsh Language (Wales) Measure (2011) saw the establishment of the Welsh Language Commissioner to promote and facilitate the use of the Welsh language in Wales (Welsh Language Commissioner, 2015). Despite providing official status for the Welsh language, this measure does not guarantee 'absolute rights' for Welsh speakers; but instead concentrates on enabling language use in its most practical sense (Parry, 2012; Vacca, 2013; Nason, 2017). This differs to the Canadian context where language rights for French speakers or Francophones are explicit (Mac Giolla Chríost, 2015, 2017; Williams, 2012). However, it could be argued, that by enforcing a particular Welsh Language Standard (along with the official status of a language) that this then creates a 'right' to speak the language. Welsh Language Pressure Group, Dyfodol (in National Assembly for Wales, 2019:14), note that the Welsh Language Measure focuses on standards rather than advocating language usage amongst speakers.

A key aspect of the Welsh Language (Wales) Measure 2011 is the Welsh Language Tribunal regarding matters of language within service provision. There is a complaints system in place if service users are unable to have their language needs met. All this has clear implications for social welfare delivery in Wales. The tribunal system can also be used to 'enshrine' a language right, by confirming the public duty placed on a public sector body. Within this Measure, Welsh language rights seem to be realised later on, as part of a wider, legislative process. Moreover, the Welsh Language Commissioner's office monitors and holds public service bodies to account if they do not comply with Language Standards that have been set (Welsh Government, 2011). The Commissioner has the power to fine bodies up to £5,000 if they do not comply with the standards set. However, critics ask whether a fine of £5,000 really makes a difference to a big organization? How much power does the Commissioner really have? Is there a risk in the Language Commissioner's office being seen as the language police, and viewed negatively for dealing with non-compliance and complaints rather than positive steps to encourage Welsh language use? According to Nason (2017) the Welsh Language Commissioner should focus on promotion and advocation of Welsh language use, rather than on a culture of complaining.

Furthermore, the relationship between the Commissioner and the Welsh Government is a key discussion point. The Welsh Language Commissioner is an independent role with certain regulatory powers, namely placing standards on public bodies (something the Welsh Language Board did not possess) (Vacca, 2013; Nason, 2017). Many have raised concerns over the independence and accountability of the Welsh Language Commissioner (Nason, 2017; Mac Giolla Chríost, 2015, 2017; Williams, 2012). The Welsh Language Commissioner scrutinises the Welsh Government via the Welsh Language Standards, how will this impact upon accountability? Could this have further knock on effects within the social welfare sector if this neutrality is lost? Who is accountable to whom?

Indeed, the Welsh Language Standards placed on the Welsh Government themselves were rejected and reworked several times calling into question the value of the standards and the independence of the Commissioner role. Moreover, on a practical level, the delay in implementing Welsh Language Standards (the health and social care standards were only initiated in 2018 and fully implemented in 2019) has also meant a loss of momentum and a transition period leaving many vulnerable service users at a disadvantage.

Language policy and planning and social welfare

Language is an all important part of our identity and forms part of a collective past, present and future (Skutnabb-Kangas, 2000). Speaking a particular language means we interpret the world in a specific way (Lewis, 2008). According to Edward Sapir (1921:7); 'language…is a purely human and non-instinctive method of communicating ideas, emotions and desires by means of a system of voluntarily produced symbols.' Communicating emotions is an important facet of receiving and providing social welfare provision. This can be even more important for speakers of minoritized languages wishing to discuss sensitive issues in their chosen language rather than the dominant language.

Informal language planning dates as far back as Roman times (Kaplan and Baldauf, 1997; Ricento, 2006); despite this, language planning as a term was coined by Einar Haugen in 1959. Language planning could be described as a way to influence the language acquisition and language behaviour of individuals and communities (Cooper, 1989). It has also been described by Kaplan and Baldauf (1997) as various laws, beliefs, rules and attitudes that create a linguistic change or stop one from occurring. Language planning can be a complicated field, often dependent on the different agendas of individuals, communities, workforce sectors, social contexts and the goals to be achieved. This complexity should be acknowledged when assessing how to meet the language needs of service users. For example, are language needs likely to be highly prioritised within an under-resourced health care sector?

Language policy is intrinsically linked to language planning and could be defined as:

> '...the more general linguistic, political and social goals underlying the actual language planning process.' (Deumart, 2009:371).

Language policy seems to be the practical platform that propels language planning into action, per se. The practical elements of implementing language strategies are all important within social welfare. For example, healthcare professionals showing language courtesy to a stroke patient who has lost the ability to communicate in English. Grin (2003), states that language policy can form part of public policy, such as other elements like health or transport. In a similar vein, Lewis and Royles describe language policy as:

> '...any intervention by government (state, regional or local) aimed at influencing the nature of a society's linguistic environment, and thus steer the language practices of individuals.' (Lewis and Royles, 2017:1)

Such macro-level language planning strategies, as discussed below, can often be at loggerheads with how individual Welsh speakers wish to use their language within their day-to-day lives, or micro-level language planning (Hodges and Prys, 2019). This dichotomy highlights the juxtaposition between state hegemonic aims and individual language ideologies based around autonomy and agency (Martyn-Jones, 1989; Armstrong, 2012).

Indeed, the Macro-Meso-Micro language planning framework (Baldauf, 2006; Liddicoat and Baldauf, 2008), could be a useful framework to understand how Welsh language policies are implemented within social welfare. Macro-level language planning is top-down, government-lead language planning, that involves constructing strategies to administer nationally. In Wales, this role is assumed by the Welsh Government. Their current Welsh Language Strategy, Cymraeg 2050: A million Welsh speakers (Welsh Government, 2017a) aims to almost double the numbers of Welsh speakers by 2050 largely through Welsh-medium immersion education. Meso-level language planning is harder to define. This could be viewed as practitioners, such as social workers, or professional associations implementing macro-level language planning on a daily-basis for service users. Lastly, micro-level language planning, is related to individual social actors which could be applied to social welfare service users. This is a meaningful framework from which to understand the relationship between the Welsh language and social welfare provision as it allows an understanding of the interplay between all levels and how services are actually implemented, or otherwise, on a daily basis. There can be vast discrepancies between the political rhetoric put forward by macro-level language planning and how these strategies are interpreted and implemented by meso-level practitioners and service agencies and how these strategies affect the day-to-day lives of service users in Wales. Indeed, the meso-level is recognised as a 'crucial language planning linchpin' (Prys, Hodges and Roberts, forthcoming) in renegotiating language policies before they are rolled out to service users. One key example is how county councils decide to interpret and implement Welsh Government strategies depending on the linguistic competence of staff and existing Welsh-medium infrastructure within the organisation (National Assembly for Wales, 2019). There is evidence that some councils prioritise certain Welsh Language Standards and cannot ensure that Welsh is treated equally to English in every single aspect of service delivery (National Assembly for Wales, 2019).

Social welfare itself can be viewed as an umbrella field providing support and protection for a number of vulnerable individuals. It also deals with the main inequalities in society such as class, gender, race and income and wealth (Spiker, 2017). The social welfare sector often serves individuals who are vulnerable members of society where their needs are usually multi-dimensional and often require assistance from multiple agencies (Alcock and Powell, 2011). For example, the role of social workers is all important in providing support and care to vulnerable, and often marginalised individuals. Promoting the social wellbeing of citizens is a crucial aspect of providing social welfare provision.

Historically, the social welfare sector has paid very little attention to the needs of Welsh speakers in Wales. May (2011:265-266) notes; '…the controversy has focused on whether speakers of minority languages have the right to maintain and use that particular language in the public, or civic realm.' Moreover, failing to acknowledge the language rights of minority language speakers, effectively means stigmatising and disadvantaging those speakers (Kymlicka, 2001). Minority languages are then often consigned to private domains only. This is an important consideration, in terms of how service users in Wales receive services, and if they choose to take up the Welsh language social welfare services available to them. It is important for service users to feel appreciated and respected regarding the language(s) they choose as a means of communication (Roberts, 1994; Misell, 2000, Roberts *et al.*, 2004). Welsh language services need to be mainstream, normalised and expected by the use of forward planning, as not viewed as an ad-hoc add-on (Davies, 2011).

Devolution, the Welsh language and social welfare provision

Devolution and the de-centralisation of government power is often a positive move for minoritized languages, as this provides additional autonomy to create legislation. Wales is a case in point, as the 1997 Referendum on devolution marked an important milestone for Wales and the Welsh language (Davies, 2014). This signalled the beginning of a unique social policy direction centred around a rhetoric of nationhood, or 'a clear red water' as described by the Former First Minister of Wales, Rhodri Morgan (Moon, 2012:1). Furthermore, since the 2011 Referendum on the law-making powers of the National Assembly for Wales; Wales now has primary law-making powers in devolved areas such the Welsh language and health and social care (National Assembly for Wales, 2011). The Welsh Government's Welsh Language strategies (along with other key strategic frameworks and policies) highlight important developments in terms of the bilingual services offered within the field of social welfare.

Iaith Pawb (Everyone's Language) (Welsh Assembly Government, 2003) was the Welsh Government's first Welsh language strategy and advocated bilingualism and inclusivity, which encouraged language ownership for Welsh speakers and non-Welsh speakers in Wales. It specifically noted the importance of meeting the language needs of vulnerable individuals receiving social welfare provision. *Iaith Pawb* could be viewed as a watershed moment as the Welsh Government referred to Welsh language rights for the first time within this strategy. Furthermore, the concept of language choice is prominent within this strategy recognising the, 'importance of being able to deliver services in the service users' language of choice in key service areas such as health and social care' (Welsh Assembly Government, 2003:47). However, one particular criticism could be that the Welsh Assembly Government's focus on bilingualism could actually dilute the drive for normalising the use of the Welsh language, by providing additional powers to protect the use of English, the dominant lingua franca in Wales.

Following this, the Welsh Government's Welsh Language Strategy, *Iaith fyw: iaith byw* (A living language a language for living (Welsh Government, 2012a) re-affirms the official status of Welsh as an official language in Wales and emphasises the shift from language choice to language need within the field of social welfare. This stronger emphasis could mean the difference between life and death within health and social care. Strategic Aim 5 within the strategy highlights Welsh Language Services and notes the aim to increase and improve Welsh language services to citizens (Welsh Government, 2012a:16). Moreover, the Welsh Government themselves recognise that health and social care is a priority field in which to provide Welsh language services and they also concede that the linguistic choices within the field are often ad-hoc:

> *'Strengthening Welsh-language services in health and social care is regarded as a priority since, for many, language in this context is more than just a matter of choice – it is a matter of need…it is evident that the provision of Welsh-language services remains piecemeal and too often it is a matter of chance whether people receive Welsh-language health and social care service.'* (Welsh Government, 2012b:42)

It is also within this strategy that the Welsh Government set out it's aims to create a strategic framework for Health and Social Care, acknowledging how crucial this field is and how linguistically under-resourced and under-valued it has been. Indeed, the Welsh Government's strategic framework within the field of health and social care in

Wales, *More Than Just Words* (West Government 2012b, 2016) aims to mainstream and normalise the use of Welsh in the health and social care sectors systematically and practically at the point of delivery, but also during the planning phases (Welsh Government, 2012b:3). The following are pinpointed as reasons to strengthen Welsh language services in health and social care – improving quality of care, maintaining professional standards, meeting the language needs of users, complying with legal and statutory requirements (Welsh Government, 2012b:7). This framework crystallises the conceptual shift from language choice to language need as epitomised by the active offer principle:

> *'…the concept of language need also has to become an integral part of care services. This means moving the responsibility from the user to ask for services through the medium of Welsh, to the service which must ensure it provides them.'* (Welsh Government, 2012b:12)

More Than Just Words: Follow On 2016-2019 (Welsh Government, 2016) also underlines the importance of quality of care and meeting individual language needs based on safety and dignity within the field of health and social care in Wales. This is an interesting statement, macro-level language planning discussing the importance of the micro-level language planning. However, is this consideration any more than pure political rhetoric?

Cymraeg 2050: A million Welsh speakers is the Welsh Government's current Welsh Language Strategy and it aims to: increase the number of Welsh speakers, increase the use of Welsh, and create favourable conditions regarding infrastructure and context for the Welsh language (Welsh Government 2017a:4). It is within the second theme, increasing the use of Welsh that services such as those offered by social welfare are included. The strategy mentions the need to strategically plan the workforce to provide fully bilingual services for service users and highlights the importance of the active offer principle. Moreover, the health and social care sectors could be an important way to contribute to the numbers of Welsh speakers who use the language in Wales. An active offer of services could potentially give individuals the added confidence to use the language within these sectors which, in turn, could help realise the Welsh Government's target of reaching one million Welsh speakers by 2050. This strategy is built largely upon creating 'new' Welsh speakers (Hodges, 2014; Hornsby, 2015) through the education system in Wales, those who might not have spoken Welsh were it not for Welsh-medium education. Moreover, education is crucial for language capacity building and language capacity strengthening (Wagoner, 2017) within the fields of health and social care in Wales. Education helps sustain a bilingual workforce by replenishing bilingual staff. The Basque Country have invested heavily in Basque-medium vocational courses to secure Basque speakers in fields such as education and health (Armstrong *et al.*, 2011). However, more research needs to be done in how this could be systematically improved and young people targeted to follow a career in social welfare. Linguistic progression from education to the workplace is an all-important language planning strategy that needs more investment in order to secure a confident, bilingual workforce to support service users language needs.

Furthermore, The White Paper *Sustainable Social Services: A Framework for Action* (Welsh Assembly Government, 2011) and The Social Services and Wellbeing Act (2014) also highlight the importance of giving service users who need care and support greater autonomy over the services they receive. Indeed, to receive support in their chosen language is all important for their mental health and wellbeing (Welsh Assembly Government, 2011; Welsh Government, 2014). The Welsh Language is clearly becoming a stable feature of social policy documents, especially in recent years and the Well-being of Future Generations (Wales) Act 2015, highlights the important role of language within the well-being goals of the Act. Furthermore, *A Healthier Wales* (Welsh Government, 2018) action plan identifies the Welsh language as an area of priority within service provision. Together, this is further evidence of mainstreaming Welsh language policy within wider social policy as noted by Williams (2011) and Lewis and Royles (2017). However, what about the daily practicalities and realities that impact upon real life social welfare service delivery?

Legislation and policies versus daily practicalities

Despite clear legislative developments, there is a juxtaposition between the legislation and government-led Welsh language strategies, and what actually happens within the social welfare sector on a daily basis. Macro-level language planning by Welsh Government is often interpreted and implemented differently at meso-level that ultimately affects the experiences of bilingual service users at a micro-level. For example, service users do not readily receive bilingual services due to local government language capacity of Welsh-speaking staff (Wrexham Council originally queried the Welsh Language Standards set for them, such as providing training to staff through the medium of Welsh, and the ability to use Welsh in 'sensitive' meetings (Golwg 360, 2015). Moreover, a growing body of key research has amassed during recent years that builds the case for language sensitive service provision and that addresses the language needs of service users in social welfare (Davies, 2011). Language is an expression of identity, solidary, resistance, and belonging to a language community, and is far more than simply a mode of communication (Lanehart, 1996). Indeed, language use for bilingual service users can be multi-dimensional and complicated as factors such as fluency, confidence, context and power relations are all at play. Bilingual services allow individuals to feel comfortable and secure in the knowledge that they are expressing themselves unreservedly in their favoured language. Issues pertaining to the authenticity and meaningfulness of linguistic exchanges between professionals, practitioners and service users and the relationships with their language needs are at the heart of providing bilingual social welfare (Davies, 2011). This highlights the need to fully consider micro-level language planning and the daily language needs of service users.

Misell's seminal research (2000) recognised four key service user groups for whom communication in one language rather than the other is a matter of necessity rather than an optional requirement. These are children, older people, mental health service users and people with learning disabilities (Misell, 2000); essentially individuals who are most likely to use social welfare provision in Wales. Misell's research highlighted the invisibility of the Welsh language when providing health and social care services. The four key service user groups are at a constant linguistic and service-based disadvantage. Despite the Welsh Government's subsequent attention in this area, this section of the chapter highlights the need for more research into the experiences of service users on a micro-level. Iaith (Welsh Centre for Language Planning) were commissioned in 2012 to conduct research into Welsh speakers' experiences of health and social care services on behalf of Welsh Government, and the Care Council for Wales. This research highlights the challenges faced by vulnerable service users when attempting to access Welsh language services. A key research finding notes three levels of Welsh-medium service delivery. The 'optimum level', where all aspects of the service are delivered through the user's preferred language and 'the least favourable option' where all services are delivery through the medium of English, without an acknowledgment of the user's preferred language (Welsh Government and Care Council for Wales, 2012:4). The third level is the 'compromise model' where the user's language is acknowledgement by professionals. This research highlights the vast differences between different levels of Welsh language service delivery within the field of health and social care and clarifies the need for language capacity building within the sector. Furthermore, Wagoner (2017) calls for language capacity building to increase the bilingual workforce within health and social care but also language capacity strengthening where current staff's language competence is strengthened by training and development in order to deliver effective bilingual services for service users of social welfare in Wales. The need for staff with language competence and confidence to use Welsh so that the 'optimum level' of service provision (Welsh Government and Care Council for Wales, 2012:1) can be provided. According to one of the research participants of the 2012 study, the lack of communication between patients and professionals means that services are seriously lacking:

> *'We receive other services where the worker speaks no Welsh at all... X isn't able to take part in discussion, he can't express an opinion directly... the worker can't get to know him as an individual, because they have to communicate through us as his parents. Whatever the professional standard of this kind of service, it can't be a good service essentially because one key factor is missing – the ability to communicate with the patient himself.'* (Welsh Government and Care Council for Wales, 2012:15)

Roberts *et al.* (2004), studying Welsh Language awareness among healthcare workers in Wales, also found that Welsh language services were restricted, largely due to the small numbers of Welsh-speaking staff to carry out these services. Another significant finding was the culture of indifference created by service providers regarding the Welsh language. This could highlight the discrepancy between language and other areas of the diversity agenda. Further research highlights that Welsh-speaking service users have not always had their language needs met. Insufficient Welsh-speaking staff capacity, lack of resources and specialist knowledge in Welsh, time pressures, attitudes and perceptions of key workers in the sectors are all deemed key barriers within this field (Davies, 1999; Davies, 2011; Roberts, 1994; Misell, 2000; Madoc-Jones and Dubberley, 2005). Indeed, according to Davies (2011:52): 'bilingual users continued to face the dual block of low personal expectations and correspondingly low levels of actual bilingual provision'.

Low expectations on the part of the users highlight how peripheral the Welsh language has been within (and continues to be in some cases) these formal spheres. Furthermore, this could emphasise what Ferguson (1959), Fishman (1967) and others have described as the diglossia where two language varieties often live side by side within a language community. This has particular resonance for minoritized languages as power relationships often determine what languages are used with whom, where, why and when (Fishman, 1965). There are high value and low value languages used in different situations (Wardhaugh, 2006; Holmes, 2008). Spolsky (2008), among others, describes the non-prestige, informal, low variety of some languages compared to high-variety, prestigious and formal languages. This can often lead to power struggles and clear language differentiation. This is a useful concept for the Welsh language in Wales as derogatory historic milestones have often meant that Welsh has been associated with a low value, informal language used in social situations but discarded from formal, prestigious situations. Madoc-Jones, Parry and Hughes (2012) highlight two types of diglossia within their research on language non-use in services settings in Wales; diglossia between Welsh and English and diglossia that exists between different types of Welsh used (formal and informal contexts). The opportunities to use Welsh within a social care and health setting were not only limited, but not always utilized due to preconceptions relating to this diglossia:

> *'Existing research about Welsh language use and non-use in service settings in Wales uniformly identifies diglossia between the English and Welsh languages as the primary barrier to minority language use and it promotes more fulsome service provision as the key to greater use.'* (Madoc-Jones, Parry and Hughes, 2012:251)

It is no surprise then, that user expectations are low if the Welsh language (as happens with other minoritized languages), is cast aside for wider, hegemonic aims of the lingua franca (Martyn-Jones, 1989). Recent research highlights that Welsh speakers' take up of Welsh-language services can be influenced by a range of factors, such as, how visible and accessible the service is, speakers' perceptions about the quality of the provision and, and behavioural choices (Citizens Advice Bureau, 2015). These factors are equally as important as the developing and enhancing social welfare provision. There is a need for further research into the psychological reasons why there can be low take up of services by Welsh speakers in different localities and what can be done to overcome this.

One field where there is limited research regarding Welsh language services is the field of mental health, which in itself, needs addressing. What little research exists, highlights the shortcomings of Welsh-medium provision within this field (Madoc-Jones, 2004; Hughes, 2018). Research by Hughes (2018) teases out the difficulties in receiving mental health therapy through your second language and how the whole process places added strain on, the already vulnerable, service user. Over-vigilance and caution from service users when discussing feelings and sensitive issues are key themes to be explored further:

> *"I'm pretty wary…I can't always explain it properly to her [therapist] about how it makes me feel because it's in English…these might not be the correct English words."* (Hughes, 2018, para. 8)

The way forward and conclusions

This chapter highlights the clear language need for Welsh language and bilingual services in the social welfare sector in Wales. What is clear, is that it is no longer feasible to simply state that there is no call for bilingual services in some localities in Wales. Regardless of demand, the onus is on providers to ensure the language needs of service users are met across different localities in Wales as noted by Misell (2000). Language planning and policy at different service levels can deliver these services in conjunction with current language legislation that places Language Standards on public service providers in Wales (Welsh Government, 2011). However, there is a need for holistic language policy and planning that recognises the complex nature of delivering social welfare across Wales. Social welfare services, are often administered by a system of mixed welfare, involving not only the public sector but also the private and voluntary sectors. This adds a level of complexity to the delivery of bilingual social welfare services and calls for greater joined-up thinking between key sectors.

The Macro-meso-micro framework (Baldauf, 2006; Liddicoat and Baldauf, 2008) could be useful in studying the interplay between Welsh language services across different language planning levels within social welfare. Despite the important role of the Welsh Government in language planning in Wales, macro-level language planning strategies are not always fully realised by the time service users experience these at a micro-level. There needs to be a greater understanding of the importance of individual service users' linguistic needs within the field of social welfare, especially at a meso-level where macro-level policies are often interpreted before they are implemented. This field can be of a sensitive nature and affect the most vulnerable within society, therefore, meeting language needs can make a real difference to the mental and physical health of service users on a daily basis.

Moving forward, clear developments in the field of social welfare and Welsh language service delivery in Wales, have been witnessed during the past twenty years of devolution. However, we could also argue that there is still a way to go in order to ensure that full language equality and language sensitivity are implemented on a daily basis. The active offer epitomises the crucial conceptual shift from language choice to language need, and acknowledges the onus placed on public bodies to actively offer these services to service users. The Welsh Language (Wales) Measure (2011) places duties on public bodies rather than the onus being on individuals to ask for bilingual services. The Welsh Government (2012) themselves described Welsh language services within health and social care 'as piecemeal' and some key research has also highlighted the limitations of certain services available in Welsh (Hughes, 2018; Madoc-Jones *et al.*, 2012) Moreover, despite the multitude of legislation, language strategies and social policies in place, attitudes are often deeply embedded in our psyche and are more difficult to change.

> '… just as speed limits do not guarantee that all cars abide by them, so a language law does not guarantee observance.' (Spolsky, 2012:5)

The Welsh Government's ambitious Welsh language strategy to reach one million Welsh Speakers by 2050 (Welsh Government, 2017a) is spearheaded by the need to create new Welsh speakers within Welsh-medium immersion education. However, the social welfare sector, specifically health and social care, has an important role to play in the linguistic progression of new Welsh speakers. Recent investment by the Welsh Government, via the National Centre for Learning Welsh and their 'Work Welsh' programme (National Centre for Learning Welsh and Welsh Government, 2018) means that more health and social care professionals can be released from work to learn and/or strengthen their Welsh language skills. It remains to be seen however, whether this programme will make a real difference in terms of effective bilingual service delivery. Furthermore, linguistic progression from education to the workplace is crucial in reaching the target of one million Welsh speakers by 2050. Social welfare provides key opportunities for Welsh speaking workers to use and often re-learn Welsh within their daily lives. A competent bilingual workforce will not only mean the government realise their target of one million speakers by 2050, but more importantly, Welsh language services can be actively offered to service users across Wales.

References

Alcock, P and Powell, M (2011) *Welfare Theory and Development: Part One – Welfare Theory*. London: Sage Publications

Armstrong, D, Bello, V and Spini, D (2011) (eds.) *Civil Society and International Governance. The role of non-state actors in global and regional regulatory frameworks*. London and New York: Routledge

Armstrong, T (2012) 'Establishing new norms of language use: the circulation of linguistic ideology in three new Irish-language communities'. *Language Policy* 2012 (11), pp145-168. doi: 10.1007/s10993-011-9219-2

Beatty C and Fothergill S (2013) *Hitting the poorest places hardest – the local and regional impact of welfare reform*, Sheffield: Sheffield Hallam University

Baldauf, RB (2006) Rearticulating the case for micro language planning in a language ecology context. *Current Issues in Language Planning.* 7(2-3): 147-170 doi:10.2167/cilp092.0

Citizens Advice Bureau (2015) *English by default – understanding the use and non-use of Welsh language services* Cardiff. www.citizensadvice.org.uk/about-us/policy/policy-research-topics/ citizens-advice-cymru-wales-policy-research/english-by-defaultunderstanding-the-use-and-non-use-of-welsh-language-services (Accessed 10.04.20)

Cooper, RL (1989) *Language Planning and Social Change* Cambridge: University of Cambridge Press

Crystal D. (2014) *Language Death* Cambridge: Cambridge University Press.

Davies, J (2014) *The Welsh Language: A History* Cardiff: University of Wales Press

Davies, E (1999) *The Language of a Caring Service* Cardiff: Welsh Language Board

Davies, E (2011) 'From the margins to the centre: language-sensitive practice and social welfare' in Williams, C. (2011) (ed.) *Social Policy for Social Welfare Practice in Wales* Birmingham: BASW/Venture Press

Deumart, A (2009) 'Language Planning and Policy' in Mesthrie, R, Swann, J, Deumart, A and Leap, WL (eds.) (2009) *Introducing Sociolinguistics.* Edinburgh: Edinburgh University Press, pp371-405

Dunbar, R (2009) *International Comparisons: Celtic Cousins – Language Legislation for Welsh and Scottish Gaelic* The Canadian Bar Association

Eberhard, DM, Simon, GF and Fenning, CD (eds.) (2020) *Ethnologue: Languages of the World. Twenty-third edition.* Dallas, Texas: SIL International

Ferguson, CA (1959) *'Diglossia'* Word, 15(2) 325–340. https://doi.org/10.1080/00437956.1959.11659702

Fishman, JA (1965) 'Bilingualism, Intelligence and Language Learning' *The Modern Language Journal.* Vol 49(4): 227-237 https://doi.org/10.1111/j.1540-4781.1965.tb00862

Fishman, JA (1967) 'Bilingualism With and Without Diglossia; Diglossia With and Without Bilingualism' *Journal of Social Issues* 23(2):29-38 https://doi.org/10.1111/j.1540-4560.1967.tb00573.x

Fishman, JA (2001) (ed.) *Can Threated Languages be Saved?* Clevedon: Multilingual Matters

Golwg 360 (2015) Cyngor Wrecsam am geisio herio 10 o'r safonau iaith newydd: https://golwg360.cymru/newyddion/cymru/205437-cyngor-wrecsam-am-geisio-herio-10-or-safonau-iaith-newydd (Accessed 10.04.20)

Grin, F (2003) *Language Policy Evaluation and the European Charter for Regional or Minority Languages* Basingstoke: Palgrave Macmillan

HMSO (1993) Welsh Language Act 1993 (c38). London: HMSO

Hodges, R (2009) 'Welsh Language Use among Young People in the Rhymney Valley'. Contemporary Wales 22(1): 16-35 www.ingentaconnect.com/content/uwp/cowa/2009/00000022/00000001/art00004

Hodges, R (2012) 'Welsh-medium education and parental incentives–the case of the Rhymni Valley, Caerffili' *International Journal of Bilingualism and Bilingual Education* 15(3): 355-373. doi: 10.1080/13670050.2011.636796

Hodges, R (2014) 'Caught in the middle: Parents' perceptions of new Welsh speakers' language use: The case of Cwm Rhymni, South Wales' *Zeszyty Łużyckienr/Sorbian Revue* 48(2014): 93-113. http://zeszytyluzyckie.uw.edu.pl/wp-content/uploads/2015/07/Zeszyty-Luzyckie-48.pdf

Hodges, R and Prys, C (2019) 'The community as a language planning crossroads: macro and micro language planning in communities in Wales' *Current Issues in Language Planning* 20(3): 207-225 https://doi.org/10.1080/14664208.2018.1495370

Hornsby, M (2015) 'The 'New' and 'Traditional' Speaker Dichotomy: Bridging the Gap' *International Journal of the Sociology of Language* 231: 107-125. doi:10.1515/ijsl-2013-0045

Holmes, J (2008) *An Introduction to Sociolinguistics* London: Longman

Hughes, SA (2018) *Iechyd Meddwl a'r Gymraeg: mae'n amser deffro*. Gwerddon Fach 28.11.2018 https://golwg360.cymru/gwerddon/534234-iechyd-meddwl-gymraeg-maen-amser-deffro] [Accessed online 13.04.20]

Jenkins, GH and Williams, MA (2000) *Eu Hiaith a Gadwant: Y Gymraeg yn yr Ugeinfed Ganrif* Cardiff: University of Wales Press

Kaplan BR and Baldauf, RB (1997) *Language Planning from Practice to Theory.* Clevedon: Multilingual Matters

Kloss, H (1977) *The American Bilingual Tradition* Rowley, MA: Newbury House

Kymlicka, W (2001) *Politics in the Vernacular: Nationalism, Multiculturalism, and Citizenship* Oxford: Oxford University Press

Lanehart, SJ (1996) 'The Language of Identity' *Journal of English Linguistics* 24(4): 322-31 https://doi.org/10.1177/007542429602400407

Lewis, G (2008) *Hawl i'r Gymraeg* Talybont: Y Lolfa

Lewis, H, and Royles, E (2017) Language revitalisation and social transformation: Evaluating the language policy frameworks of sub-state governments in Wales and Scotland. *Policy & Politics.* doi:10.1332/030557317X14938075758958

Liddicoat, A and Baldauf, RB (2008) 'Language planning in local contexts: Agents, contexts and interactions' in Liddicoat, A and Baldauf RB (eds.) *Language planning and policy: Language planning in local contexts.* Clevedon: Multilingual Matters, pp3-17

Mac Giolla Chríost, D (2015) *Language Commissioners and their Independence* Bangor University Administrative Justice Conference

Mac Giolla Chriost, D. (2017) 'Language commissioners and their independence' in: Nason, S (ed.) *Administrative Justice in Wales and Comparative Perspectives. The Public Law of Wales.* Cardiff: University of Wales Press, pp107-24

Madoc-Jones, I (2004) 'Linguistic sensitivity, indigenous peoples and the mental health system in Wales' *Journal of Mental Health Nursing* 13(4): 216-44 doi: 10.1111/j.1440-0979.2004.00337.x

Madoc-Jones, I and Dubberley, S (2005) 'Language and the provision of health and social care in Wales' in *Diversity in Health and Social Care 2005* (2): 127-34

Madoc-Jones, I, Parry, O and Hughes, C (2012) 'Minority language non-use in service settings: what we know, how we know it and what we might not know' *Current Issues in Language Planning*, 13(3): 249-62, DOI: 10.1080/14664208.2012.704860

Martyn-Jones, M (1989) 'Language, power and linguistic minorities: the need for an alternative approach to bilingualism, language maintenance and shift' in Grillo, R (ed.) *Social Anthropology and the Politics of Language* London: Routledge, pp106-25

May, S (2011) 'Language Rights: The "Cinderella" Human Right' *Journal of Human Rights*, 10(3): 265-89, DOI: 10.1080/14754835.2011.596073

Misell, A (2000) *Welsh in the health service: The scope, nature and adequacy of Welsh language provision in the NHS in Wales.* Cardiff: Welsh Consumer Council

Moon, DS (2012) 'Rhetoric and policy learning: On Rhodri Morgan's 'Clear Red Water; and 'Made in Wales' health policies'. *Public Policy and Administration.* 28(3): 306-23 https//doi.org/10.1177/0952076712455821

Morgan. P (1991) (ed.) *Brad Y Llyfrau Gleision.* Llandysul: Gwasg Gomer

Moseley, C (2011) (Editor) *Atlas of the World's Languages in Danger.* Unesco Publishing [Online]: www.unesco.org/new/fileadmin/MULTIMEDIA/HQ/CLT/pdf/aboutEndangeredLanguages-WV-EN-1.pdf (Accessed 05.04.2020)

Nason, S (2017) 'Administrative justice in Wales: a new egalitarianism.' *Journal of Social Welfare and Family Law*, 39(1): 115-35

National Assembly for Wales (2011) *Results of the National Assembly for Wales Referendum 2011* Cardiff: National Assembly for Wales

National Assembly for Wales (2019) *Supporting and Promoting the Welsh Language* Cardiff: National Assembly for Wales

National Centre for Learning Welsh and Welsh Government (2018) *What is Work Welsh?* https://learnwelsh.cymru/work-welsh/what-is-work-welsh (Accessed 10.04.20)

Office for National Statistics (2012). *2011 Census: Key Statistics for Wales*. ONS. [Online]: www.ons.gov.uk/peoplepopulationandcommunity/populationandmigration/populationestimates/bulletins/2011censuskeystatisticsforwales/2012-12-1 (Accessed 26.02.2020)

Parry, RG (2012) *Cymru'r Gyfraith: Sylwadau ar Hunaniaeth Genedlaethol* Caerdydd: Gwasg Prifysgol Cymru.

Prys, C, Hodges, R and Roberts, G (forthcoming) 'Rhetoric and reality: a critical review of language policy and legislation governing official minority language use in health and social care in Wales' Minorités linguistiques et société/*Linguistic Minorities and Society*

Roberts, G (1994) 'Nurse/Patient communication within a bilingual health care setting' *British Journal of Nursing* 3(2): 60-4, 66-7

Roberts G, Irvine F, Jones P et al. (2004) *Report of a Study of Welsh Language Awareness in Healthcare Provision in Wales*. Bangor: University of Wales

Sapir, E (1921) *Language: An Introduction to the Study of Speech*. New York: Harcourt, Brace & World Inc.

Skutnabb-Kangas, T (2000) *Linguistic genocide in education – or worldwide diversity and human rights?* Mahwah, NJ & London, UK: Lawrence Erlbaum Associates

Skutnabb-Kangas, T (2007) 'Linguistic Human Rights in Education?' In García, O and Baker, C (eds) *Bilingual Education. An Introductory Reader*. Clevedon, Buffalo & Toronto: Multilingual Matters, pp137-144

Skutnabb-Kangas, T and Harmon, D (2018) 'Biological diversity and language diversity: parallels and differences' in Penz, H & Fill, A (eds) *Handbook of Ecolinguistics* New York: Routledge, pp11-25

Spiker, P (2017) *Arguments for Welfare: The Welfare State and Social Policy*. London: Rowman and Littlefield Publishers

Spolsky, B (2008) *Sociolinguistics* Oxford: Oxford University Press

Spolsky, B (2012) (ed.) *The Cambridge Handbook of Language Policy* Cambridge: Cambridge University Press

Thomas, H and Williams, CH (2013) (eds.) *Parent, Personalities and Power: Welsh-medium Schools in South-east Wales* Cardiff: University of Wales Press

United Nations (1948) Universal Declaration of Human Rights: www.un.org/en/universal-declaration-human-rights (Accessed 05.04.2020)

Vacca, A (2013) 'Protection of minority languages in the UK public administration: A comparative study of Wales and Scotland' *Revista de Llengua i Dret* 60(1): 50-90

Wagoner, C (2017) *Language capacity building and strengthening in the Welsh statutory education and health and social sectors*. PhD Thesis, Cardiff University

Wardhaugh, R (2006) *An Introduction to Sociolinguistics* London: Blackwell Publishing

Welsh Assembly Government (2003) *Iaith Pawb: A National action plan for a bilingual Wales* Cardiff: Welsh Assembly Government

Welsh Assembly Government (2011) *The White Paper Sustainable Social Services: A Framework for Action* Cardiff: Welsh Assembly Government

Welsh Language Board (1996) *Welsh Language Schemes: Their preparation and approval in accordance with the Welsh Language Act 1993* Cardiff: Welsh Language Board

Welsh Language Commissioner (2015) "The Commissioner's functions include." www.comisiynyddygymraeg.cymru/english/Pages/Home.aspx. (Accessed 30.01.2020)

Welsh Government (2011) *Welsh Language (Wales) Measure* London: HMSO

Welsh Government (2012a) *A living language: a language for living – Welsh Language Strategy 2012-2017* Cardiff: Welsh Government

Welsh Government (2012b) *More than just words: Strategic Framework for Welsh Language Services in Health, Social Services and Social Care* Cardiff: Welsh Government

Welsh Government (2014) *The Social Services and Wellbeing Act (2014)* Cardiff: Welsh Government

Welsh Government (2016) *More than just words: Follow-on strategic framework for Welsh Language in Health, Social Services and Social Care.* Cardiff: Welsh Government

Welsh Government (2017a) *Cymraeg 2050 - A million Welsh Speakers* Cardiff: Welsh Government

Welsh Government (2017b) *Technical report: Projection and trajectory for the number of Welsh speakers aged three and over, 2011 to 2050* Cardiff: Welsh Government

Welsh Government (2018) *A Healthier Wales: Our Plan for Health and Social Care* Cardiff: Welsh Government

Welsh Government and Care Council for Wales (2012) *Welsh Speakers' Experiences of Health and Social Care Services* Cardiff: Welsh Government

Welsh Government and Welsh Language Commissioner (2015) *National Survey for Wales, 2013-2014. Welsh Language Use Survey* Cardiff: Welsh Government and Welsh Language Commissioner

Welsh Statutory Instruments 2018 No. 441 (W. 77) WELSH LANGUAGE: The Welsh Language Standards (No. 7) Regulations 2018 www.legislation.gov.uk/wsi/2018/441/made (Accessed 26.03.2020)

Williams, CH (2011) 'Paradigm Shifts, Geostrategic Considerations and Minority Initiatives' *Treatises and Documents: Journal of Ethnic Studies* 66: 8-23 http://orca.cf.ac.uk/id/eprint/24644

Williams, CH (2012) 'In defence of language rights: language commissioner in Canada, Ireland and Wales in Brohy, C et al. (eds.) *Law, Language and the Multilingual State: Proceedings of the 12th International Conference of the International Academy of Linguistic Law.* Bloemfontein: SUN MeDIA. 45-71

Williams, G and Morris, D (2000) *Language Planning and Language Use: Welsh in a Global Age* Cardiff: University of Wales Press

Wyn Williams, I (2003) (ed.) *Our Children's Language: The Welsh-medium Schools of Wales 1939-2000* Talybont: Y Lolfa

Chapter 8

Climate Change and Social Welfare: Exploring Environmental Social Work

Holly Gordon

Introduction

On the 29th April 2019 a climate emergency was declared in Wales by the Minister for Environment, Energy and Rural Affairs. This proceeded organised protests and several Local Authorities in Wales declaring their own climate emergencies amid local residents organising and petitioning for the declaration to be made. Cardiff was one of five UK cities identified as 'centres of disruption' by the non-violent direct-action group, Extinction Rebellion as part of a five-day national campaign. Protests organised by the movement included a mass cycle ride during rush hour a few days prior to the declaration being announced. Protests continued across Wales after this time as part of a 'summer uprising' with Extinction Rebellion calling on the Welsh Government to dramatically accelerate efforts to address the crisis. The climate emergency declaration was made in the context of unequivocal scientific evidence of the climate system warming (IPCC, 2014) and in recognition that climate change is the defining challenge of our time. Yet despite the overwhelming evidence of climate change and the observed effects on humans, social welfare professions have been slow to address environmental issues (Coates *et al.*, 2006) having been referred to as 'isolated' from key debates and environmental action (Marlow and Van Rooyen, 2001). This chapter draws on environmental social work literature, which holds relevance to all social welfare professions. For social welfare professions, much discussion on the 'environment' has only referred to the social environment (Närhi and Matties, 2016), with the proximal, interpersonal environmental facets, such as family and school dominating. This has occurred despite a well-established understanding that people's physical environment significantly affects their life experience and matters relating to equity and justice (Kemp, 2011).

Climate change can affect humans in a multitude of ways, including increased mortality and morbidity from heat waves, fires and food and water borne disease spread (Pacheco, 2020). The current data illustrates that the planet is 1.1°C warmer than pre-industrial periods (WMO, 2020). Since the 1980s, each successive decade has been warmer than any preceding one since 1850. There is a high probability that this increased warming is the result of human activity since the mid-20th century (at least 95 per cent probability) (IPCC, 2014). This increase is already creating visible changes such as a rise in flooding, droughts, heat waves, tropical storms and rising sea levels. Sea levels are rising at a rapid pace with around 90 per cent of this excess heat being absorbed by the Earth's oceans causing an increase in water volume and subsequent advanced glacial and ice sheet melt which contributes to sea level rise. Rising sea levels are exposing islands and low-lying areas to increased risk of flooding. Across the planet, countries are experiencing heat waves and prolonged periods of drought. In recent years there have been wild fires on an unprecedented scale, such as those in Australia between 2019-2020, which as of March 2020 had seen 46 million acres burnt and an estimated one billion animals killed, including some species which were driven to extinction (Redfearn, 2020).

In Wales, the impact of climate change is predicted to impact soil conditions, bio-diversity and landscapes due to warmer, drier summers. A decline in native species and increased number of invasive species is expected as well as deaths and illnesses from hotter weather and coastal and inland flooding affecting homes and infrastructure (Natural Resources Wales, 2020). The impact of climate change will leave communities vulnerable, particularly in coastal areas and agricultural land will be at risk from flooding storm damage and water shortage. From the weight of scientific data available, it can only be concluded that the evidence for rapid climate change is compelling. It is in this context of increased scientific certainty and an upsurge in interest in the environmental movement, that a developing field known as 'environmental social work' has emerged which holds vast potential for all social welfare professions.

Environmental social work

In the early stages of a growing environmental awareness, interest was limited to a small group of academics who repeatedly asserted the need for social work to engage in environmental issues. It was not until 1981 that social work academics Germain (1981) and Weick (1981) 'raised the alarm' in relation to a bio-physical absence in the social work agenda, and over the following decades more academics with an awareness of a pending environmental crises joined the debate. The ground breaking publication edited by Hoff and McNutt (1994) entitled *The global environmental crisis: Implications for social welfare and social work* gave social work its first comprehensive text calling for the profession to fully recognise the connection between planetary and human well-being. Contributions made by Rogge (1994), Tester (1994) and Shubert (1994) offered persuasive arguments relating to social work's lack of foresight on environmental issues, recognising the breach in social work ethics and values involving the well-established aim of upholding social justice. These early pioneers sought to raise awareness of the impact of climate change, environmental degradation and the potential engagement of social work. The need to raise awareness of the social work role in climate change spans decades and to a large extent still continues. However, it became increasingly recognised that early publications did not offer any vision of what this form of social work intervention may look like in practice (Molyneux, 2010; Kemp, 2011). In addition, it was noted that there was reluctance from the profession to transform practice to include environmental justice (Coates *et al.*, 2006; Zapf, 2005a; Zapf, 2005b).

There has been a lack of practical application in environmental social work, leaving social workers with little insight into what it looks like in practice. Commentators have noted that whilst social workers are asked to create a new vision, contributions to this subject are often 'abstract', 'devoid of detail' and 'detached from everyday interaction with service users' (Molyneux, 2010). For example, such vagueness can be seen in the work of Coates (2000) who urges social workers to support people in recognising that all life is sacred and to develop supportive social structures which promote wellbeing. Molyneux (2010) concludes that such offerings present more like a prophecy than a practice method, causing readers to be motivated but unable to apply this directly into practice. However, since the 2010s onwards, eco-critical discussions have grown and transformed global debates. This has been supported by several international conferences and publications. These discussions hold common features which challenge mainstream social work and call for a paradigm shift whilst critiquing current structures. Närhi and Matthies (2016) view these discussions as having a global perspective whilst creating models for local action focusing on community resilience. Examples of this can be seen in the work of Rambaree (2013), who argues for a stronger focus on social justice within sustainable development and the need for social workers to analyse both social and cultural impacts. Additionally, Dominelli critiques industrialisation and urbanisation adopted in the West leading to intensified environmental pressures and takes a globalised perspective which includes a critique of neoliberalism, and poses societal and community based sustainable solutions in her ground-breaking text *Green Social Work* (Dominelli, 2012) These publications have supported the development of social works efforts in responding to the climate emergency.

Ramsay and Boddy (2017) have further contributed to the field by using a concept analysis framework to identify characteristics of environmental social work. This involved a systematic literature review with Table 4 containing a total of 117 articles. This supports the move towards an 'operational definition' by identifying four common themes to improve clarity (Ramsay and Boddy, 2017). The identified themes consist of: using social work skills creatively, openness in values and practice, transformation and interdisciplinary working. This approach moves away from theoretical disparities and focuses on commonalities within the subject. The table below identifies the prominence of each theme/sub theme in this analysis:

Table 8.1: Number of articles that state attributes

Themes	No. of articles	%
Creatively apply existing skills to environmental concepts	67	100
Openness to different values and ways of being or doing		
Shift practice, theory and values to incorporate the natural environment	67	99
Learn from spirituality and indigenous cultures	28	41
Incorporate the natural environment in social work education	17	25
Appreciate the instrumental and innate value of non-human life	22	32
Adopt a renewed change orientation		
Change society	60	88
Critique hedgemony	58	85
Work across boundaries and in multiple spaces		
Work in multidisciplinary teams	58	85
Work with communities	45	66
Work with individuals	38	56

(Ramsay and Boddy, 2017)

Ramsay and Boddy's (2017) analysis showed that within the last 15 years publications have tripled on two occasions which could be indicative of a professional shift.

Over the last decade the enhanced focus on practice has led to publications making an increased effort to develop practice-based case studies which offer examples of environmental social work from around the world. Gray *et al.*'s (2013) text *Environmental Social Work*, contains case studies covering the areas of community gardens and activism, working with drought affected families, challenging corporate ethics and an environmental project for young offenders. This publication supports the move towards a more practice orientated focus by writers and improves our understanding of what environmental social work practice might entail. Other case studies include Evans *et al.*'s (2010) Social Care Institute for Excellence (SCIE) commissioned research project which drew on case studies to highlight how adult social care in the UK can become more sustainable in its service provision. The paper outlined Swansea Council's co-production model which utilised time banking systems of skill exchange. The main drive of the initiative was to reduce carbon emissions and therefore reduce costs. Additionally, Lysack's (2015) Canadian based case study demonstrates that public policy is an area which environmental social work can engage with and influence. The case study offers an example of policy engagement in relation to coal in Alberta, Canada where political agreement to phase out the use of coal was achieved through the work of a network involving health professionals, NGO staff, and academics. The group gathered evidence relating to the health and economic costs to the community and applied pressure to gain a political commitment for change. Whilst examples of practice still appear to be scant (Ramsay and Boddy, 2017), and there is scope for a wider array of case studies, particularly from the UK, it is clear that some recent efforts have been made.

Given the current climate emergency and the known impact on the human population, it is critical for social welfare professions in Wales to renew their commitment to social justice and to rapidly adapt. This requires a challenge to the mainstream paradigm, which suggests that environmental social work has similarities with critical, feminist and radical perspectives (Närhi and Matthies, 2016) which are already present in social welfare professions. However, significant barriers to its emergence are present, firstly, the subject is marginalised in social welfare literature and lacks perceived importance within managerialist employment structures. Secondly, although a professional interest has now been established, those in direct practice need guidance e.g. workshops/case studies, to support environmental incorporation into practice and thirdly, the university curriculum needs attention in relation to the connections between social and environmental justice and sustainability to promote the transition (McKinnon, 2008). If environmental practice in social welfare professions in Wales is to flourish, further attention will be required in culturally specific models, interventions and research. Whilst it is acknowledged that environmental social work is in its fledgling stage in Wales, further consideration will now be given to the potential reach of environmental social work within policy, education and activism for social welfare professions in a Welsh context.

Environmental policy and social welfare professions

The climate emergency facing the planet requires innovation and commitment from every citizen and holds challenges for practitioners, academics and policy makers. Policy development on climate change involves multiple stakeholders, which includes social welfare professions. Social welfare professionals hold expertise on social issues and will bear witness to the effects on the communities they work alongside. They are well placed to vocalise the realities of climate change on the ground and should be involved in policy development, implementation and monitoring in this area. Engagement with policy makers and lobbying for change can occur at a local, national and international level (Dominelli, 2011). The global agenda of Sustainable Development Goals offers social workers an opportunity to redefine practice through centralising socioeconomic development, environmental sustainability and human rights. In Wales, legislative change has provided an opportunity for the country to begin to transform society by ensuring that a long-term vision is applied in practice. These are important to social welfare professionals as they will underpin current and future efforts and provide an opportunity for transformative change. Policy practice involves social welfare professionals using their skills to support the development and transformation of policies to achieve ecological justice. Such practice holds great merit in the challenge of climate change for both adaptation and mitigation.

The Future Generations (Wales) Act 2015 addresses the wellbeing of people across social, economic, environmental and cultural domains through the introduction of seven wellbeing goals. The public sector in Wales is now required to consider the long-term impact of any decision making on future generations, recognising the extent of current and future challenges of climate change, poverty, employment and health. Sustainable development must be incorporated into the work undertaken by public bodies. This includes the publishing of wellbeing objectives to enable wellbeing goals to be reached. Public bodies must act to ensure they meet their set objectives which will be evidenced in local wellbeing plans and be subject to annual review. The Act gives social welfare professionals a way to legitimately engage with public bodies to monitor and review progress and to lobby against policies which are incongruent to the Act's principles. The Act has implemented a 'sustainable development principle' which must be adhered to by public bodies to meet the duties imposed by the Act. In accordance with the sustainability principle, the Act establishes Public Service Boards (PSBs) in each Local Authority. PSB members include the Local Authority, Local Health Board, the Fire and Rescue Authority and Natural Resources for Wales. The following approaches ensure better joint working, learning lessons and tackling long term challenges. Public bodies must consider five factors to demonstrate adherence to the sustainability principle:

1) Long term: creating a balance between short term community needs and ensuring long term needs are safeguarded
2) Prevention: preventing problems in the first instance or mitigating problems to ensure they don't worsen
3) Integration: consider how wellbeing objectives affect each of the wellbeing goals
4) Collaboration: collaboration both within bodies and between bodies to support achieving wellbeing objectives
5) Involvement: involving stakeholders and ensuring that those involved reflect a diverse range of people in that area

Figure 8.1 : Principles of the Future Generations (Wales) Act 2015

Goal	Description of the goal
A prosperous Wales	An innovative, productive and low carbon society which recognises the limits of the global environment and therefore uses resources efficiently and proportionately (including acting on climate change); and which develops a skilled and well-educated population in an economy which generates wealth and provides employment opportunities, allowing people to take advantage of the wealth generated through securing decent work.
A resilient Wales	A nation which maintains and enhances a biodiverse natural environment with healthy functioning ecosystems that support social, economic and ecological resilience and the capacity to adapt to change (for example climate change).
A healthier Wales	A society in which people's physical and mental well-being is maximised and in which choices and behaviours that benefit future health are understood.
A more equal Wales	A society that enables people to fulfil their potential no matter what their background or circumstances (including their socio economic background and circumstances).
A Wales of cohesive communities	Attractive, viable, safe and well-connected communities.
A Wales of vibrant culture and thriving Welsh language	A society that promotes and protects culture, heritage and the Welsh language, and which encourages people to participate in the arts, and sports and recreation.
A globally responsible Wales	A nation which, when doing anything to improve the economic, social, environmental and cultural well-being of Wales, takes account of whether doing such a thing may make a positive contribution to global well-being

Reproduced from Well-being of Future Generations (Wales) Act 2015: The Essentials (2015, p6)
https://gov.wales/sites/default/files/publications/2019-08/well-being-of-future-generations-wales-act-2015-the-essentials.pdf

The Future Generations (Wales) Act 2015 is the first law of its kind in the world and holds enormous potential. It is supported by more specific legislation on the management of natural resources. Approaches to sustainable management of natural resources in Wales are set out in the Environment (Wales) Act 2016, to support the adaptation and mitigation of the impact of climate change. The health of natural resources is considered to enable future resilience. This includes a duty placed on Welsh ministers to ensure that greenhouse emission targets are being met and that interim targets are monitored to assess progress in meeting the 2050 goal. Interim targets are monitored at five yearly intervals, which Welsh ministers must report on to the National Assembly for Wales. The Act affords a flexible approach so targets can be adapted as scientific findings on climate change evolve. If amendments are to be made in regard to carbon emission targets, Welsh ministers must seek advice from the advisory body which supports ministers. In March 2019, the initial delivery plan *Prosperity for all: A low carbon Wales*, was published in accordance with the requirements of the Environmental (Wales) Act 2016. The delivery plan includes a collection of 76 policies and 24 new proposals, which provide details of how Wales is to meet its emission reduction targets and gives a vision for a low carbon Wales.

Whilst Wales has already developed ambitious plans to tackle the climate emergency, there is a role for social welfare professions in Wales to ensure that policies and legislation are fully implemented. Policy makers should be held to account for not acting quickly or robustly enough to tackle climate change and the policy landscape in Wales offers social welfare professionals a mechanism to do this. However, prior to social welfare professionals engaging in environmental action for change, the role of education must be considered to ensure social welfare professionals are equipped to engage in climate change concerns.

Environmental social work education

This section focuses on social work education as an example, but recognises that community and youth work-based education programmes would also benefit from increased environmental inclusion. The need to integrate the environment into social work education is a common theme present in environmental social work literature (see Gray and Coates, 2015; Melekis & Woodhouse, 2015; Jones, 2008; McKinnon, 2008) and whilst a global lack of engagement from universities remains, efforts in recent years have increased. McKinnon (2008) has discussed the need for social works 'on-going relevance' by having a focus on social sustainability within the education curriculum of both pre and post qualification courses. However, it has been argued that for a transformative change to occur in the profession a paradigm shift needs to happen within social work education which would;

> '*provide a way forward for developing a different frame of reference for understanding Earth as a holistic entity and for taking action towards a more sustainable environment.*'
> (Boetto, 2016:63)

Such efforts are presented in Gray *et al*.'s (2013) publication: *Environmental Social Work*, which holds five chapters on education as well as the special edition on environmental education in the *Journal of Social Work Education* (Gray *et al*., 2015). Yet despite some encouraging steps forward, incorporating environmental social work into the social work curriculum is still in the early developmental stages. The inclusion of social work education in the literature on environmental social work, highlights the impact it can have towards transformation. Whilst the extent to which social work education includes the natural environment is unknown (Harris and Boddy, 2017), some insights have been gleaned from Australia, north America and Wales, however considerable gaps in understanding course content remain.

An updated content analysis of tertiary social work education in Australia undertaken by Harris and Boddy (2017), illustrated a little engagement with the subject. The 44 social work degree courses analysed contained a total of 937 subjects of core and elective subjects. All mandatory subjects were included. 31 subjects being taught across 15 universities contained terms related to the natural environment. Three universities were found to have designed subjects specifically devoted to the natural environment. Subject specific content was found on 'Gender, climate change and social sustainability' and 'Green Justice: Environment and Social Issue'. It is recognised that this 2017 analysis shows some increase since Jones' (2008) findings. Similarly, Kemp (2011) refers to the marginalisation of environmental content in the social work curriculum in the USA, and asserts that where such content is present, it is due to specific faculty members interests. The area of education has also been focused on by researchers. An example of this is Lucas-Darby's (2011) study. This research centred on a community practice course with 'greening' as its theme, with students spending a semester undertaking a community based green project, and concluded by stressing the critical need to include such content.

Wales currently has six universities which deliver social work programmes. A 2015 survey exploring environmental content in the social work curriculum showed that whilst teaching does contain a distinct social justice focus which includes international social work perspectives, subjects relating to environmental social work and ecological justice were not being explicitly taught. One university acknowledged the importance of the subject by including Dominelli's (2012) Green Social Work text in their list of potential book reviews for students graded assignment. Whilst the importance of the subject was not dismissed, lecturers commented on the pressures on content relating to individualised casework as one reason why this had not been included. In 2015, a stand-alone lecture was offered to universities in Wales on climate change and social work with two universities responding positively to this offer. A post lecture evaluation form was developed to capture the students' views on the subject and their view on the validity of including this subject in the social work curriculum. A total of 32 students attended the lectures. The evaluation showed that students' knowledge on the subject prior to the lecture was low but did include some understanding of community activism and the therapeutic value of nature. A large majority felt the subject should be incorporated into the curriculum, although some were concerned about lack of space in the current curriculum. The extent to which the students felt the subject should be incorporated into the curriculum varied. The majority thought that a one-off lecture was suitable. However, the majority of students stated that they would like to learn more about the subject and enjoyed the learning which had occurred. This review of social work education in Wales highlights both the lack of attention given to the climate emergency as well as the potential to progress this critical area.

Integrating the environment into social work education was not evident across Wales and globally the inclusion of the environment into social work programmes has been 'peripheral' and 'piecemeal' (Melekis and Woodhouse, 2015). However, some innovative departments in Australia, North America and Europe have developed modules and interdisciplinary courses which are pioneering future developments in this area (Drolet *et al.*, 2015). Such examples offer insight into how universities can further support such endeavours by developing a cultural commitment to sustainability, developing curriculum and guidance for staff and students and creating interdisciplinary departments (Melekis and Woodhouse, 2015). Whilst some practical barriers to incorporating the natural environment exist, the impact of neoliberalism on social work education should be recognised. The commercialisation of universities and competitive environment between departments and institutions has been widely recognised (Connell, 2013). Managerialism has ushered in a focus on efficiencies and economic performance which has impacted on how decisions on content are made (Harris, 2014). This may be a significant force impeding the inclusion of the natural environment within social work education according to Harris and Boddy (2017). Harris and Boddy (2017) draw attention to the disparity between the extent of social work literature now available on the natural environment and the inadequate level of its inclusion within social work education and suggest a time-lag has led to curriculum content not being updated to reflect rapidly changing contexts. Education for social work students and qualified social workers must be centred on current knowledge which is relevant to the field of practice which includes the impact of climate change. A distinct lack of efforts in this area could be harmful for those requiring support services (Yaffe, 2013) and the profession itself (Melekis and Woodhouse, 2015).

Action for change

This section will consider how alternative practice methods for social welfare professionals practicing in Wales can be implemented which incorporate politicised action and change involving a re-engagement with local communities and social movements as well as an inclusion of the environment into practice. This area has previously been identified as a gap in environmental social work literature from global north scholars (Närhi and Matthies, 2016). As Dominelli states:

> *'The complexities arising from the financial and environmental crises require practitioners to look for new paradigms for practice, and give greater priority to social and community development within an ecological framework that cares for the environment as well as the people living within it.'* (Dominelli, 2010:603)

Whilst considering such practice methods, it is important to highlight the essential features required of such practices which includes the importance of acknowledging ecological justice alongside social justice, a critique of neoliberalism and collaboration which will support an alternative vision of social welfare professions.

Whilst individualised practice methods can incorporate the environment, the benefits of integrating the environment into practice which is situated within community development would have more transformative outcomes. Social welfare professionals based in practice and education repeatedly assert the relevance of community work approaches within practice (Barron and Taylor, 2010: Healy, 2012) and whilst such practice methods aren't widespread in the West, research by Forde and Lynch (2014) found that social work contributions to communities often goes hidden and unacknowledged. There is much to learn from social welfare professions in the global south who may have stronger associations with community development and more intense direct experiences of climate change. Some academics have looked to Cuba for examples of empowering practice within an anti-capitalist context (Backwith and Mantle, 2009), as Cuba has a strong grasp of sustainable development, triggered by rapid resource depletion (from the fall of the USSR and years of sanctions), Cuba may hold valuable insight for environmental social work. For Ife (1998) community-based practice engages in bottom up processes, not found within managerialism. This discourse has a social justice focus working alongside marginalised groups seeking community and societal level changes, informed by critical perspectives. However, if social welfare professions in Wales are to remain committed to their definitional aims of social justice, they must incorporate ecological justice into discourse.

The emergence of Transition towns offers a strong example of a grassroots, community-led response to neoliberal practices by focusing on sustainable and localised responses to the climate emergency (Gordon, 2017). The first transition town in Wales emerged in 2007 in Llandelio with a focus on several aspects of transitional systems relating to food, energy and economics. This hub is part of the wider transition movement which has become one of the most influential movements across the Global North (Sage, 2014). Environmental social work can also learn from alternative lifestyles and livelihoods in Wales, such as the development of ecovillages. The world-renowned Ecovillage of Lammas in Pembrokeshire, contains collective smallholdings and low impact dwellings. The Ecovillage has adopted traditional farming and building methods. Such initiatives offer environmental social work insight into alternative communities and could offer practice learning opportunities for student social workers in Wales and sites for post qualifying training.

Feygina (2013) illustrates the interconnectedness of ecological and social injustice stressing that they both emerge from and are upheld by socio-economic processes and hierarchal power structures which uphold the dominant paradigm. For Feygina (2013), right wing authoritarianism e.g. political conservatism and the promotion of the free market, upholds the existing paradigm and attempts to prevent strides towards equality and redistribution. This not only exacerbates injustices to humans but also contains considerable disregard for the environment. Thus Feygina (2013) asserts that the ideological roots of social injustice and anti-environmental sentiment, exist within the same paradigm. This understanding has importance in considerations of how to effect change (Feygina, 2013). Critical researchers highlight a number of structural factors such as gender and class which impact on human experience, but they also engage with issues of consumerism and environmentally harmful practices (Denzin, 2002). Feygina (2013) suggests that given the connection between social and environmental (in)justice, enlarging the theoretical landscape of justice is of great value and concludes by suggesting that without the amalgamation of social and environmental justice considerations, sustainability may be beyond reach.

Environmental social work requires an understanding of structural issues on both a local and global scale. Globalisation has begun to intensify its pace facilitated by technological advancements, the increasing presence of Multi-National Corporations and diminishing trade barriers (Ellwood, 2001). This global growth is transforming capitalist relations and structures, spreading specific ideologies (particularly neo-liberalism) and commodities. It has been recognised that environmental injustice stems from resource inequality and environmental degradation which occurs through normal industrialisation processes:

> *'Unsustainable models of development, unequal power dynamics and unequal distribution of resources, central to the current global socio-economic system of neo-liberalism, exacerbate structural inequalities and affect most poor and low-income people.'* (Dominelli, 2013: 431)

Ramsay and Boddy (2017) stress the pervasiveness of neoliberalism, whereby individuals can internalise and act out neoliberal values without having an awareness of this. For example, it has been argued that, social work practices which support people to participate in society – a society which exploits nature and promotes competition and individualism, is aligning itself with the neoliberal agenda (Coates, 2003). It has also been raised that those who stand in opposition to neoliberal practices may find themselves isolated and vulnerable if they are situated within bureaucratic systems (Ramsay and Boddy, 2017). This raises dilemmas for both environmental theorising and practice in relation to ensuring that environmental social work stands firm in its commitment to justice by challenging existing structures and not colluding with them. Having an understanding of neoliberalism would appear necessary for a move towards transformation which entails a rejection of consumerism and a move towards a sustainable society (Boetto, 2016). This highlights the importance of involving neoliberal critique in the subsequent research and practice methods for environmental social work.

Environmental social work calls for a wide range of partnerships and a broad interdisciplinary knowledge base (Gray *et al.*, 2013). Environmental social work, by its very nature expands to social welfare professions and involves many disciplines and communities from around the world as all species rely on the Earth's systems and resources for survival. Progression in this field will require unusual interdisciplinary partnerships, which Kemp (2011) refers to as 'strange bedfellows' and local community collaboration where daily life consists of environmental threats. Other disciplines will need to be leaned upon by social welfare professions, such as the area of pedagogy, agriculture and science. Taylor (2013) offers a unique practice example of collaboration when working within the area of marine science and another case example of collaboration can be seen in the Gilesgate energy initiative, UK. This project aimed to developed renewable energy sources to create affordable energy and create employment opportunities to tackle fuel poverty. It involved a community social worker, local residents, interdisciplinary academics, private businesses, social workers, policy makers and housing providers. They held public meetings, exhibited renewable technologies, undertook energy audits in households and informed residents of available grants. This led to homes being adapted which lowered fuel costs. The long-term aim of the project was to become energy self-sufficient. The community social worker supported the co-ordination of stakeholders, meetings and exhibitions and played a central role in the project (Dominelli, 2012).

Community initiatives involving energy affords another area for environmental social work engagement. Local initiatives such as the 'energy club' based in Bethesda, north Wales, provides low cost power to residents through a local hydropower scheme. This supports power to be used locally and the reduction in travel miles produces lower energy bills. Such initiatives would benefit from social welfare engagement and would also offer sites for training and education in environmental social work practice. Kemp (2011) draws attention to the benefits of engaging with urban planning and geography. This includes the use of participatory approaches currently used in these areas. Such approaches bring together professionals, researchers and community stakeholders to undertake community based participatory research. This would allow for collaborative action plans to achieve change and can be adopted into practice, policy and research (Kemp, 2011).

Environmental social work in Wales can draw upon and engage with the environmental movement to further its cause. The drive for justice is strongly identifiable with such movements, which have offered an alternative to so called 'legitimate' political parties. Thompson (2002) asserts that Anti Discriminatory Practice partly developed from social movements. This has taken the form of challenging dominant individualised approaches to practice, such as psychodynamic interventions. Social movement influence has allowed for a reconsideration of sociological factors affecting service users enabling the integration of social justice concepts (Thompson, 2002). This originated with an analysis of class, progressing gender and race then moving on to disability and sexuality. Whilst acknowledging the historic context of social welfare professions involvement in social movements, Ferguson (2008) identifies radical social work as a product of great social movements, referring to the 1970's era of civil rights, women's rights and anti-war protest. In relation to climate change, Extinction Rebellion holds potential for environmental social work's engagement in action for change. The group causes disruption and financial cost to the state in an attempt to pressurise the government to take urgent action on climate change. Extinction Rebellion has already seen engagement from social welfare professions across the world, but more could be done to demonstrate solidarity with the movement's cause. Social welfare professionals and families accessing support have been encouraged to engage with the movement, stressing the importance of acting in solidarity with those most affected by climate change (Morton, 2019).

Conclusions

This chapter has presented the key areas which require attention if an identifiable environmental social work movement in Wales is to emerge beyond the realm of theory. The effects of environmental degradation and resource depletion on marginalised people highlight the importance of social welfare professions engagement in this area. By understanding the need to stand in solidarity with communities to tackle climate change and how this relates to the very essence of social welfare professions, developments can progress within education and practice learning opportunities, policy engagement and community-based practice which is transformative. This chapter will conclude with recommendations which emerged from this chapter's discussions.

- It is important that social, community and youth work students are educated to understand the responsibilities they hold in relation to ecological justice, as well as social justice. Therefore, this subject should be taught within education and training programmes as part of modules focusing on community development.
- Social, community and youth work education departments can collaborate with community organisations and other university departments to develop interdisciplinary modules and practice learning opportunities. This requires educators to challenge the dominant neoliberal ideology which gives attention to managerialism and compliance.
- Social work education departments and social work bodies could facilitate a national working group to develop core competencies and curriculum resources on ecological justice.
- The development of an environmental social work network in Wales to support with policy engagement, networking opportunities and awareness raising.

It is vital that social welfare professions in Wales recognise the valuable skills the profession can contribute to this area involving mitigation and adaptation to prevent the catastrophic effects of climate change. Whilst such a transformation holds many challenges, the cost of not advancing these efforts is high. Social welfare professions are uniquely placed to take action and challenge unsustainable practices and as such, for them to remain relevant, they must ensure that tackling the climate emergency becomes an integral part of practice.

References

Backwith, D and Mantle, G (2009) 'Inequalities in health and community-oriented social work: Lessons from Cuba.' *International Social Work* 52(4): 499-511

Barron C and Taylor B J (2010) 'The rights tools for the right job: Social work students learning community development' *Social Work Education* 29(4): 372-85

Boetto, H (2016) 'A Transformative Eco-Social Model: Challenging Modernist Assumptions in Social Work' *British Journal of Social Work* 47(1): 48–67

Coates, J (2000) From Modernism to Sustainability: New Roles for Social Work. Retrieved from www.ecosocialwork.org/jcoates2.html

Coates, J (2003) *Ecology and Social Work: Towards a new paradigm* Halifax: Fernwood Books

Coates, J, Gray, M, and Hetherington, T (2006) 'An 'ecospiritual' perspective: Finally, a place for indigenous approaches', *British Journal of Social Work* 36(3): 381-99

Connell, R (2013) 'The neoliberal cascade and education: an essay on the market agenda and its consequences' *Critical Studies in Education* 54(2): 99-112

Denzin, N K (2002) 'Social Work in the 7th Moment' *Qualitative Social Work* 1(1): 25-38

Dominelli, L (2010) 'Globalization, contemporary challenges and social work practice' *International Social Work* 53(5): 599-612

Dominelli, L (2011) 'Climate change: social worker's roles and contributions to policy debates and Interventions' *International Journal of Social Welfare* 20(4): 430-438

Dominelli, L (2012) *Green Social Work: From Environmental Crisis to Environmental Justice* Cambridge,: Polity Press

Dominelli L (2013) 'Environmental justice at the heart of social work practice: Greening the profession' *International Journal of Social Welfare* 22(4): 431-39

Drolet, J, Wu, H, Taylor, M and Dennehy, A (2015) 'Social Work and Sustainable Social Development: Teaching and Learning Strategies for 'Green Social Work' Curriculum' *Social Work Education* 34(5): 528-43

Ellwood, W (2001) *The no nonsense guide to Globalisation* London: New Internationalist, Verso

Environment (Wales) Act 2016, Available at: www.legislation.gov.uk/anaw/2016/3/contents/enacted (Accessed 25.03.2020)

Evans, S, Hills, S and Grimshaw, L (2010) Sustainable systems of social care, Adult Services SCIE Report 35, London: SCIE UK

Ferguson, I (2008) *Reclaiming Social Work: Challenging Neo-liberalism and Promoting Social Justice* London: Sage Publications

Feygina, I (2013) 'Social Justice and the Human–Environment Relationship: Common Systemic, Ideological, and Psychological Roots and Processes' *Social Justice Research* 26(3): 363-81

Forde, C, Lynch, D (2014) 'Critical Practice for Challenging Times: Social Workers' Engagement with Community Work', *British Journal of Social Work* 44(8): 2078-94

Germain, C (1981) 'The physical environment and social work practice', Maluccio, A N (ed.) *Promoting competence in clients: A new/old approach to social work practice* New York: Free Press, pp103-24

Gordon, H L (2017) 'Climate change and food: a green social work perspective' *Critical and Radical Social Work* 5(2): 145-62

Gray, M, Coates, J and Hetherington, T (2013) *Environmental Social Work* Oxon: Routledge

Gray, M and Coates J (2015) 'Changing Gears: Shifting to an Environmental Perspective in Social Work Education' *Social Work Education* 34(5): 502-12

Harris, J (2014) '(Against) Neoliberal social work' *Critical and Radical Social Work* 2(1): 7-22

Harris, C and Boddy, J (2017) 'The Natural Environment in Social Work Education: A Content Analysis of Australian Social Work Courses' *Australian Social Work* 70(3): 337-49

Healy, K (2012) *Social Work Methods and Skills* Basingstoke: Palgrave, Macmillan

Hoff, M and McNutt, J G (1994) *The global environmental crisis: Implications for social welfare and social work* Brookfield: Ashgate Publishing

Ife, J (1998) *Rethinking Social Work: Towards Critical Practice* South Melbourne: Longman

IPCC (2014) 'Climate Change 2014 Synthesis Report Summary for Policymakers' https://ar5-syr.ipcc.ch/topic_summary.php

Jones, P (2008) 'Expanding the ecological consciousness of social work students: education for sustainable practice' in *Proceedings of EDU-COM 2008 International Conference* pp285-292. From: Sustainability in Higher Education: Directions for Change, 19-21 November 2008, Khon Kaen: Thailand

Kemp, S P (2011) 'Recentring Environment in Social Work. Practice: Necessity, Opportunity, Challenge' *British Journal of Social Work* 41(6): 1198-210

Lucas-Darby, E T (2011) 'The New Color Is Green: Social Work Practice and Service-Learning' *Advances in Social Work* 12(1): 113-25

Lysack, M (2015) 'Effective policy influencing and environmental advocacy: Health, climate change, and phasing out coal', *International Social Work* 58(3): 435–47

Marlow, C and Van Rooyen, C (2001) 'How green is the environment in social work?' *International Social Work* 44(2): 241-54

McKinnon, J (2008) 'Exploring the Nexus between Social Work and the Environment' *Australian Social Work* 61(13): 256-68

Melekis, K and Woodhouse, V (2015) 'Transforming Social Work Curricula: Institutional Supports for Promoting Sustainability' *Social Work Education* 34(5): 573-85

Molyneux, R (2010) 'The Practical Realities of Ecosocial Work: A Review of the Literature' *Critical Social Work* 11(2): 61-69

Morton, D (2019) 'Extinction Rebellion: a social worker's observation' *Critical and Radical Social Work* 7(2): 263-65

Närhi K, and Matthies, A L (2016) 'Conceptual and historical analysis of ecological social work', in J McKinnon, J Alston, M (eds.) *Ecological social work: toward sustainability* Houndmills: Palgrave Macmillan pp21-38

Natural Resources Wales (2020) https://naturalresources.wales/about-us/what-we-do/climate-change/climate-change-overview/?lang=en

Pacheco, S E (2020) 'Catastrophic effects of climate change on children's health start before birth' *The Journal of Clinical Investigation* 130(2): 562-64

Rambaree, K (2013) 'Social Work and Sustainable Development: Local Voices from Mauritius' *Australian Social Work* 66(2): 261-76

Ramsay, S and Boddy, J (2017) 'Environmental Social Work: A Concept Analysis' *British Journal of Social Work* 47(1): 68-86

Redfearn, G (2020) 'Silent death: Australia's bushfires push countless species to extinction' *The Guardian*, 3 January 2020 www.theguardian.com/environment/2020/jan/04/ecologists-warn-silent-death-australia-bushfires-endangered-species-extinction (Accessed 20.02.2020)

Rogge, M (1994) 'Environmental injustice: Social welfare and toxic waste'. In: Hoff, M, McNutt, J (eds.) *The global environmental crisis: Implications for social welfare and social work* Brookfield, VT: Avebury pp53-47

Sage, C (2014) 'The transition movement and food sovereignty: From local resilience to global engagement in food system transformation' *Journal of Consumer Culture* 14(2): 254-75

Shubert, J (1994) 'Case studies in community organizing around environmental threats', in Hoff, M, McNutt, J (eds.) *The global environmental crisis: Implications for social welfare and social work* Avebury: Brookfield

Tester, F J (1994) 'In an age of ecology: Limits to voluntarism and traditional theory in social work practice', in M. Hoff., J. McNutt (Eds) *The global environmental crisis: Implications for social welfare and social work* Avebury, Brookfield

The Future Generations (Wales) Act 2015, Available at:
www.legislation.gov.uk/anaw/2015/2/contents/enacted (Accessed 13.04.2020)

Taylor, S A (2013) 'Social science research in ocean environments: A social worker's experience', in Gray, M, Coates, J, Hetherington, T (Eds) *Environmental Social Work*, Oxon: Routledge

Thompson, N (2002) 'Social Movements, Social Justice and Social Work' *British Journal of Social Work* 32(6): 711-22

Weick, A (1981) 'Reframing the person-in-environment perspective' *Social Work* 26(2): 140–43

World Meteorological Association (2020) 'WMO Statement on the State of the Global Climate in 2019', WMO-No. 1248,
https://library.wmo.int/doc_num.php?explnum_id=10211 (Accessed 15.02.2020)

Zapf, M (2005a) 'Profound connections between person and place: Exploring location, spirituality, and social work', *Critical Social Work* 6(2): 1

Zapf, M (2005b) 'The spiritual dimension of person and environment: Perspectives from social work and traditional knowledge' *International Social Work* 48(5) pp633-42

Yaffe, J (2013) 'Guest editorial – Where's the evidence for social work education? *Journal of Social Work Education* 49(4): 525-27

Chapter 9

Social Welfare and the Scope of Human Rights

Gideon Calder

> **Prelude: Bethan's choices**
>
> Bethan is the mother of Ava, who is seven. Ava is one of around 200,000 children in Wales who lives in poverty (End Child Poverty, 2019). She has experienced periodic health problems since birth. She is smaller than her peers, and after a bright start, has begun to fall behind at school. She eats a free breakfast at school each morning (Welsh Government, 2015), but out of term-time, Bethan faces a struggle to maintain for Ava the level of nutrition and security that her being at school affords. She finds herself having to economise on heating during the winter, and often goes without food herself in order to give Ava as full a meal as possible. At the same time, she is proud of her independence as a mother, and places a very high value on being self-sufficient, and making her own choices about what is best for Ava.
>
> What have Bethan's choices got to do with *human rights*? Do human rights make a difference here? Should they? We will refer back to Bethan and Ava periodically during this chapter.

Introduction: approaching human rights in Wales

Human rights are conceived in unified, global terms – something held in common by coming up to 8 billion people in 193 countries, simply because they are human. Yet they are realised at a local level, in widely varying national settings, and in connection with lives lived in widely diverse ways. Both of these factors matter, and appreciating both is crucial to understanding what human rights can and cannot achieve. This is partly because of what goes on in the space between the international statements of those rights – such as the Universal Declaration of Human Rights (United Nations, 1948), or the European Convention on Human Rights (Council of Europe, 1950) – and on the other hand people's everyday lived experiences in what the co-author of the Universal Declaration Eleanor Roosevelt (1958) famously called the 'small places, close to home' where people like Bethan and Ava seek justice, opportunity and dignity.[1] There is a complex process of *translation* in the application of the insights of an international declaration and the national and local contexts (Frezzo, 2015:17). This translation does not take place simply through instruments of state policy, but through various institutions and levels of practice which 'in turn confine and affect the state's range of discretion' (Armaline *et al*., 2015:12). So, while the power of those grand declarations lies in their enduring directness and simplicity, the space between them and everyday life is messy, complex, shifting and contested. The realisation of human rights is fragmented and ambiguous, rather than clean and consistent. And it is there that social welfare policy and practice sits, alongside other factors which shape the concrete differences which human rights might make.

This chapter looks at all of this, in the context of social welfare in Wales since the foundation of the National Assembly for Wales in 1999 and the introduction across the UK of the Human Rights Act in 2000. At that point, then-First Secretary Rhodri Morgan predicted that the effects of that Act in Wales would be 'profound, fundamental and far-reaching' – and likened its role in protecting the rights of ordinary citizens to that, in its own time, of the medieval legal code Hywel Dda (Donnelly, 2000). It was typical of Morgan to frame the UK-wide adoption of a policy incorporating the European Convention of Human Rights in terms of its resonance with Welsh traditions. But the timing of the landing of this amplification of the role of international human rights conventions meant that tying them into a "Welsh" way of doing things was not just a piece of rhetoric. With the National Assembly in its early stages, there was an opportunity to be pioneering. The scope for finding strong and distinctive ways of incorporating human rights into policy could be counted among the potential raft of what Morgan would later refer to as 'devolution dividends' (Morgan, 2006; Drakeford, 2012). Part of our focus in this chapter is on how much, and how well, that opportunity was taken. With the Conservative general election manifesto of 2019 having given a non-specific commitment to 'update' the Human Rights Act after Brexit (previous policy having been to repeal it), the fate of the UK's relationship to the European Convention is uncertain at the time of writing (Conservative and Unionist Party, 2019:48). Even so, Welsh law will remain linked to international human rights law in particular and substantive ways.

In the UK as a whole, as we will see, the implementation of a human rights agenda has sat in an uneasy, sometimes conflicted relation with the dominance of neoliberalism – the policy implications of which often directly undermine the potential to realise human rights in the most radical and effectual of ways. Yet there is a case for saying that Wales has, at least in part, taken a distinctive, more radical path, with a stronger stress on the relationship between human rights and social welfare. Through the chapter,

---

[1] The full passage reads: 'Where, after all, do universal human rights begin? In small places, close to home - so close and so small that they cannot be seen on any maps of the world. Yet they are the world of the individual person; the neighborhood he lives in; the school or college he attends; the factory, farm, or office where he works. Such are the places where every man, woman, and child seeks equal justice, equal opportunity, equal dignity without discrimination. Unless these rights have meaning there, they have little meaning anywhere. Without concerted citizen action to uphold them close to home, we shall look in vain for progress in the larger world.' (Roosevelt, 1958).

our focus will move from theoretical questions around the conception, shape and scope of human rights to how key recent policy developments in Wales have embodied aspects of international human rights conventions. Here we find innovative thinking, groundbreaking potential, but also mixed results. This leaves work to do, in the messy contexts mentioned above. If for Roosevelt the first challenges of this work lay in making human rights 'real' in the small places, among people like Bethan and Ava, that remains the case in Wales today. We start, though, at the theoretical level.

The very idea of human rights

The point about human rights is that they are universal: 'rights inherent to all human beings, whatever our nationality, place of residence, sex, national or ethnic origin, colour, religion, language, or any other status' and to which we are all equally entitled. (OHCHR, no date). In the abstract, there is little to dislike about them. There may even be a degree of complacency about them, and a presumption that they are what they are, and *obviously* important (Woods, 2014:2). As abstractions they can seem distant, and bleached out. But it's often when they are brought down to earth, and invoked in this or that case, that any such complacency is replaced with a sense of controversy. While we may generally like the idea of human rights as an achievement of the modern world, this does not mean that this or that person benefitting from them is popular. In fact they are often associated with unpopular causes; with being wheeled out to protect those perceived as a threat, or as a drag on "mainstream" society, or as the authors of their own misfortune. Yet as Jonathan Wolff has put it, 'that is their *whole point* – to protect people in difficult times when sentiment is against them' (Wolff, 2019). This reflects, in part, the circumstances in which contemporary frameworks of human rights were conceived: in the aftermath of two world wars, the Nazi holocaust, and in awareness of the potential in modern societies for human-caused harms on an unprecedented scale. Human rights 'are there to constrain governments' (Hale, 2018: 245). They are *fundamental*, in the sense that their violation or neglect is the most serious of political accusations (Williams, 2005:72).

And partly because they are fundamental, the foundations of human rights are contested. Some disputes surround what they are based on, or whether they can be grounded at all (Calder, 2018). For some, they hinge on the identification of shared human attributes, such as rationality or sentience, or more recently distinctive human capabilities (see e.g. Nussbaum, 1997, 2006; Vizard, 2007, 2016; Burchardt and Vizard, 2011). For others, that link between rights and shared, "objective" human needs or capacities is inherently specious and biased. From this perspective, rather than capturing deep truths about human nature or what is most vital for our flourishing, human rights merely reflect the values and hopes embedded in a particular kind of modern, liberal, Western worldview (Rorty, 1998; MacIntyre, 2016). This is a worldview which, with the rise of right-wing populism and the fading of Western influence in the world, is arguably in retreat and may ultimately be remembered as a passing historical moment. Meanwhile, there are questions around how rights relate to duties. It is one thing to say that a human right exists, and another to identify whose duty it is to honour that right – which government, which agency, which individual(s). (Disputes along these lines have recently become especially visceral in connection with the rights of migrants and asylum seekers – in which case they can literally become a matter of life and death.) And then there are disagreements about who has rights in the first place, and what basis they have: whether groups might have rights as well as individuals, for example, or whether newborns or those in a coma have rights in the same way as the fully rational adult, or whether future generations of people might have rights at all (Woods, 2014).

And there are conceptual tensions between the fact that while rights (even as presented in national-level policy such as the Human Rights Act) are couched in universal terms, the modern nation state is based 'on an idea of exclusive membership' (Goodhart, 2005: 156) which effectively already gives a local bias to the rights they install. As citizens and taxpayers, we are often assumed to owe more to those nearby, or to our fellow citizens, than those further away. Then again, there is a dominant discourse which presents human rights themselves as a kind of foreign imposition. In March 2020, the *Daily Express* ran a news story on the Brexit trade talks with a headline beginning: 'EU demands UK keeps their human rights' (MacRae, 2020). Here, human rights are presented as if there are different versions of them, so that certain rights might 'belong' to the EU in some way which makes them 'theirs', rather than 'ours', and so there is a threat in them being imposed on people as a 'demand'. There are fierce internal tensions in this kind of narrative. Human rights are strongly associated with autonomy – with the value of people having control over their life and circumstances, exercising freedom of thought and expression, protected against 'slavery or servitude' (United Nations, 1948 – see e.g. articles 4, 18 and 19). They are conceived precisely as attaching equally to everyone, already, rather than something which might belong to some more than others. But the point remains that their take-up, and how much differences they make in the 'small places', depends on effective implementation at the national level – so in the case of the UK, within the four nations which currently compose it, as well as via the Westminster government.

All these questions are deep and substantial, and shape the scope of what rights might mean. They lie beneath the surface of the negotiation of the relationship between human rights and social welfare. But they may not seem to intrude there in a direct way. What *does* feature upfront in social welfare policy and practice is debates about the wording of specific rights, their implications, and which apply to which situations in which ways. To see how this goes, it is helpful to look at different forms which rights may take, and different jobs they may do.

Forms of human rights

Human rights are typically presented as working in two ways. On the one hand, they protect against abuse, coercion, exploitation or exclusion. Such rights are known as *negative* rights, in that they work by negating potential harms: so the right to bodily integrity is a right not to be physically violated; the right to free speech is a protection against being silenced; and the right to life is not a right to live life in some designated way, but a right not to have one's life taken away. On the other hand, rights may work *positively*, by entitling people to goods. These rights will require active intervention by governments or policymakers. They may include food, housing, healthcare, education and social security. These positive rights are in the foreground of debates about social welfare, and are contentious in particular ways. This is a major part of why the space between formal declarations and Bethan and Ava is messy and contested.

For a sense of how such contestation takes shape, it is helpful to break down positive rights along the lines identified by T.H. Marshall (1950). (Under these headings we find negative rights too, but they are especially helpful in showing the different forms which positive rights might take).

> *Civil rights* – rights 'necessary for individual freedom' (Marshall, 1950:10) – such as the right to own property, and to receive justice.
> *Political rights* – rights required to 'participate in the exercise of political power' (Marshall, 1950:11) – such as the right to vote, and to stand for political office.
> *Social rights* – rights connected with the distribution of economic and social welfare – such as the right to health, education and social security.

An important aspect of Marshall's account is that the impacts and focal points of social rights range very widely, from access to resources to the benefits of participation as a citizen, and also that they are importantly contextual – what they amount to depends partly on 'the standards prevailing in the society' (Marshall, 1950:11). What's also important for him is that social rights are, historically, the last to arrive on the scene: he saw the establishment of welfare states during and after World War II – so in the UK's case, what is often referred to as the 'classic' welfare state – as the moment when they emerged to take their place. On the one hand, though the rights of the European Convention are generally negative (Hale, 2018), positive social rights are right at the heart of the United Nations Declaration of 1948, which includes rights to 'realization … of the economic, social and cultural rights indispensable for … dignity and the free development of … personality' (article 22), to work and just remuneration (article 23), a 'standard of living adequate for health and well-being' and 'security in the event of unemployment, sickness, disability, widowhood, old age or other lack of livelihood' (article 25), education (article 26), and participation in 'the cultural life of the community' (article 27).

While the original promise of the framing of human rights indicated a full spectrum – negative and positive, civil, political and social – the social versions of positive rights have typically been delayed in their arrival, and often overtly resisted. Their achievement has been scrappy and fragile. This matters, because one way of interpreting the ways human rights have been incorporated into policy in Wales since devolution is that there has been an attempt to make up for some of that lost time. While there are differing accounts among historians, sociologists and lawyers of why that time has been lost (see e.g. Frezzo, 2015; Hale, 2018; Moyn, 2018; Vizard, 2016; Whyte, 2019), most sooner or later home in on the role played by the neoliberalism which can be taken to have dominated debates about social welfare in many national contexts, Wales's included, since the 1970s.

Neoliberalism and the place of human rights

Neoliberalism can be succinctly defined as 'the elevation of market-based principles and techniques of evaluation to the level of state-endorsed norms' (Davies, 2017:xiv). Since the advent of Thatcherism in the UK, it has involved a combined promotion of the market (through deregulation, privatisation, and the liberation of financial markets) and restriction of the state (through a preference for lower taxation, cuts to social welfare spending, and a retraction of the state's role as a social actor). But going by Davies' account, this does not simply mean that the state's role is taken up by that of the market. It also involves the reform of non-market institutions (for example, the public and voluntary sectors) so that they behave more like businesses, and the blurring of the line between the state and private enterprise. (A process epitomised in the UK government's response to the COVID-19 pandemic in 2020, which repeatedly pivoted towards the commissioning of private enterprises to deliver key measures designed to mitigate the effects of the virus, even while badging such measures as if they were part of the NHS – such as the infamously patchy, suboptimal and hugely expensive Test and Trace system, run by Serco.) Neoliberalism's entrenchment has continued since the 1970s, through changes of government after the late 1980s high-point of Thatcherism – including, albeit in more selective and sometimes ambiguous ways – in the New Labour years, where the market continued to appropriate and deplete the public realm (Marquand, 2013; Hindmoor, 2018).

This background matters to our understanding of how human rights have been adopted in UK law and policy. Historically, the rise of neoliberalism and the increasing prominence of human rights – the passing over of the term from talk at the level of the United Nations and European Court to widespread public usage – can be seen as running in parallel from the 1970s onwards. For some critics, this has meant the co-opting of the human rights agenda in the name of neoliberalism – if not explicitly, then certainly in practice (Moyn, 2018; Whyte, 2019). So, it is those aspects of the human rights agenda which sit most easily with the running of society as if it were a business which are promoted most easily in a neoliberal environment. Negative rights which can be presented as protecting against state intervention and coercion become unexceptional, and in some cases amplified. Meanwhile positive rights requiring 'a claim on the resources of others through the tax system' (Plant, 1988), and particularly social rights in Marshall's sense – rights to resources, welfare and full economic, political and cultural participation in society – have been neglected or denied, as instead of an assumption that the welfare state will promote such expectations, 'people are encouraged to create supportive relationships among themselves' (Dominelli, 2019:26). Welfare increasingly comes to operate according to market principles, with what Daniel Edmiston has called an 'accelerated commodification of civic status, participation and duty' (Edmiston, 2020:38).

In such a climate, the scope and impacts of human rights will be squeezed, and expectations lowered. Article 25 of the United Nations Declaration states that:

> *'Everyone has the right to a standard of living adequate for the health and well-being of himself and of his family, including food, clothing, housing and medical care and necessary social services, and the right to security in the event of unemployment, sickness, disability, widowhood, old age or other lack of livelihood in circumstances beyond his control.'*

And that

> *'all children… shall enjoy the same social protection'* (United Nations, 1948)

These remain aspirations; as rights, their realisation has been patchy at best, and in some senses is in decline. Consider the 2018 verdict of the UN's Special Rapporteur on Extreme Poverty and Human Rights, Philip Alston:

> *'Although the United Kingdom is the world's fifth largest economy, one fifth of its population (14 million people) live in poverty, and 1.5 million of them experienced destitution in 2017…Close to 40 per cent of children are predicted to be living in poverty by 2021. Food banks have proliferated; homelessness and rough sleeping have increased greatly; tens of thousands of poor families must live in accommodation far from their schools, jobs and community networks; life expectancy is falling for certain groups; and the legal aid system has been decimated.'* (Alston, 2019)

So there has been a drastic falling-short, the consequences of which Bethan and Ava are living day-to-day. We could say that Ava's very physical and social development has been shaped by the very absence of any guarantee that she might 'enjoy the same social protection'.

While the causes are long-term and complex, when viewing this in terms of a failure to realise human rights, one key factor is that social and economic rights have been consciously absented from landmark pieces of UK legislation with the potential to cement them. The Human Rights Act was widely criticised for not including social rights (Joint Committee on Human Rights, 2008). The Equality Act 2010, combining a series of previous acts concerning equality and anti-discrimination around factors such as gender, race and disability – not a piece of human rights legislation *per se*, but one with substantive implications for how relevant aspects of law and policy would play out – included a section on socio-economic inequality which was notoriously not then enacted by the incoming Coalition government (though see the next section). It is not by coincidence that the decades of neoliberal dominance have coincided with an exponential rise in income inequality in the UK, and a confirmation of its place among the most unequal societies in the world (Wilkinson and Pickett, 2009, 2018). There is a sense in which the very legitimacy of the state in seeking to tackle such structural inequalities is undermined. Social problems become privatised, domesticated and individualised (Hartas, 2014:122-3; see also Marquand, 2013). Aspects of the human rights agenda which might have reversed this process have been set to one side. And while much of this is conducted by omission – by leaving out welfare-oriented rights – it sits alongside explicit rejection of the human rights agenda. Conservative governments at Westminster have made an explicit habit of associating such priorities with the undermining of the national interest, and with what Prime Minister Boris Johnson has termed the 'lefty' agendas of 'activist' lawyers (Johnson, 2020). At the UK level, the 2000s have been a mixed period in terms of the facilitation of human rights by the welfare state.

A 'Welsh' approach to human rights?

So has the story in Wales been different? Has Wales found ways of realising human rights which are deeper and less attenuated than the strictures of a neoliberal welfare state will allow? I will suggest that there are three clear respects in which it has, and another, just as clear, in which it has not.

On the one hand, at a procedural level, Wales has as a matter of course been more overt and affirmative in its commitment to human rights principles than the UK government, especially since 2010. The successive revisions and extensions of the original devolution settlement under the Government of Wales Act 2006 and Wales Act 2017 stipulate that Welsh ministers have no power to enact legislation incompatible with any of the rights set out in the European Convention, and set into UK law under the Human Rights Act (HM Government, 2006; 2017) – with the Wales Act providing new scope to 'shape equality and human rights outcomes' (Equality and Human Rights Commission, 2018). (This will add an extra edge of contention to any proposed reforms of the latter at UK level.) Steps have been taken to sustain and deepen the reach of existing commitments on human rights – for example, through a collaborative Steering Group for Advancing and Strengthening Equality and Human Rights, established in 2019, and an exploration into how to incorporate further UN conventions – including the convention on the rights of disabled people – into Welsh law, expected to amount to a more substantial assessment of the options by the end of 2020 (Hutt, 2019). These steps signal the inclination to supplement formal adoption of human rights principles with the provision to improve their 'bite' at ground level – with 'social rights accountability' – the empowerment of civil society and its involvement in the processes through which the implementation of principles has been realised (Casla, 2020). The existence of rights at legal level does not itself realise them at the level of lived experience. There is a recognition of this – necessary, if not sufficient, to ensure that human rights make the differences they promise.

Secondly, Wales has seen the introduction of policies which, at least in parts, have pushed further than their UK-level counterparts in seeking to realise human rights in the 'small places', drawing on existing conventions and legislation but applying them innovatively in the Welsh context. There are two particularly prominent examples of this, both of direct relevance to the position of Bethan and Ava. In a genuinely groundbreaking way, the Rights of Children and Young Persons (Wales) Measure 2011 requires that decision-making by Welsh ministers has due regard for the UN Convention on the Rights of the Child. In 2004, the then National Assembly had unanimously adopted the UNCRC as the formal basis of policy making for children. This is the most prominent articulation of the human rights of children, with radical implications for how children might be regarded as citizens, with positive rights to (for example) participation and equal treatment under the law alongside negative protections against (e.g.) discrimination and unwarranted separation from parents (Williams, 2013). The introduction of the Measure followed ten years after the establishment of the office of Children's Commissioner for Wales, the first of its type in the UK, with the role of promoting and safeguarding the rights and welfare of children in Wales. The role of the Commissioner is to listen to children – be accessible to them, as much as to act in an expert capacity on their behalf. These again are steps which can be seen as attempts to put 'teeth' into formal appeals to human rights, to translate them from rhetoric to ground-level action. Something similar can be said about the implementation of the socio-economic duty – that's Part 1 of the Equality Act 2010, left uncommenced at UK level by the incoming Cameron government of 2010. This is due to come into force in Wales in March 2021. Its aim is to require that those taking strategic decisions assess their potential impacts in terms of socio-economic disadvantage, and take on board the views and needs of those affected (Welsh Government, 2020). It is the part of the Equality Act which carries the heaviest weight in terms of positive and social rights – and so carries the potential to fill gaps in the neoliberal 'version' of the human rights agenda, as we mentioned earlier. Arguably, addressing these gaps is preconditional to the effective pursuit of much of the rest of the menu of human rights – a point to which we will return in closing.

Thirdly, Wales since devolution has seen creative, sometimes groundbreaking policies which have helped reconceive how human rights might be realised, and for whom. Thus, at the formal level, the Social Services and Well-Being (Wales) Act requires ministers to have due regard both for the UNCRC and the UN Principles for Older Persons. But the detail of the legislation amounts in many ways to an elaborate thinking through of how the potential benefits of such principles might be realised among the users of social services, and among carers. The prioritisation of co-production, hearing the voices of those involved, and the provision of advocacy services are core elements of the proposed reorientation of social services provision along more participative and dialogue-focused lines. This again amounts to a means of escaping the charge that human rights may end up seeming abstract and anaemic from the ground if the tools by which they might be picked up and used are not there, and genuinely accessible. Parts of the Act, both in spirit and substance, can be read as an attempt to redress that gap. And it is arguable that the trailblazing Well-Being of Future Generations (Wales) Act 2015 provides as joined-up a basis on which to provide for the real achievement of human rights as any piece of Welsh or other recent legislation. By requiring public bodies in Wales to address long-term impacts of their decisions and to think in preventative (rather than curative) terms about poverty, health inequalities and climate change, the Act has the potential to help furnish the conditions in which human rights might better be protected and enjoyed – or in more sober terms, to prevent the erosion of those conditions which will follow on from any large-scale environmental depletion (see Chapter 8). While the interests of future human beings are not directly addressed in human rights conventions, there are strong reasons to argue that they should.

These steps were not taken without resistance: they were characterised by conflict, as well as cross-party collaboration (Williams, 2013). Neither have they been uniformly effective, or achieved everything they might have. There have been grounds on which each has been criticised for not going far enough, or for remaining too close to existing, limited ways of working. But they can be seen as clear, substantial, and potentially significant attempts to make good on the promise of a human rights agenda – and specifically, to expand out the range of applications of human rights from their thinner, more legalistic or negative senses so that they are enhancing human flourishing at the level of lived social experience. There is a greater chance that human rights will reach Bethan and Ava in tangible, difference-making ways, when fleshed out along these lines.

And yet there is a fourth sense in which the position of Bethan and Ava has not been affected by the positive appropriation of a human rights agenda in Wales. Consider this statement:

> *'Our duty as a Government is to use our powers to their maximum potential and effect on behalf of those children who face poverty in their daily lives in Wales. It is a matter of both entitlement and social justice. Freedom from poverty is a basic human right.'*
> (National Assembly for Wales, 2005:34)

Used as a yardstick against which to measure progress since, it serves as a burning reminder of Wales's human rights deficit in this respect (see Chapter 4). While poverty is not something which is simply under the purview of Welsh Government, even with the extension of powers since 1999 – as so many of the levers of economic policy, along with social security remain at UK level – there has been a consistent priority on reducing its effects. Yet in 2017-18, Wales was the only nation to see a rise in child poverty – with just under 30 per cent of children in Wales living in poverty at that stage (End Child Poverty, 2019). In their most recent report on whether Wales is getting fairer, the Equality and Human Rights Commission (2018) found that while there have been clear steps forward, the most persistent deficits or reverse trends lie in the areas of socio-economic disadvantage, with particularly stark knock-on effects for children and disabled people. Against this background, it seems naïve, if not downright misleading, to romanticise the extent to which Wales might serve as a beacon for the realisation of the social rights which UK policy has tended to neglect. These trends and numbers tell us much about how things are going in the 'small places', and the everyday shape of the lives of Bethan and Ava.

Conclusions: human rights work in an unequal society

Human rights have been a crucially important feature of how social welfare has been conceived, framed and practiced in Wales since devolution. Their prominence in key policies has contributed to the development of a distinctive and often pioneering agenda in the areas where the terms of devolution have provided room for manoeuvre. They have served as a vehicle for the articulation of progressive aims, and a lever through which those aims have been given purchase. And they have been an important element in how social policy in Wales has diverged, where it has, from neoliberal dogma. That divergence looks likely to grow, at the time of writing – with the details of the post-Brexit settlement still to be decided and a steady narrative during the Covid-19 pandemic and policy responses to it of how governments of Wales, Scotland and Northern Ireland have departed from the Conservative line in London. Welsh Governments have been much readier to pick up the vocabulary of human rights, and of the European Convention and the United Nations Declaration, than their recent counterparts at Westminster. Yet a 'headline' role for human rights in policy will never be sufficient, by itself, to bring about fundamental progressive change.

This is partly because of the distance of the 'small places' from the grand declaration, and the messiness of the space between. It is also because of the persistence of poverty, and inequalities of income and wealth, and other structural factors which the machinery of human rights has not been able to tackle. It also reflects tendencies towards the individualisation and domestication of the realm of the 'small places', and their dislocation from structures of constructive intervention and support. It is also because of the limits of rights, and of human rights discourse. They are potentially highly effective in identifying the minimal requirements for human flourishing, for ensuring a kind of equality of status, and providing tools for the protection of individuals from discrimination and the arbitrary exercise of power. But they cannot by themselves furnish good relations or conducive domestic space, or build the public realm, or promote the kind of everyday, lived fairness which R.H. Tawney called practical equality – the realistic exercise of choices and taking of opportunities, the achievement of which 'depends not only upon an open road, but on an equal start' (Tawney, 1964:143). The road is more open in Wales than in 1999. The equalisation of the positions from which people set out still needs substantial work.

References

Alston, W (2019) *Report of the Special Rapporteur on Extreme Poverty and Human Rights on his Visit to the United Kingdom of Great Britain and Northern Ireland* United Nations Human Rights Council. Available at: https://undocs.org/A/HRC/41/39/Add.1

Armaline, WT, Glasberg, DS and Purkayastha, B (2015) *The Human Rights Enterprise: Political Sociology, State Power, and Social Movements* Cambridge: Polity Press

Burchardt, T and Vizard, P (2011) 'Operationalising the capability approach as a basis for equality and human rights monitoring in twenty-first century Britain' *Journal of Human Development and Capabilities* 12(1): 91-119

Calder, G (2018) 'Grounding human rights: what difference does it make?' in Moseley, A and Norman, R (eds.) *Human Rights and Military Intervention* London and New York, Routledge, pp15-31

Casla, K (2020) 'Freedom and Social Citizenship: Public Services and Social Rights' in Harrop, A, Murray, K and Nogarede, J (eds.) *Public Service Futures: Welfare States in the Digital Age* London: Fabian Society, pp43-50

Conservative and Unionist Party (2019) *Get Brexit Done: Unleash Britain's Potential* London, Conservative and Unionist Party

Council of Europe (1950) *European Convention on Human Rights*. Available at: www.echr.coe.int/Documents/Convention_Eng.pdf

Davies, W (2017) *The Limits of Neoliberalism: Authority, Sovereignty and the Logic of Competition* London: Sage

Dominelli, L (2019) 'Reconceptualising poverty in Europe: exclusion, marginality and absolute poverty reframed through participatory relational space' in Gaisbauer, HP, Schweiger, G and Sedmak, C (eds.) *Absolute Poverty in Europe: Interdisciplinary Perspectives on a Hidden Phenomenon* Bristol: Policy Press, pp17-38

Donnelly, R (2000) 'New Human Rights Act in Britain' *Irish Times*, 3 October. Available at: www.irishtimes.com/news/new-human-rights-act-in-britain-1.1105059

Drakeford, M (2012) 'Devolution and the welfare state: the case of Wales' in Calder, G, Gass, J and Merrill-Glover, K (eds.) *Changing Directions of the British Welfare State* Cardiff: University of Wales Press

Edmiston, D (2020) *Welfare, Inequality and Social Citizenship* Bristol: Policy Press

End Child Poverty (2019) *Local Indicators of Child Poverty, 2017-18* Loughborough: Loughborough University

Equality and Human Rights Commission (2018) *Is Wales Fairer? The State of Equality and Human Rights in 2018*. Available at: www.equalityhumanrights.com/sites/default/files/is-britain-fairer-2018-is-wales-fairer.pdf

Frezzo, M (2015) *The Sociology of Human Rights* Cambridge: Polity Press

Goodhart, D (2005) 'Britain's glue: the case for liberal nationalism' in Giddens, A and Diamond, P (eds.) *The New Egalitarianism* Cambridge, Polity Press, pp154-10

Hale, B (2018) 'Social justice and human rights' in Craig, G. (ed.) *Handbook on Global Social Justice* Cheltenham, Edward Elgar, pp241-49

Hartas, D (2014) *Parenting, Family Policy and Children's Well-Being in an Unequal Society* Houndmills: Palgrave Macmillan

Hindmoor, A (2018) *What's Left Now? The History and Future of Social Democracy* Oxford, Oxford University Press

HM Government (2006) *Government of Wales Act 2006*. Available at: www.legislation.gov.uk/ukpga/2006/32/contents

HM Government (2017) *Wales Act 2017* Available at: www.legislation.gov.uk/ukpga/2017/4/contents/enacted

Hutt, J (2019) 'Oral Statement in the Siambr by the Deputy Minister and Chief Whip: An Update on Advancing Equality and Human Rights in Wales'. Available at: https://record.assembly.wales/Plenary/5664#A51598

Johnson, B (2020) Speech to Conservative Party Conference, 6 October. Available at: www.conservatives.com/news/conservative-party-conference-2020-speeches

Joint Committee on Human Rights (2008) *A Bill of Rights for the UK* London: The Stationery Office

MacIntyre, A (2016) *Ethics in the Conflicts of Modernity* Cambridge: Cambridge University Press

MacRae, G (2020) 'EU demands UK keeps their human rights despite failing own 'crucial' living standards' *Daily Express*, 13 March. Available at: www.express.co.uk/news/politics/1254604/EU-ECHR-Brexit-trade-talks-latest-news-human-rights-living-standards-Michel-Barnier

Marquand, D (2013) *Mammon's Kingdom: An Essay on Britain, Now*. Harmondsworth: Penguin

Marshall, TH (1950) *Citizenship and Social Class* Cambridge: Cambridge University Press

Morgan, R (2006) *Wales Can Do It*, Cardiff: Welsh Assembly Government

Moyn, S (2018) *Not Enough: Human Rights in an Unequal World* Cambridge, Mass.: Harvard University Press

National Assembly for Wales (2005) *The Official Record of the National Assembly for Wales, 09/02/05* Cardiff: National Assembly for Wales

Nussbaum, M (1997) 'Capabilities and human rights' *Fordham Law Review* 66, pp273-300

Nussbaum, M (2006) 'Capabilities as fundamental entitlements' in Kaufman, A (ed.) *Capabilities Equality: Basic Issues and Problems* New York and London: Routledge, pp44-70

OHCHR (no date) 'What are human rights?' Available at: www.ohchr.org/en/issues/pages/whatarehumanrights.aspx

Plant, R (1988) *Citizenship, Rights and Socialism* London: Fabian Society

Roosevelt, E (1958) Speech at the United Nations, New York, Thursday 27 March. Passage available at: www.walesforpeace.org/una/human-rights.html

Rorty, R (1998) 'Human rights, rationality and sentimentality', in his *Truth and Progress* Cambridge: Cambridge University Press

Sen, A (2009) *The Idea of Justice* Cambridge, Mass.: Harvard University Press

Tawney, RH (1964) *Equality*, 4th edn London: George Allen and Unwin

United Nations (1948) *Universal Declaration of Human Rights*. Available at: www.un.org/en/universal-declaration-human-rights

Vizard, P (2007) 'Specifying and justifying a basic capability set: Should the international human rights framework be given a more direct role?' *Oxford Development Studies* 35, issue 3, pp225-50

Vizard, P (2016) 'The human rights and equalities agenda' in Dean, H and Platt, L (eds.) Social Advantage and Disadvantage Oxford, Oxford University Press, pp42-61

Welsh Government (2015) *Free Breakfast in Primary Schools* Cardiff: Welsh Government. Available at: https://gov.wales/sites/default/files/publications/2018-03/free-breakfast-in-primary-schools.pdf

Welsh Government (2020) *Socio-Economic Duty: An Overview*. Available at: https://gov.wales/socio-economic-duty-overview#section-42134

Whyte, J (2019) *The Morals of the Market: Human Rights and the Rise of Neoliberalism* London and New York: Verso

Wilkinson, R and Pickett, K (2009) *The Spirit Level: Why More Equal Societies Almost Always Do Better* London: Allen Lane

Wilkinson, R and Pickett, K (2018) *The Inner Level: How More Equal Societies Reduce Stress, Restore Sanity and Improve Everyone's Well-being* London: Allen Lane

Williams, B (2005) 'Human rights and relativism' in *In the Beginning was the Deed: Realism and Moralism in Political Argument* Princeton, NJ: Princeton University Press, pp62-74

Williams, J (2013) (ed.) *The United Nations Convention on The Rights of the Child in Wales* Cardiff: University of Wales Press

Wolff, J (JoWolffBSG) (2019, 26 February) 'Human rights are often popular in abstract, but very unpopular in their particular application. But that is their *whole point* - to protect people in difficult times when sentiment is against them.' Retrieved from https://twitter.com/JoWolffBSG/status/1100296764249255936

Woods, K (2014) *Human Rights* Basingstoke: Palgrave Macmillan

Chapter 10
Advancing Equalities and Social Justice post 2010

Charlotte Williams and Teresa Crew

Introduction

The UK Equalities legislation and framework for implementation is considered world leading. Across the devolved legislatures there are, however, significant distinctions in the interpretation and implementation of the law. This geo-diversity reflects context-specific factors, such as historic politics, policy development, institutional practices and structures, as well as size and cultural considerations, all of which influence and shape approaches to equalities (Chaney, 2012; Hankivsky *et al.*, 2019). Whilst there is considerable scope for cross jurisdiction learning and the sharing of goals, methodologies, experiences and pilots, developing a distinctive approach, tailored to the needs and realities of the nation is critical to advancing equalities.

The equalities landscape in Wales today is influenced by three key pieces of legislation. The Equality Act 2010 which unified, simplified and strengthened forty years of British anti-discrimination law, provides legal protection for the 'protected characteristics' of age, disability, gender reassignment, race, religion or belief, sex, sexual orientation, marriage and civil partnership, and pregnancy and maternity (Feast and Hand, 2015). The Welsh Government has continued to demonstrate its distinctive equality agenda, through a further two key pieces of legislation. 'The Wales Act 2017', which included the requirement that every four years, all public bodies should publish a *Strategic Equality Plan* that considers the effect of their policies on people with 'protected characteristics', and to reduce the inequalities of outcome that result from socio-economic disadvantage. In addition, the 'Well-being of Future Generations (Wales) Act 2015' put in place seven well-being goals, overseen by a sustainability commissioner, that include: global responsibility, community and culture, Welsh language, and equality (Welsh Government, 2019).

The Equality Act 2010 instituted the approach of *equality mainstreaming*, placing a specific public sector equality duty on *all* central and local government departments. Mainstreaming, a concept widely discussed, requires that an equality perspective is incorporated in the design, development and evaluation of all policies at all levels and at all stages (see Parken *et al.*, 2019). As Williams (2011) noted in the previous edition of this text, this signalled "a fundamental shift from '*negative* equality duties' to '*positive* equality duties" which required public authorities to actively advance and promote equality in service provision rather than simply reacting to discrimination or reported inequalities (p114). As such this approach differs markedly from former equality legislation which has in different eras focused on equal treatment, anti-discrimination and positive action (Bagihole, 2009). Williams argued this forthright approach meant that 'there can be nowhere in the country where issues of equality are not ringing in the ears of public servants' (p114).

The unique specific duties which came into force in 2011 required the Welsh Government to undertake equality impact assessments of policies, strategies, action plans, practices and budgetary spend. This would necessarily entail, astutely identifying and highlighting inequalities and carefully collecting and analysing the data necessary for strong equality plans. An additional unique aspect of the Welsh framework requires public bodies to engage widely with and consult those with individuals, groups and organisations with protected characteristics when designing equality policy. The ambition is to enable more 'participative-democratic' approaches to policy making (Chaney, 2012). In this way partnership and collaboration across sectors and with actors in civil society becomes a powerful lever for change. Monitoring and reviewing performance are also mandated as public sector organisations have a duty to publish their equality objectives, equality plans, data and to assess the impact of their plans. Perhaps most significant in progress towards equality in Wales is the fact that Equalities and Human Rights forms part of the Deputy First Minister's portfolio (see also Chapter 9). This means that all elements of the equalities regime have her oversight and can be integrated, including recognition of groups, protection of their rights and redistribution to tackle inequality.

Wales therefore provides an impressive example of a mainstreamed equalities commitment in public service provision. This cross-cutting approach underpins the Strategic Equality Plan 2016-2020 *Working Towards A Fairer Wales*, which focusses on eight broad public service goals: engaging those with protected characteristics to be involved in the design and delivery of services; enabling substantive rights through the provision of accessible advice, information and advocacy; reducing pay inequalities; reducing violence and abuse; enabling greater diversity in public appointments; strengthening cohesion; reducing poverty; and the Welsh Government standing as an exemplar in the pursuit of equality.

There have been many positive developments. Hankivisky *et al.* 2019 argue that the devolved states offer examples of '*innovative equality mainstream initiatives*' (p144) citing Wales as having provided 'an impressive and thoroughly mainstreamed commitment to public service provision' (p148) with highly advanced monitoring duties linked to equality outcomes.

This chapter builds on its previous iterations in the 2007 and 2011 versions of this text, focussing here on developments in the *post*-Equality Act era. It will consider some of the successes and opportunities of the recent decade and the key challenges for advancing greater equality in Welsh society.

The Equalities challenge in Wales

Equalities work is a tough call. There can be little doubting the complexity of the task of creating a more equal society. Even with the strong infrastructural arrangements in place, making equality happen remains a challenge. Wales is the poorest country in the United Kingdom and one in which there are prevalent and ongoing inequalities (see Chapter 3). Complexities in implementation, moving targets, changing political and popular climates, the emergence of new dimensions of inequality and the attrition of expertise and resources all serve to compound the difficulties of achieving equality goals. In addition, unprecedented and serendipitous world events such as the current Covid-19 pandemic can have profound and disproportionate impacts on sections of the community vulnerable by virtue of protected characteristics and on the economic welfare of all.

Tackling equalities demands, in the view of some commentators, being in for the long haul, engaging with experimentation and reflexive learning (Parken, 2018; Parken *et al.*, 2019) and a sustained and persistent effort on the part of all – politicians, civil servants and policy makers, academics, key stakeholders in civil society, practitioners and those who make use of public services as 'experts by experience'. Research by Hankivsky *et al.* (2019) argues that strategies must be tailored and adapted to national realities and needs if they are to realise their transformatory potential.

The challenges in Wales are considerable. Poverty and socio-economic disadvantage in Wales are deep and widespread and the Welsh labour market provides limited opportunities. Whilst the equalities focus is on groups with certain individual characteristics it has increasingly been recognised that low socio-economic status interacts to compound their inequality. People with protected characteristics are much more at risk of living in a low-income household, are more at risk of poorer health, education and poor employment outcomes. Inequalities in outcomes in employment, earnings and income first evidenced in Wales by Davies *et al.*, 2011 *An Anatomy of Economic Inequality in Wales* are confirmed by Davies and Parken's (2017) more recent review and as discussed by Beck in this volume. Davies *et al.*'s 2011 review noted that those groups protected by anti-discrimination law face more disadvantage in Wales than in the UK as a whole. They provided evidence to demonstrate disadvantage in education, employment and earnings amongst the young, disabled people, specific ethnic groups and of women in each of these groups being particularly disadvantaged (Davies *et al.*, 2011). It is worth considering the nature of inequality and some of the challenges identified for specific groups in more detail.

Women

Women in Wales, represent a specific and compelling example of the issues of tackling inequality. They are concentrated in low pay, low skilled sectors of the economy which produces a precariarity that results in poverty in older age. The number of women in poverty has changed little in the last ten years (Winckler, 2019) as women hold 80 per cent of all part-time jobs (Parken, Pocher and Davies, 2014). Women are presumed to 'prefer' such part-time employment (a key influencing factor of the Gender Pay Gap), due to the gendered dynamics of household relationships. But part-time employment is problematic for women, as it is over associated with the five C's: cleaning, catering, clerical, customer service and caring - all of which are low paid sectors (EHRC, 2018). Rather than women preferring flexibility as cited by Farrell (2005), Parken (2018) comments that women take on these roles because they are the only ones available on a part-time basis.

In addition, nearly half of mothers in Wales say they are mainly responsible for childcare, compared with just four per cent of fathers (WEN Wales and Oxfam, 2019). While 13.8 per cent of women in Wales (the highest in the UK) provide unpaid care to an adult relative, neighbour or other person because of long-term physical or mental ill health or disability, or old age (Bevan Foundation, 2015).

The gender pay gap (GPG) is seen as a critical factor in understanding women's poverty (Winckler, 2019). Calculated as the difference between average hourly earnings (excluding overtime) between women and men (Smith, 2019), this pay differential is understandable as women only account for six per cent of chief executives of the top 100 businesses in Wales (Fawcett Society, 2019). Statistics by Chwarae Teg (2019a) show that the Welsh GPG increased to 14.5 per cent in 2019. While this remains below the UK average of 17.3 per cent, the GPG varies enormously across Wales. Ranging from 2.3 per cent in Conwy to 25.6 per cent in Torfaen, out of the twenty-two local authorities, all but two had a GPG. When comparing the GPG of large companies in Wales there is a mixed picture. Some Welsh firms have large GPGs, where men are paid up to 40 per cent more than women on average, there are also those where the GPG does not exist at all (Mosalski and Miller, 2018). But Andrews (2018), from the Institute of Economic Affairs, argues that these calculations do not distinguish between full-time and part-time employment, and do not provide like-for-like' comparisons (p1). Without detailed statistical data, we cannot assess if the GPG is an example of discrimination or factors, such as "job, age, education level, or experience" (Andrews, 2018:2).

Tackling the GPG remains high on the agenda of the Welsh Government. The Welsh Public Sector Equality duty led to the legal requirement for organisations with 250 or more employees to publish annual pay gap data between their male and female employees. This approach highlights obvious problems such as comparing 'like for like' (Andrews, 2018) and, whilst the EHRC is responsible for enforcing GPG reporting rules (Government Equalities Office, 2017), a freedom of information request by *The Guardian* showed that no companies have been fined to date despite many failing to file their gender pay gap figures on time (Perraudin, 2019).

In addition to low pay, several issues are identified as compounding gendered inequalities, including violence and domestic abuse, caring responsibilities and lack of political participation and representation. The issue of women's representation in decision making bodies in Wales is monitored by the Equality and Human Rights Commission (EHRC) and their reports *Who Runs Wales?* have indicated slow progress over time. The 2017 report stated '*Women make up the majority of the public sector workforce in Wales, this is not generally reflected in positions of power'* (EHRC, 2017:4).

The Welsh Government's Gender Equality Review, conducted by Chwarae Teg, concluded in July 2019. The subsequent *"Deeds not Words"* (Chwarae Teg, 2019b) report and roadmap sets out the actions the Welsh Government should take to achieve its bold vision for gender equality in Wales. Although the Review focused on gender, it clearly advocates for an intersectional approach, and recognises that it is important to consider all aspects of equality and the protected characteristics.

Disabled citizens

In terms of disability the evidence in equally stark. The percentage of disabled people varies across the UK, but Wales is reported to have the highest levels, at 26 per cent (Papworth Trust, 2018; Davies and Parken, 2017). Scope (2019) found that on average, people with disabilities face extra costs of up to £583 a month, although for one in five disabled people, this was more than £1,000 a month. On average, a disabled person's extra costs are equivalent to almost half of their income (not including housing costs). A JRF report, *Poverty in Wales 2018* (JRF, 2018), found that 39 per cent of disabled people in Wales are in poverty, the highest in the UK, compared with 22 per cent of non-disabled people (Barnard, 2018). Wales also has the largest number of disability related benefit claimants and the widest employment gap with non-disabled people of anywhere in the UK) (Disability Wales, 2018). Employment is a difficult route out of poverty for people with disabilities as they tend to have fewer formal qualifications, or as is the case for 18 per cent of the working-aged disabled population in Wales, hold no qualifications. (National Survey for Wales 2018 cited in Disability Wales, 2019). If a lack of formal qualifications is paired with low confidence, people with disabilities are even more likely to experience labour market disadvantage (Robinson, 2000 cited in Grant, 2012).

The Welsh Government's *Framework for Action on Independent Living* (2014) found disabled people in Wales experienced physical barriers such as access to transport, buildings and housing, and digital barriers when organisations only advertised vacancies online. There are concerns that employers may also have unconscious biases towards people with disabilities. Scope (2014) found that 36 per cent of the public tend to think of disabled people as 'not as productive' as everyone else and that a quarter of disabled people felt other people expected less of them because of their disability (Aiden and McCarthy, 2014). Immense barriers in access to service exist for disabled people in Wales as evidenced in the annual reports published by Disability Wales (www.disabilitywales.org).

Ethnic minorities

With 5.9 per cent of the Welsh population being from a Black and Minority Ethnic (BAME) background (StatsWales, 2019b), Wales is one of the least ethnically diverse parts of the UK (Owen *et al.*, 2015). BAME groups in Wales report persistently higher unemployment rates compared with White Welsh groups. Some groups being at particular risk, e.g. Bangladeshi men are over seven times more likely to be in low-paid jobs than otherwise comparable White men. More than 50 per cent of BAME women are projected to remain unemployed up to 2020 (Nicholl, Johnes and Holtom, 2016).

As with women and people with disabilities, some ethnic minorities cluster in low-skilled occupations. This could represent discrimination from other forms of employment or stereotyping into particular jobs (Catney and Sabater, 2015). Taking one ethnic minority as an example of a group that has experienced widespread discrimination, Gypsy Travellers experience high levels of poverty. But there is still limited information on the receipt of benefits and tax credits among Gypsy Travellers in Wales (Powell, *et al.*, 2019). While Travellers are presumed to have a propensity for self-employment, it could be, that like other BME communities, Travellers turn to self-employment as a response to poor employment opportunities (Broughton, 2015). As negative attitudes towards Gypsies, Roma and Traveller communities are still widely held (EHRC, 2016a), anecdotal evidence suggests Traveller communities experience discrimination when they claim welfare benefits.

The government's Strategic Equality Plan 2020-2024 notes '*Recent spikes in hate crime have affected Black Asian and Minority Ethnic (BAME) people, since 73% (2018/19 figures) of recorded hate crimes and incidents are motivated by racial or religious prejudice. Recent meetings of the Wales Race Forum and our All Wales BAME Engagement Programme have starkly highlighted racism in our communities, including schools and workplaces, and the need for concerted action to promote racial equality*'. (Welsh Government, 2020a:12)

At the time of writing the Welsh Government is poised to produce its Race Equality Action Plan based on a rigorous evidence review of key policy fields carried out by the Welsh Centre for Public Policy.

LGBTIQ

While the pattern and persistence of inequality by gender, race and disability have been subject to considerable monitoring, the additional fields of inequality have been more significantly profiled following the 2010 Equality Act. Data from the ONS on sexual orientation, for example, found that the proportion of the population in Wales that identify as lesbian, gay or bisexual (LGBT) has increased from 1.3 per cent in 2012 to 2.4 per cent in 2018 (Sanders, 2020). This small increase may be due to public attitudes towards sexuality becoming generally more positive over the last twenty years. As part of the Changing Face of Wales season, 1,000 people in Wales were asked how they felt about adult same-sex relationships. The vast majority (83 per cent), said they were either quite or very comfortable. Yet, 15 per cent said they were not at all or not very comfortable, and 2 per cent were 'not sure' (Pollock, 2019).

A key issue for the LGBTI community relates to hate crimes. The Welsh Government commits to supporting communities to be well connected and safe (Welsh Government, 2019:47). This is vital for LGBTI groups as research from a number of sources report high levels of hate crime. The National Union of Students (NUS) (2014), which included respondents from Wales, found that overall, LGBT students tend to feel less safe on their campus than heterosexual students. One in five LGBTIQ students and one in three trans students reported experiencing at least one form of bullying or harassment on their campus. Hate crimes related to sexual orientation doubled in Wales over the last five years: 751 incidents occurred in 2018/19, compared with 270 in

2014/15 (Home Office, 2014 and 2019). These increases can be in part explained by improvements in crime recording by the police' (Home Office, 2019) however, research by Stonewall (2017) also finds high levels of hate crimes. Based on a sample of more than 1,200 LGBT people in Wales, this study revealed almost one in four LGBT people (23 per cent) had experienced a hate crime or incident relating to their sexual orientation within the last 12 months. Alongside this, half of the trans people surveyed (52 per cent) reported experiencing a hate crime or incident because of their gender identity within the last 12 months. Reporting was low, as four out of five LGBT people (82 per cent) who experienced a hate crime or incident did not report the incident to the police. While not specific to Wales, research by the Government Equalities Office (2018) found that most LGBT respondents avoided being open about their sexual identity in public because they feared a negative reaction from others. When asked, 40 per cent of survey respondents had experienced a least one negative incident involving someone they did not live with in the last 12 months.

LGBT groups face specific barriers to existing services. Harvey *et al.* (2014) reports three structural and cultural barriers when attempting to access appropriate support: assumed heterosexuality in service provision; gender-binary (women-only or men-only) service provision and inadequate level of staff diversity, knowledge and skills. These hetro-centered services can mean that LGBT communities may feel that these services aren't suitable for them (Harvey *et al.*, 2014). But it is not just about improving services, there is a serious need to not only develop and extend support provision, but also to increase services available to LGBT people in Wales. Maegusuku-Hewett, Raithby and Willis (2015) found that the concentration of services in larger towns and cities meant they had to travel long distances on public transport. North and Mid- Wales in particular have a lack of LGBT specific services where resources are patchy and subject to a 'postcode lottery'.

Religion and belief
The relationship between religion and disadvantage is more difficult to establish. The emergence of British Muslims as a group widely recognised as subject to systematic discrimination, harassment and abuse is clearly recognised in an era of growing Islamophobia. The Davies *et al.* (2011) report did enable some extrapolation, noting Muslim women as twice as likely as those of Christian faith in Wales to have no qualifications. The 2015 UK wide report by EHRC (Mitchell *et al.*, 2015) looking at workplace and service provision found a complex and differential picture of the experiences of religious minorities and suggested (p16) *'better signposting to, and navigation of, practical guidance, including the compilation of checklists of factors that employers or service providers should take into consideration. Greater clarity on how to make complaints, especially in relation to the provision of goods, services and facilities, was also required'*. In 2016, the EHRC published *Religion or Belief: Is the Law Working?* (EHRC, 2016b). The research found the Equality Act and the Human Rights Act does provide sufficient protection for individuals with and without a religion or belief, religion or belief organisations and other groups protected by the Equality Act.

Age

One of the major challenges of the devolved legislature is responding to the needs of older people. Wales is an ageing population and this is set to continue. Currently 27 per cent are 60 and over and this is projected to rise to 33 per cent by 2030 (State of the Nation Report, Older People's Commissioner for Wales, 2019). Older people in Wales face considerable barriers in access to services and service discriminations. The 2019 State of the Nation report indicates stark inequalities that exist within the older population and the areas where things are getting worse for older people. Poverty, having fallen, is now rising and healthy life expectancy between the least and most deprived areas in Wales varies by as much as 18 years. The report details that significant numbers of older people are not able to access the local services they need; do not know their rights; and are not able to age well. The report highlights considerable issues of abuse, workplace discriminations and deep inequalities in access to services.

One step forward, two steps back?

The Equality and Human Rights Commission (EHRC) produced their statutory quinquennial report on progress on equality and human rights in Wales since 2010. They published the report *Is Wales Fairer?* in December 2015 (EHRC, 2015) and it is supported by a wealth of data and evidence. It shows good progress has been made in key areas in Wales, including a fall in homelessness, reduction in hostility towards lesbian, gay and bisexual people and an increase in the proportion of pupils achieving five GCSE's grades A*-C. However, it also found areas where there has been little or no progress. For example, in education where significant inequalities remain between different groups of people. The report has also found young people are significantly worse off in many ways including income, employment, poverty and housing. Estyn (2014) found that between 20 per cent and 50 per cent of pupils in Wales had experienced bullying at some point in their school lives, at risk were pupils with disabilities and LGBT pupils. Of concern were statistics from 2014 that demonstrated that hate crime motived by sexual orientation was the second most commonly reported hate crime (Ibid:27).

The 2015 report noted that the number of marriages and civil partnerships increased, divorces fell, but in 2013, there was a positive step as we saw the introduction of same-sex marriage (p7). The gender pay gap narrowed from 20 per cent to 17 per cent but this was due to men's average pay declining more than women's increasing (EHRC, 2015:14).

The third *Is Wales Fairer?* (2018) reported some progress. Up until 2010, the proportion of 16-18-year olds who were not in education, employment or training (NEET) stayed around 12 per cent (StatsWales, 2012). By 2018, this had fell to 10 percent (StatsWales, 2019a). For 19-24-year olds, between 1996 to 2008, the rate ranged between 16-20 per cent, before climbing to 23 per cent in 2010 (StatsWales, 2012). In 2018, the proportion of 19 to 24-year olds who were NEET fell to around 16 per cent (StatsWales, 2019a).

The EHRC (2018) also refers to increasing numbers of women in Wales engaging in democracy as in 2017, the rate of female voters was higher in Wales than in England (p112). Most recently there has been attention given to promoting diversity in public appointments given then significance in the delivery of public services. In launching a Strategy to address greater inclusion in appointments the Minister said: '*Whilst progress has been made in recent years – for example in 2018-19, women made up 63.5% of all Ministerial appointments and re-appointments in Wales – a renewed approach is needed in order to improve the wider diversity of public leaders and particularly to widen appointments drawn from BAME groups and disabled peo*ple' (Welsh Government, 2020b). In 2018-19, 3 per cent of appointments were of BAME people despite them making up 5 per cent of the population. Out of 170 appointments to public bodies by Welsh ministers in that period, fewer than six were from black, Asian and minority ethnic (BAME) backgrounds (BBC, 2019).

These are heartening developments but there is clearly a long way to go. Up until 2017, policy to address Wales' long history of deeply entrenched poverty, proceeded separately from equalities policy focused on individual characteristics. The Wales Act 2017 devolved the power to Welsh Ministers to enact the socio-economic duty of the Equality Act 2010 so when public bodies take strategic decisions, they are required to have due regard to the inequalities of outcome that result from socio-economic disadvantage (Welsh Government, 2019). Further to this, the Well-being of Future Generations (Wales) Act requires all public bodies to apply the 'sustainable development principle' (Welsh Government, 2015).

This integration of policy provides a strong foundation for tackling inequality. Yet for the past decade, the Welsh Government's equality aims have been restricted by the UK Government's austerity programme, a neo-liberal agenda which has included sustained reductions in public spending, tax rises and a reduction of public services (Malin, 2020). Between 2009/10 and 2013/14, total identifiable public expenditure on services in Wales fell in real terms by £822 million, a fall of 2.58 per cent (HM Treasury, 2015). While total public sector spending for Wales increased by 8.3 per cent from 2013-14 to 2017-18, total spending remained below its 2011-12 level, both in real terms and on a per person basis. UK austerity policies have had a clear impact in Wales (Ifan, Sion and Poole, 2019). According to the Office of National Statistics (ONS) (2016) Quarterly Public Sector Employment Survey, between the second quarter 2010 and the second quarter 2016, 23,700 fewer people were employed by councils in Wales. This equates to the loss of 17,600 permanent jobs as well as 6,100 temporary/casual jobs and 6,900 fewer men and 9,200 fewer women employed full-time, as well as 2,000 fewer men and 5,400 fewer women in part-time employment (cited in Unison Cymru, 2016). This has had a significant impact on equality and social justice in Wales.

Advancing equality – everybody's business

The breadth and multi-dimensional nature and complexity of inequality demand approaches that tackle change across the range of social policy spheres in an integrated way and that draw on a range of methods and stakeholders in the change effort. The *post*-Equality Act era represents a significant engagement with the issues of implementation, with commentators beginning to identify the key challenges of mainstreaming and implementing equalities.

Whilst relatively little research evidence exists analysing the progress of equality mainstreaming in the devolved legislatures, work by Chaney (2012), Havkinsky *et al.* (2019), and Parken (2018) provide useful insights on the successes and challenges of implementation.

The Havkinsky *et al.* study, based on interviews with key stakeholders across the devolved legislatures, recognises considerable successes in Wales through its mainstreamed commitment to advancing equality in public policy. They cite the example of work on closing the pay gap within a broader framework that has also initiated strategies to reduce violence against women and domestic abuse and monitor gender diversity in public appointments. This is a bold example of the Welsh Government strategy to tackle integration of the broad sweep of disadvantage with a long term inter-generational ambition.

When the Equality Act was in development a considerable groundswell of opinion from key stakeholders raised questions about the intersectional approach on which it is built. Many feared a dilution of effort on the specifics of racial disadvantage, or by gender or disability within the broad-brush approach. The critique suggested some forms of discrimination would get more attention and resources than others, especially those with a long institutional history such as gender and race, leading to competition between the various strands (Squires, 2009). The Act recognises the interlocking nature of inequalities and demands a focus on the very intersections that form disadvantage. This approach has undoubtedly brought with it a number of challenges for implementation, being a difficult concept to translate into practice, and difficult to quantify in terms of outcomes. There are challenges in gathering data on intersectional disadvantage and issues with embedding and institutionalising this approach into everyday practices of public servants and others. Parken (2018) argue this is a steep learning curve and puts forward the importance of facilitating workshops that promote looking at key policy areas from an intersectional perspective (p8). For instance, Parken (Parken *et al.*, 2019) offers models for reflective learning and provides extended examples of how to tackle intersectional policy development.

There needs to be good training and education for policy makers enabling them to free up their mindsets and engage with equality issues not as peripheral or marginal to what they are doing (Parken *et al.*, 2019).

Resistance to this type of thinking might relate to lack of expertise and experience but it also is hampered by a siloed approach to policy areas and path dependencies that are difficult to shake off. Havinksy *et al.* note policy actors still thinking in terms of discrete protected characteristics and funding structures that favour projects based on specific protected characteristics where is it easier to produce clearer and more quantifiable outcomes.

The literature has now quite strongly identified the precursors to successful mainstreaming (Chaney, 2012; Parken, 2018). Strong leadership, at the highest level and an increase in the diversity make-up of that leadership is important to these developments. Opportunities for members of diverse groups to have a direct influence on decision making is critical. High participatory engagement (Chaney, 2012) and strong coalition building between government, academics and civil society actors is crucial to policy development and momentum. Strong enforcement measures with clear sanctions for lack of accountability is important. There needs to be good training and education for policy makers enabling them to free up their mindsets and engage with equality issues not as peripheral or marginal to what they are doing (Parken *et al.*, 2019). The data dearth requires systematic tackling and there is a need for evidence of all kinds – both quantitative and qualitative implying a key role for researchers. This implies a multi-actor, multi-sectorial approach to the issues at hand, indeed advancing equalities as everyone's business. Strategic visioning and engaging and convincing the wider public of the equality imperative becomes important to its resourcing and its progress; advancing the notion that a more equal society is unequivocally beneficial for all (Wilkinson and Pickett, 2009).

Conclusions

The enabling environment for equality practice in Wales is second to none, at both central and local level. Local authority obligations are clear in terms of the push towards greater user engagement and participation, clear identification and auditing of issues of inequality and being held accountable for proactive strategies of redress. Opportunities for social welfare professionals to take a more proactive stance on social justice issues are being opened up within a wider culture in Wales of equitable public service delivery. Within this values-based framework, participation, rights-based welfare and progressive universalism are the mainstays, all of which resonate with the values and social justice ambitions of professional practice. Many of the barriers to progress are now clearly signposted and there is recognition of the fact that experiential learning is the key to sustainable changes in practice. What is clear is that policy makers cannot achieve change alone and that the legislation and the infrastructure supporting it will always be weak without wider cultural engagement and commitment. Equality strategies require the energy and commitment of a range of actors, the policy makers, the academics and researchers, groups and organisations in civil society and professional groups on the frontline of delivery and the public at large.

While opportunities for further progress on equalities in Wales have been severely hampered by the UK Government's programme of austerity, there have been noted advances in Wales. There is evidence of small steps towards tackling long standing inequalities such as poverty, the gender pay gap and public health concerns such as suicidal behavior amongst men and more. At the same time the path towards an equal society in Wales remains unclear, as the world is experiencing a worldwide pandemic. We are experiencing a transformed society with disturbing death tolls, 'social distancing', empty streets and shops, and a natural world recovering from the damage inflicted by humankind. As a result, Britain faces an unprecedented recession and this will undoubtedly have reverberations in rising to the challenge of equality in years to come.

References

Aiden, H and McCarthy, A. (2014) *Current attitudes towards disabled people* Scope

Andrews, K.(2018) The Gender Pay Gap Reporting Measures. *The Institute of Economic Affairs*. London

Bagilhole, B (2009) *Understanding equal opportunities and diversity: The social differentiations and intersections of inequality* Bristol: Policy Press

Barnard (2018) *Poverty in Wales 2018* York: Joseph Rowntree Foundation

BBC (2019) *BAME appointments: Welsh Government 'must do more'. 27th June 2019* . Available online: www.bbc.co.uk/news/uk-wales-politics-48771948

Bevan Foundation (2015) *Women's Equality Now: The Position in Wales Today on Unpaid Care* Cardiff: Wales Women's Equality Network

Broughton, N (2015) *Self-employment and ethnicity: an escape from poverty?* York: Joseph Rowntree Foundation

Catney, G and Sabater, A (2015) *Ethnic minority disadvantage in the labour market* York: Joseph Rowntree Foundation

Chaney, P (2012) New legislative settings and the application of the participative-democratic model of mainstreaming equality in public policy making: evidence from the UK's devolution programme. *Policy Studies* 33(5): pp455-76

Chwarae Teg. (2019a) *Wales' Gender Pay Gap increases to 14.5%*. 7th November 2019. Available online: https://chwaraeteg.com/news/wales-gender-pay-gap-increases

Chwarae Teg. (2019b) *Deeds not Words: Review of Gender Equality in Wales (Phase Two)*. Available online: https://chwaraeteg.com/projects/gender-equality-review/#phase-two

Davies, R, Drinkwater, S, Joll, C, Jones, M, Lloyd-Williams, H, Makepeace, G, Parhi, M, Parken, A, Robinson, C, Taylor, C, and Wass, V (2011) *An Anatomy of Economic Inequality in Wales, A report prepared on behalf of the Wales Equality and Human Rights Commission* Cardiff: EHRC p215

Davies, R and Parken, A (2017) "Devolution, Recession and the Alleviation of Inequality in Wales", Fée, D and Kober-Smith, A (eds.) *Inequalities in the UK* Emerald Publishing Limited, pp323-40.

Disability Wales (2018) A national disgrace: the high price of disability poverty in Wales. Available online: www.disabilitywales.org/national-disgrace-high-price-disability-poverty-wales

Disability Wales (2019) Press Release – The Future is Now! Available online: www.disabilitywales.org/press-release-the-future-is-now

EHRC (Equality and Human Rights Commission) (2015) *Is Wales Fairer? The state of equality and human rights 2015* Cardif: EHRC

EHRC (2016a) *Is Britain Fairer?': Key facts and findings on Gypsies, Roma and Travellers* London: EHRC

EHRC (2016b) *Religion or Belief: Is the Law Working?* London: EHRC

EHRC (2017) *Who Runs Wales?* Cardif: EHRC

EHRC (2018) *Is Wales Fairer? The state of equality and human rights 2018* Cardiff: EHRC

Estyn (2014) *Action on bullying – A review of the effectiveness of action taken by schools to address bullying on the grounds of pupils' protected characteristics*. Cardiff: Estyn. Available online: www.estyn.gov.wales/system/files/2020-07/Action%2520on%2520bullying%2520-%2520June%25202014.pdf

Farrell, W (2005) *Why Men Earn More and What Women Can Do About* New York: Amacom

The Fawcett Society (2019) *Gender Pay Gap and Causes Briefing*. Available online: www.fawcettsociety.org.uk/Handlers/Download.ashx?IDMF=e1d6747c-4cde-4a3a-9bee-6b0da9670757

Feast, P and Hand, J (2015) Enigmas of the Equality Act 2010 – "Three uneasy pieces", *Cogent Social Sciences*, 1:1, 1123085

Grant, A (2012) Barriers to work for Incapacity Benefit claimants in Wales *Contemporary Wales* 25, 173-90

Government Equalities Office (2017) Gender pay gap reporting: overview. Available online: www.gov.uk/guidance/gender-pay-gap-reporting-overview

Government Equalities Office. (2018) LGBT Survey. Research Report. Available online: https://assets.publishing.service.gov.uk/government/uploads/system/uploads/attachment_data/file/721704/LGBT-survey-research-report.pdf

Harvey, S, Mitchell, M, Keeble, J, McNaughton Nicholls, C and Rahim, N (2014) *Barriers faced by Lesbian, Gay, Bisexual and Transgender People in Accessing Domestic Abuse, Stalking, Harassment and Sexual Violence Services* Cardiff: Welsh Government Social Research

Hankivsky, O, de Merich, D and Christoffersen, A (2019) Equalities 'devolved': experiences in mainstreaming across the UK devolved powers post-equality act 2010. *British Politics*, 14(2):141-61

HM Treasury (2015) *Public Expenditure Statistical Analyses (PESA)* London: Her Majesty's Stationery Office

Home Office (2014) *Hate crimes, England and Wales 2013 to 2014*. Data tables. Available online: www.gov.uk/government/statistics/hate-crimes-england-and-wales-2013-to-2014

Home Office (2019). *Hate crimes, England and Wales 2018 to 2019*. Data tables. Available online: www.gov.uk/government/statistics/hate-crime-england-and-wales-2018-to-2019

Ifan, G, Sion, C and Poole, E (2019) *Government Expenditure and Revenue Wales 2019* Cardiff: Cardiff University

Joseph Rowntree Foundation (JRF) (2018) *Poverty in Wales 2018* York: JRF. Available at: www.jrf.org.uk/report/poverty-wales-2018

Maegusuku-Hewett, T, Raithby, M and Willis, P (2015) 'Life in the Pink Dragon's Den: mental health services and social inclusion for LGBT people in Wales'. In *Lesbian, Gay, Bisexual and Trans Health Inequalities. International Perspectives in Social Work* edited by Fish, J and Karban, K. Bristol: Policy Press

Malin, N (2020) *De-Professionalism and Austerity: Challenges for the Public Sector* Bristol: Policy Press

Mitchell, M, Beninger, K, Donald, A and Howard, E (2015) *Religion or belief in the workplace and service delivery. Findings from a call for evidence*. Manchester: Equality and Human Rights Commission

Mosalski, R and Miller, C (2018) *The gender pay gap: The companies in Wales with the biggest gap between men and women's salaries* WalesOnline [5 April 2018]. Available online: www.walesonline.co.uk/business/business-news/gender-pay-gap-companies-wales-14494090

National Union of Students (2014) *Education Beyond the Straight and Narrow LGBT students' experience in higher education* NUS

Nicholl, A, Johnes, C and Holtom, D (2016) *Breaking the links between poverty and ethnicity in Wales*. York: Joseph Rowntree Foundation

Older People's Commissioner for Wales (2019) *State of the Nation 2019*. Available online: www.olderpeoplewales.com/Libraries/Uploads/State_of_the_Nation_e_-_online.sflb.ashx

Owen, D, Gambin, L, Green, A and Yuxin, L (2015) *Projecting employment by ethnic group to 2022* York: Joseph Rowntree Foundation

Papworth Trust (2018) Facts and Figures, 2018. Disability in the UK.

Parken, A, Pocher, and Davies, R (2014) *Working Patterns in Wales: Gender, Occupations and Pay* Cardiff: Cardiff University

Parken, A (2018) *Putting equality at the heart of decision-making Gender Equality Review (GER) Phase One: International Policy and Practice* Wales Centre for Public Policy, Cardiff University

Parken, A, Davies N, Minto, R and Trenow, P (2019) Equality Mainstreaming: Policy Development Model. Available online: https://chwaraeteg.com/wp-content/uploads/2019/09/Equality-Mainstreaming-Policy-Development-Model.pdf

Perraudin, F (2019) 'What is gender pay gap reporting, and what does it mean?' *The Guardian* [28 February 2019]

Pollock, I (2019) LGBT attitudes in Wales: 'Huge distance' travelled in 30 years. BBC News [15 March 2019]. Available online: www.bbc.co.uk/news/uk-wales-47569273

Powell, A. Barton, C, Garton-Grimwood, G, Cromarty, H, Brown, J, Roberts, N, Kennedy, S, Powell, T (2019) Gypsies and Travellers *Commons Library, Parliament* [9 May 2019]. Available online: https://commonslibrary.parliament.uk/research-briefings/cbp-8083

Sanders, S (2020) Sexual orientation, UK: 2018. Office of National Statistics. Available online: www.ons.gov.uk/peoplepopulationandcommunity/culturalidentity/sexuality/bulletins/sexualidentityuk/2018

Scope (2019) *The disability price tag 2019*. Scope. Available online: www.scope.org.uk/campaigns/extra-costs/disability-price-tag

Smith, R (2019) *Gender pay gap in the UK: 2019* Office of National Statistics. Available online: www.ons.gov.uk/employmentandlabourmarket/peopleinwork/earningsandworkinghours/bulletins/genderpaygapintheuk/2019

StatsWales (2012) *Further Analysis of data related to Young People Not in Education, Employment or Training (NEET)* Available online: https://gov.wales/sites/default/files/statistics-and-research/2019-03/further-analysis-of-data-related-to-young-people-not-in-education-employment-or-training.pdf

StatsWales (2019a) *Young people not in education, employment or training (NEET) Year to 31 March 2019* Available online: https://gov.wales/sites/default/files/statistics-and-research/2019-08/young-people-not-in-education-employment-or-training-neet-2018-to-2019-649.pdf

StatsWales (2019b) *Ethnicity by area and ethnic group*. Available online: https://statswales.gov.wales/Catalogue/Equality-and-Diversity/Ethnicity/ethnicity-by-area-ethnicgroup [accessed 08.02.2020]

Stonewall (2017) *LGBT in Wales. Hate Crime and Discrimination* Stonewall Cymru

Squires, J (2009) Intersecting Inequalities, *International Feminist Journal of Politics*, 11(4): 496-512

Unison Cymru (2016) *Local Government Wales: Audit of Austerity 2016*. Unison Cymru Wales

Welsh Government (2014) *Framework for Action on Independent Living* Cardiff: Welsh Government

Welsh Government (2015) *Well-being of Future Generations (Wales) Act 2015 The Essentials* Cardiff: Welsh Government

Welsh Government (2019) *A More Equal Wales – Commencing the Socioeconomic Duty. Consultation Document* Cardiff: Welsh Government

Welsh Government (2020a) *Strategic Equality Plan 2020-2024: Equality Aims, Objectives & Actions* Cardiff: Welsh Government

Welsh Government (2020b) *Written Statement: Launch of the Diversity and Inclusion Strategy for Public Appointments in Wales (2020 – 2023)*. Cardiff: Welsh Government. Available online: https://gov.wales/written-statement-launch-diversity-and-inclusion-strategy-public-appointments-wales-2020-2023

Wilkinson, K and Pickett, R (2009) *The Spirit Level: Why More Equal Societies Almost Always Do Better* London: Allen Lane

Williams, C (2011) 'Equalities and Social Justice in a Devolved Wales' in *Social Policy for Social Welfare Practice in a Devolved Wales* Birmingham: BASW/Venture Press

Winckler, V (2019) *Trapped: Poverty amongst women in Wales today*. Chwarae Teg

WEN Wales and Oxfam (2019) *Cymru Feminist Scorecard 2019, Tracking Welsh Government action to advance women's rights and gender equality* Cardiff: Women's Equality Network (WEN) Wales & Oxfam Cymru

Chapter 11

Child and Family Services: Welsh policy developments 2010-2020

Jen Lyttleton-Smith

Introduction

In the late 1990s and 2000s, the UK nations saw an upsurge in child-centred policy throughout the Labour Governments of Tony Blair and Gordon Brown. Now, a decade after the conclusion of the New Labour political era, and with a Labour-dominated Welsh Government maturing under devolution, Wales' aspirational approach to child and family services policy is notable in its contrast to the direction of UK Conservative-led Governments. Taking the premise of children's rights as a concrete underpinning of policy, the narrative strength of public services as nurturing support structure focused on the voices, well-being, and futures of vulnerable children in Wales is exceeded in the UK only by Scotland. In terms of rhetoric and ambition, it is hard to identify international competitors on this issue outside of Scandinavia and the Netherlands[1]. However, while ambition is strong in the key pieces of legislation of this era relating to disadvantaged children, full-scale implementation and accurate measurements of success continue to challenge public services, and it is uncertain how their effects will emerge in the coming years.

Meanwhile, Westminster-led austerity economics, rising inequality, under-employment[2], and shifts within social work practice cultures have significantly impacted the Welsh capacity to care for vulnerable children and families through welfare policy and practice. While children's social care funding is protected from reduction, the dramatic increase of children cared for by the state ('looked-after') over the past ten years has inflicted budgetary pressure on child and family services. At the time of writing, there are 6,845 children looked-after in Wales, compared to 5,160 in 2010[3] (StatsWales, 2019a). Despite these difficult circumstances, over the same period a range of new and developed policy-driven activities have produced a progressive landscape

---

[1] New Zealand has also been taking great strides in a rights-based approach, though their implementation of their rhetoric is challenging to trace through their welfare practice.
[2] Distinct from 'unemployment' as the rise of, so-called, 'zero-hour contract' allots employment to those without reliable work and, often, with insufficient earnings.
[3] Meanwhile, children receiving care and support in Wales (which includes children to be receiving other forms of support from child and family services but usually requiring less provision than looked-after children) rose from 18,865 in 2010 to over 20,000 in the mid-2010's, but dropped in 2015-16 back to just under 19,000[3] (StatsWales, 2019b).

of national and local provision. This chapter provides an overview of this national policy and practice guidance, its application in preventative and interventionist work, and how it has developed over the past decade.

Policy context and strategic development

Welsh policy has centralised children's rights throughout all key policy areas since devolution, particularly in child and family services, and has sought to integrate this basis throughout child and family services through embracing practice and policy innovation. Examples of this include the establishment of Integrated Family Support Services (IFSS), the early adoption of the Children's Commissioner role, and comprehensive advocacy support for all children. In this, Wales demonstrates a clear lineage of ambitious rhetoric observable government policy dating back to the early 2000s (Butler & Drakeford, 2013; Pithouse, 2011). In another timeline, this may have supported the Welsh achievement of the UK Government ambition of ending child poverty by 2020 (Welsh Assembly Government, 2005), reducing the burden on child and family services and enabling them to focus more efforts on preventative, rather than interventionist work. Instead, the financial crash of 2008 heralded an entirely different context of austerity and rising poverty in the UK which came to dominate the next decade. Despite devolved social care budgets and policy, the impact of this was powerfully felt in Welsh child and family services through economic constraints and rising inequality. Child referrals to social services rose steadily over the decade, eventually flattening out in around 2016 (see Chapter 4) challenging budgets and resource capacity. Despite this substantial challenge, Wales continued to develop its own approach to child and family social care policy distinct from England.

Opening the decade with a radically different economic, political, and social landscape to that of the past years, Welsh Government continued to foster innovation under straitened budgets and rising numbers of referrals to child and family services. This complemented an openness to innovation and change in child and family social work that was emerging in the UK during the publication of the England-focused Munro Review of child protection practice (Munro, 2011), Allen Review of Early Intervention (Allen, 2011), and the UK Family Justice Review (Norgrove, 2011), and it was at this point that Wales began to publish its own innovative strategies to develop child and family services. Note that prior to the national referendum in 2011, Wales was not permitted to produce its own legislative Acts so policy was legislated through 'Measures' that were granted Royal Assent; in this period Welsh Government produced the Children and Families (Wales) Measure of 2010 (Welsh Government, 2010), and the Rights of Children and Young Persons (Wales) Measure 2011 (National Assembly for Wales, 2011)[4].

---

[4] After 2011, Wales was permitted to legislate through Acts of the National Assembly for Wales.

The Children and Families (Wales) Measure 2010

This measure provides a basis for the policy and practice developments in child and family services throughout the next decade, containing the seeds of key policy themes like early intervention, targeted parenting and childcare support, and children's voice and rights. Despite the difficult financial situation, the Children and Families (Wales) Measure (Welsh Government, 2010) set out an ambitious plan to eradicate child poverty through a plethora of strategies and responsibilities placed on local authorities, including: raising the income and employability of parents; reduce child inequalities in education, culture, health and housing; to support parenting (and while this is just one mention of parenting support in a long list of aims, this single point achieves great prominence in policy in the years following), and to build strong, cohesive communities (Part 1:1). It also requires local authorities to ensure that 'sufficient' play facilities and opportunities exist for its child population, and states that these should be assessed regularly. Briefly, but importantly, it sets expectations that children and young people will be involved in local authority decision making in decisions that affect them (Part 1:12), and this chapter will return to this subject below. Part 2 sets out registration, regulatory, and inspection processes for independent childcare providers. Part 3 provides the necessary legislation to underpin the nationwide establishment of Integrated Family Support Teams to deliver IFSS, also discussed further below. Extending the theme of early intervention and identification of children in need of care and support, it also includes provision for children's need to be assessed should their parents access social or health support services, enabling the early identification of vulnerable children. The Measure sets the tone for a child-centred approach to delivering welfare policy, complemented by the Rights of Children and Young Persons (Wales) Measure that followed the next year.

Rights of Children and Young Persons (Wales) Measure 2011

This Measure put Wales at the forefront of children's rights implementation internationally, by requiring that the United Nations Convention on the Rights of the Child (United Nations, 1989) be considered in relation to every act of policy delivered, even if that policy has no direct relevance to children and families. It states that the UNCRC must be actively promoted in Wales to the public, including children, and that respect for their identity, their wellbeing, and protection from harm is the responsibility of the state. In relation to voice and advocacy, it gives "the child who is capable of forming his or her own views the right to express those views freely in all matters affecting the child, the views of the child being given due weight in accordance with the age and maturity of the child" (Article 12:1), including the right to be heard in legal proceedings. It also protects the right to children and young people's freedom of expression, access to culture, and care for disability. The Measure has been praised for Welsh Government's high level of engagement with the UNCRC Committee, and the opportunities it creates for children and young people to have genuine influence in policy making (Williams, 2012; 2013). Williams (2013) and Rees (2010) argue that the Measure positioned children's rights as a defining characteristic of Welsh devolution, locating Wales at the forefront of child wellbeing policy in the UK and internationally, though later commentary questions whether this rhetoric found its way to full implementation in the eight years following its publication (Hoffman, 2019).

Sustainable Social Services: A Framework for Action (2011)

Continuing the trend for centralising the public's voice and views, the policy context for devolved national approach was heralded by the publication of *Sustainable Social Services* (Welsh Government, 2011a) which placed citizen involvement, including children and young people, at the heart of social care policy and practice. Other key narratives emerging included greater third sector involvement in designing and delivering core child and family support and care services, with a 'multi-agency approach' emerging as one of the defining concepts of the decade and requiring unprecedented levels of co-operation and communication between organisations – sometimes in the format of a Multi-Agency Safeguarding Hub (MASH), but also in multiple other formal and informal ways. Alongside this, citizen participation and voice became a standard fixture of almost all policy documents, with a level of stakeholder consultation now nearly universal to all policy developments. The degree to which such consultations are conducted in a transparent and accessible way remains a matter of debate, as the processes by which consultation and participation occurred were often opaque – under-described in documents purporting to share their results – however the value placed upon their prominence in decision-making led to the evolution of 'participation' into 'co-production' (Pestoff *et al.*, 2013)[5]. This concept had slowly but steadily gained traction in policymaking throughout the 2000s and was enthusiastically adopted by Welsh Government as the zenith of involving citizens in decision-making. These approaches were unified and cemented in the defining legislative development of devolved Welsh social care thus far: The Social Services and Well-Being (Wales) Act 2014.

Key legislative developments

The measures described above led to the development of The Social Services and Well-Being (Wales) Act 2014 (hereafter 'The SSWB Act'), the defining piece of legislation guiding social care services in Wales, representing a step away from Westminster driven policy and producing a distinctly Welsh approach to providing care and support to children and adults. A second piece of legislation of lesser but still substantial relevance to child and family care and support is the Well-Being of Future Generations (Wales) Act 2015 (hereafter 'The WFG Act'), and this is also discussed briefly here.

---

[5] The degree to which policy is co-productive, rather than participative is also a controversial matter. Co-production implies not only expressing views but having genuine power over decision making to a meaningful degree (Arnstein, 1969; Bovaird et al., 2015). Whilst there are many examples of this occurring in adult services, the degree to which children and young people are involved in actual decision making in Wales under 'co-production' is not yet clear but given the paucity of examples promoted with any detail there is reason to be suspicious as to whether policy continues to be participative, rather than co-productive (Public Health Wales and Co-production Wales, 2015).

Social Services and Well-Being (Wales) Act 2014

This was first published in 2014, having been in active development for approximately four years, and was enacted in April 2016. Partly a realisation of ideological goals established during the creation of the Welsh Assembly, and partly an amelioration of the above strains on financial and resource capacity, the SSWB Act and its associated guidance sets out a vision for social care focused on citizen participation, multi-agency collaboration, and a holistic approach to well-being as the purpose of social care. In relation to children, this latter point shifts focus away from child protection and risk assessment towards a promotion of social policy as seeking to improve the lives of families in need (though the degree to which this is occurring in practice is under debate).

This legislation, in planning since devolution and in active development from 2010, represented a concerted step away from the prior necessity of following in the footsteps of Westminster, embedding multi-agency working, co-production, a preventative approach and outcomes-focused practice in policy. The degree to which practice is enacting those principles is yet to be ascertained; this is currently the focus of a government-funded evaluation of the policy implementation looking at both child and adult services. The SSWB Act is described at length elsewhere, so I will focus this discussion on its particular ramifications for child and family services.

The first critical difference between the Welsh legislation and its UK predecessor (and current English counterpart) is that the SSWB Act in Wales applies to both adults and children, whereas in England only adults are covered by the Care Act (2014). This sets out a precedent for practice that children's rights and expectations regarding social care should not differ from the standards offered for adults. The Act does dedicate a specific section (Part 6) to care and support for looked-after children, acknowledging the specific role it holds as corporate parent to these children and the ramifications of this for its responsibility, however the overall merging of adult and child policy has important practical and symbolic effects, which are discussed further below.

From its title and throughout, the SSWB Act centralises the concept of well-being within care and support, with significant implications for the direct practice approach of social workers and support workers. The Act demands that social care not just protect children and adults, but also promote their overall wellbeing, providing the tools and resources for them to flourish. Enacting the requirements of the earlier measures, the Act contains extensive legislation around public voice and control, though in relation to children and young people it contains the clause that their voices will impact decision making only where they are deemed capable of contributing. This latter clause creates a notable 'judgement gap' where decision-making still, in reality, lies with adults, making it important to have processes in place to scrutinise whether such judgements of capability are fair and reasonable. Independent Reviewing Officers are expected to perform this role, though the efficacy of this role in England has been questioned due to their frequently sporadic personal contact with the children they serve (Diaz *et al.*, 2019). In addition, safeguarding policy is clarified and extended. A key change in the law here includes a statutory duty on commissioned services to report safeguarding concerns regarding children (and adults) to the local authority. Assessments of need are restructured to mandate more regular reassessment, including of wellbeing, with reference to the National Outcomes Framework (discussed below).

The Well-Being of Future Generations (Wales) Act 2015
Developed concurrently, The Well-Being of Future Generations Act 2015 ('the WFG Act') is closely tied to the SSWB Act. As the name suggests, this is a forward-thinking piece of legislation that seeks to ground current policies and action in a view of global and local developments that impact on the national interest. Though not exclusively relating to children per se, the WFG Act acts to orientate and solidify the ethos of Welsh welfare services (among other aspects of governance) within the framework of wellbeing, prevention-over-intervention, and the involvement of citizens in decision making. All these approaches directly mirror those contained within the SSWB Act and expand their relevance to the broader population outside of those who need care and support. In this sense, the WFG Act extends the reach of Welsh health and social care policy to those children not currently in receipt of services.

To oversee the outcomes of these policies a Ministerial Advisory Group for Improving Outcomes for Children, formed in 2016, and has a particular focus on children in or on the edge of care. The details of their sessions, in which they scrutinise the implementation and development of the above policies, are published regularly on the Welsh Government website and offer helpful insight into current priorities and debates.

Policy themes of the 2010s for child and family services

Within the Measures and Acts discussed above, there are seven key areas that clearly emerge to produce the narrative of policy development for Welsh child and family services in the 2010s.

1. A rights-based conceptual understanding of childhood
As demonstrated within the Rights of Children and Young Persons (Wales) Measure, Wales has sought to expand upon the UNCRC conception of children's rights and embed them throughout all government policy. This aspirational approach is not new to Wales: a whole hearted commitment to children's rights has been visible since the start of devolution (Butler, 2011; Butler and Drakeford, 2013), observable in *Children and Young People: A Framework for Partnership* (National Assembly for Wales, 2000) and *Children and Young People: Rights to Action* (Welsh Government, 2004). The language applied aspires to ensure that children are not just protected but helped to flourish through policy innovation and involvement in decision-making. The SSWB Act brings these enhanced set of rights and expectations to bear directly on the lives of children and families receiving social care services and in doing so it draws a clear distinction between Wales and England.

First, the SSWB Act replaced Part 3 of the Children Act (1989) with the effect that all children, regardless of assessment or background, have a right to expect the same living standards and wellbeing. Further expectations of the role of the state where it holds parental responsibility, as it does in the case of looked-after children, are set out in a separate Part 6. Second, the SSWB Act is distinct from English policy in the negating of any personal responsibility for the child's own support – no contributions to care may be sought from the child until they reach the age of 18 (p88), while in England they can, theoretically, be sought from age 16 (Mitchell, 2015). The conceptual shift here is important as the Welsh approach attempts to protect the child from the consequences of circumstances beyond their control into early adulthood, recognising that the negative impact of early life may delay the readiness of care-experienced children for adult responsibilities. Third, the SSWB Act brings together child and adult care policy under 'one roof' to reflect family/relationships based approach, with the effect that children and adults are legislated to receive the same care and support. This is particularly noticeable when the National Outcomes Framework is accounted for, which stipulates the same well-being outcomes for both adults and children.

2. *Mandatory advocacy and participation*

The participation of children and families in decision making around their care and support is writ large in all the above policies, while publically funded organisations such as Co-Production Wales and Young Wales (who published the Children and Young People's National Participation Standards in 2018) have been formed in recent years to ensure the implementation of policy goals relating to participation[6]. The SSWB Act legislates that professionals "in so far as is reasonably practicable, ascertain and have regard to the individual's views, wishes and feelings… [and] have regard to the importance of providing appropriate support to enable the individual to participate in decisions that affect him or her to the extent that is appropriate in the circumstances" (Welsh Government, 2014a:7), including looked-after children (with IROs responsible for "ensuring that any ascertained wishes and feelings of the child concerning the case are given due consideration by the local authority" (*ibid* p76)). These principles are reinforced in practice guidance for child and family services, which centralise the importance of participation in decision making (AFA Cymru, 2018; Welsh Government, 2016).

While there are clearly limits to this participation, dictated by a professional's own assessment of capacity and 'appropriateness', and the degree to which advocates (whether independent or IRO) are well-informed enough to accurately express a looked-after child's wishes and feelings, this approach to involving vulnerable citizens – including children – in decision making emerges as one of the defining features of Welsh social care in this decade. As a result of this legislation, most local authorities in Wales either already have in place, or are currently developing plans to involve children and young people receiving care and support in decision making and departmental planning via consultation and participation groups (Lyttleton-Smith *et al.*, 2018) – though the extent of this work remains highly variable.

---

[6] Funky Dragon, a previously prominent contributor to children and young people's participation in government policy, had its funding withdrawn in 2014 and subsequently the project ended.

3. Family support and early intervention services

Churchill and Sen (2016) identify a general trend over the past two decades towards increased family support services and 'early interventions' to try and diminish what is perceived as 'welfare dependency' and reduce the number of children entering care. This is prominent, for example, in the Munro Review (2011) which advocates 'early help'[7] for parents who are struggling, and in the parallel Allen Review (2011). Under the devolved social care system, policy language, target population, and implementation are closely married to the local political landscape; in the case of early help and intervention, this enacts ideological beliefs regarding the relationships between family and state, and structural responsibility for social issues (Cameron *et al.*, 2007). Welsh Government's position, informed by its dynastic Labour majority, was already clear, having established plans in the 2000s to offer comprehensive support services for families experiencing difficulties of various kinds, including poverty, mental illness, addiction, and domestic violence. Since then, Wales has demonstrated an increased focus on family support throughout the 2010s, primarily through the Integrated Family Support Service (IFSS), introduced in 2010 within the Children and Families (Wales) Measure, and rolled out nationally in 2014 – alongside broader preventative work such as Flying Start, Families First, and Communities First (the latter now defunct). These activities are discussed further below. Throughout this, Welsh Government has characterised parents in need of care and support as vulnerable victims of systemic poverty and inequality: this contrasts starkly with the approach of the 'Troubled Families' programme in England, which was a deficits-based approach delivered to address 'problem behaviours' within families, described as "crime, anti-social behaviour, truancy and unemployment" (Bate & Bellis, 2017). Such difference within policy language clearly demarcates the approaches of the neighbouring countries.

Welsh policy has demonstrated an ongoing commitment to preventative policy to reduce the number of children and families in need of support from social services. Much of this work is covered by Chapter 4 in relation to the nation's anti-poverty strategies, however here a brief discussion of key policies salient to child and family services is provided. Welsh Government opened the decade with a clear statement of intent relating to such preventative work, presenting a 'Rainbow Model' of 'Prevention-Protection-Remedy' (Figure 11.1) to "drive the development of structured ways to pre-empting, identifying and addressing problems at the earliest possible opportunities using the most appropriate interventions" (Welsh Government, 2011b). This has taken the form of a plethora of policies ranging from face-to-face targeted work for those with identifiable risk factors, to broad population measures designed to reach all children

---

[7] Distinct from 'intervention' in that it better supports a strengths-based approach – see Featherstone et al., 2014. There are distinct conceptual difficulties of defining exactly what constitutes an 'early intervention', as the term is applied broadly and, often, interchangeably with 'family support' or 'intensive family support' to describe radically different services. In many uses, 'early' is used to refer to interventions that prevent further escalation of existing issues in families, but in the Allen Review (2011) the term is used to refer specifically to family support for parents with 0-5 year olds, with 'early' describing the child's age. Welsh Government applies the definition that early intervention constitutes support 'to prevent young people and families with children of all ages from developing problems which are difficult to overcome' (Welsh Government, 2017:3). For a full and nuanced discussion of this complex matter see Churchill and Sen (2016).

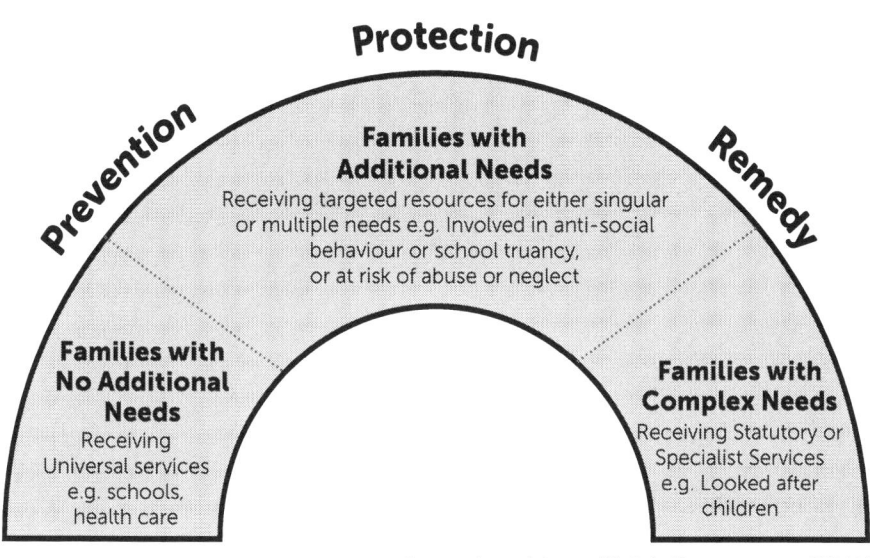

Figure 11.1: Welsh Government Approach to Family Services

Protection

Prevention

Remedy

Families with Additional Needs
Receiving targeted resources for either singular or multiple needs e.g. Involved in anti-social behaviour or school truancy, or at risk of abuse or neglect

Families with No Additional Needs
Receiving Universal services e.g. schools, health care

Families with Complex Needs
Receiving Statutory or Specialist Services e.g. Looked after children

Reproduced from Welsh Government (2011)

and families in the hope of producing equal experiences of childhood wellbeing for all. Targeted approaches introduced or significantly developed and expanded in the 2010s include: IFSS, Flying Start, Families First, and Reflect.

Integrated Family Support Services: IFSS was introduced as a pilot scheme in 2010 in three Welsh areas, and was gradually rolled out nationally, reaching full coverage in 2014. The initial focus of the scheme was on supporting families with parental substance misuse problems, though latterly other concerns were also addressed, such as domestic violence. IFSS received a broadly positive mixed-methods evaluation in 2014 after three years of study, which encompassed its Phase One pilot sites and national roll-out (Welsh Government, 2014b). Short-term outcomes measured by Goal Attainment Scaling, the Strengths and Difficulties Questionnaire (SDQ) and Warwick Edinburgh Mental Well-being Scale were found to be improved for families engaged with the service. The evaluation found positive impressions of the service amongst parents and professionals, though the research team caution that IFSS appears to work best for families approaching a crisis point, with an escalation of existing issues occurring, rather than those families who have already reached a significant crisis. Other limitations noted included that the length of support was too short for some families, and that service quality was dictated by the quality of professionals delivering support (though this is universal to all forms of care and support).

Flying Start: Flying Start was launched by Welsh Government in 2006 as part of its strategic approach to early intervention with vulnerable families. It aimed to accomplish this through free childcare, parenting support, enhanced health visitor support, and speech and language development support focused on children under four years old.

The service is delivered in areas judged to have very high levels of disadvantage based on the Index of Multiple Deprivation and Free School Meal entitlement. Later, in 2012, an outreach programme was incorporated (Welsh Government, 2012). As of 2019, 22,576 children were receiving Flying Start services, with 20 per cent of children under four in Wales receiving Flying Start health visitor support (Welsh Government, 2019a). Qualitative evidence has indicated that there may be positive outcomes for family wellbeing and child development (Thomas *et al.*, 2018; White and McCrindle, 2010), and this was recently confirmed via a linked-data intervention evaluation which found positive outcomes relating to health, education, and social care.

Families First: This family support programme that shares a name with many varied iterations of supporting disadvantaged families worldwide, and was designed to complement and extend the work conducted under Flying Start for families with older children. It focuses on families with lower levels of need, with the intention of preventing relatively minor problems from escalating. It was introduced in Wales in 2011 to contribute to the national Child Poverty Strategy in three ways: reducing the number of families living in workless households; improving the skills and employability of parents and carers in low-income households, and improving outcomes for children by reducing and countering inequalities (Welsh Government, 2011b).

Reflect: This service conducts direct therapeutic work with parents who have had children removed in care proceedings to support this vulnerable group, reduce rapid repeat pregnancies, and try to prevent further child protection concerns with any future children. A positive evaluation of the pilot scheme in 2018 accompanied the national expansion of the project (Roberts *et al.*, 2018).

4. The Improvement of Placement Quality and Capacity for Looked-After Children

A central focus of the Ministerial Advisory Group for Improving Outcomes for Children has been raising the standards of care for looked-after children. Amidst strong collaboration between a number of organisations in Wales, many local and national initiatives have been identified to progress this work. Particular examples include:

Residential care: There has been much discussion within Local Authorities and government regarding the children's residential care sector in Wales, with a range of research commissioned in the latter part of the decade to investigate how best to move forward in improving quality and capacity. This work revealed a "lack of emergency or crisis provision, including remand, and residential care for children at the highest end of the continuum of need" (Welsh Government, 2019b). As a result of this, alongside concerns regarding costs and profiteering within the independent sector, there have been moves by many Local Authorities to consider expanding public provision within their areas, and several have already conducted preparatory work for this to develop (Lyttleton-Smith *et al.*, 2018).

Fostering Framework: In order to encourage better partnership working, improved standards, transparency, and to support fostering capacity in Wales, a National Fostering Framework began to be developed in collaboration by Welsh Government and a number of third sector organisations in 2015 (National Fostering Framework, 2017). This programme addresses commissioning, branding, kinship care, fees and allowances, training, and best practice guidelines (informed by new fostering regulations enacted in 2019) (Social Care Wales, 2019). Currently in the final stages of development, the ramifications of this work, if implemented effectively, could have a strong positive impact on the quality and capacity of fostering in Wales over the next decade. Other significant developments in Welsh fostering include the Confidence in Care project, which is delivering a UK programme of training, 'Fostering Changes', including to all 22 Welsh Local Authorities, the evaluation of which (due to be delivered by Cardiff University in 2020) may produce further substantial impact on the sector.

5. A 'well-being' centred approach and outcomes-focused practice

Wales has seen a notable shift towards 'well-being' policy discourse that focuses on the agency and relationships of individuals in a strengths-based model that embraces the role of communities and rights in promoting positive outcomes. This shift is closely tied to (and is sometimes used interchangeably with) 'outcomes focused care'. The National Outcomes Framework (NOF), promised in Sustainable Social Services (Welsh Government, 2011a) was delivered alongside the SSWB Act, and applies shared standards of wellbeing to both adults and children in need of care and support. The 14 outcomes listed broadly cohere with the available literature on well-being and quality of life, including securing rights and entitlements, protection from abuse and neglect, education, and social and economic well-being. The fact that the NOF does not generally delineate between the well-being needs of adults and children is potentially problematic: children in care have often experienced severe trauma and loss in the critical early years of life, and will have difficulties achieving well-being that are quite distinct from those of many adults receiving care and support. The criteria for them to achieve a good standard of well-being may, in many cases, be more complex and extensive than those supplied within the NOF, making its use for child and family services somewhat limited. The Welsh Assembly Public Accounts Committee Report for Care-experienced Children and Young People has noted the need to form a new set of well-being indicators specifically focused on the things that matter to young people, highlighting the Bright Spots survey and supporting work (Selwyn & Briheim-Crookall, 2017) as a guide to what factors should be included, such as placement and social worker changes (National Assembly for Wales, 2018).

6. Broad child and family population measures

Wales has implemented a wider range of broad population measures to counter socio-economic disadvantage and curtail the development of complex needs within vulnerable families. This forms part of an overall preventative strategy to reduce the number of children in need and in care. Initiatives include free childcare, and breakfast clubs.

- **Free breakfast clubs**: Wales has been providing free breakfasts in local authority primary schools since 2004 (Welsh Government, 2015), having enthusiastically implemented a nationwide programme as a method of reducing child inequality and supporting vulnerable children. Breakfast clubs are intended to benefit disadvantaged children by providing no- or low-cost healthy meals, childcare, and socialisation, and analysis of the Welsh programme has evidenced positive outcomes (Murphy *et al.*, 2011; Moore *et al.*, 2014). According to a 2014 audit of UK breakfast club provision, Wales have the highest breakfast club availability in the UK, with 96 per cent of primary and secondary schools covered, and 86 per cent offering completely free meals (compared to an average of 45% across the UK). In addition, 75 per cent of school clubs are Welsh Government funded; this is significantly higher than all other UK countries, with just 2 per cent of English clubs being government funded (Kellogg's, 2014).

- **Free childcare**: Welsh Government currently offers 30 hours of free childcare per week across 48 weeks per year for 3- and 4-year-old children of working parents. This was expanded from an existing offer of 10 hours in 2017, and supports parents to seek work who may otherwise have needed to stay at home. The offer extends the universal preschool education offer within state-funded facilities that was already in place.

7. Curtailed marketization in favour of partnership working

While English social care has continued to escalate the privatisation of social care instigated in the 1980s by Thatcher's Conservative government, and expanded in the 1990s under the Blair Labour government, the other nations of the UK, including Wales, have resisted this within their devolved policy remit (Jones, 2015a). In the 2010s, England has aggressively pursued the privatisation of children's social care, embracing controversial providers such as G4S and Serco to deliver services on behalf of local authorities (Jones, 2015b). Instead, Wales has placed an emphasis on partnership working between adult and child social care and alongside health, police, education, and third sector services, which particularly thrive in the delivery of specialised services such as Child Sexual Exploitation (for example, Barnardo's and the NSPCC) and fostering support (The Fostering Network). This is sometimes labelled, jargonistically, as a 'whole-systems approach'. Private organisations delivering services for profit are visible in Wales, notably in the children's residential home sector and fostering, however their role across child and family services is considerably limited compared to in England. Partnership working is highlighted as a key principle of the SSWB Act and the '4Cs' Children's Commissioning Consortium Cymru partnership is one pertinent example of how this approach emerges in practice.

By drawing together a number of local authority commissioners in one body and running shared tendering services, the intention of 4Cs is to reduce costs of commissioning private care for children, better meet children's needs by providing an overview of all available care contexts and resources before commissioning a placement setting, and raise the quality of independent provision through a competitive but restricted marketplace. In this latter sense, 4Cs attempts to gain the 'best of both worlds' in relation to the balance of private and public sector provision: public services impose direction and funding on a case-by-case basis, while benefitting from the diversity and flexibility of independent providers. The outcomes of 4Cs have been reported favourably by stakeholders, particularly in relation to cost savings and its collaboration on frameworks in Wales for fostering and residential children's placement services to guide and regulate independent providers (Smale, 2016).

Conclusions

As the number of children in care continues its bumpy rise, child poverty continues to escalate, and the situation is exacerbated by the unfolding consequences of the 2020 COVID-19 pandemic, the degree to which Welsh policy can counter the substantial risks to the well-being of vulnerable children and families is uncertain. We have some indicators as to how the next decade of child and family policy may be shaped: the findings of the Care Crisis Review across England and Wales (Thomas, 2018), and those of the Child Welfare Inequalities project (Bywaters *et al.*, 2020) are likely to impact Welsh policymaking in the coming years. Meanwhile, despite their controversial and contested status (Children's Commissioner for Wales, 2018), the discourse of Adverse Childhood Experiences has been established throughout the health and social care sectors as a basis for understanding and acting on trauma (Bellis *et al.*, 2015). The ACE framework can now be identified as a basis for Welsh policy and practice in relation to child and family services (see, for example, Welsh Government, 2017) and its narrative dominance in the sector may continue to rise in the wake of the COVID-19 pandemic as policymakers rush to implement effective strategies to combat the trauma associated with the phenomenon. Above all else, the potentially huge increase in the number of children and families suffering with moderate to severe economic and mental health problems brought by the economic consequences of the pandemic will frame the unfolding of the next decade, and Welsh Government are likely to find their child poverty targets further adrift than ever before.

If optimism is to be found, it is in the strong rights-based and participatory approach that Welsh Government have already established in legislation that will ensure the voices and interests of vulnerable children and families cannot be side-lined in the country's response to these convergent crises. There is still substantial work needed to support the full implementation and development of well-being-focused policy; for example, on the lack of national collation of subjective wellbeing outcomes from children and families in local authority care[8]. Instead, the primary measures of 'success' for child and family service delivery is children coming into care and numbers of placement changes. These are both measures which, particularly in the case of the former, are likely to at least

---

[8] There is no current national strategy on data collation here: practitioners independently assess wellbeing outcomes via simple distance travelled ratings but this is not collated centrally, making the impact evaluation of well-being policy difficult.

partially reflect socio-economic factors outside of the control of local authorities and even Welsh Government itself. These do not reflect the focus of the SSWB Act nor the actual quality of services, and this lack of knowledge around how wellbeing is or is not improving for children and families accessing social services stymies our understanding of how well Welsh Government is supporting local authorities to deliver on these policy initiatives. This will need to be corrected to report positively on the outcomes of child and family policy in any review of the next decade.

References

AFA Cymru (Association for Fostering and Adoption) (2018) Practice standards and good practice guide: Reviewing and monitoring of a child or young person's Part 6 Care and Support Plan. Available at: www.afacymru.org.uk/wp-content/uploads/2019/09/IRO-Exec-Summary_E.pdf

Allen, G (2011) Early intervention: the next steps, an independent report to Her Majesty's government by Graham Allen MP. The Cabinet Office. London: The Stationery Office

Arnstein, S (1969) 'A ladder of citizen participation', *Journal of the American Institute of Planners* 35(4): 216-24

Bate, A and Bellis, A (2017) House of Commons Briefing Paper Number CBP 07585: The troubled families programme (England). London: Parliament/House of Commons Library

Bellis, M A, Ashton, ., Hughes, K, Ford, K, Bishop, J and Paranjothy, S (2015) Welsh Adverse Childhood Experiences (ACE) Study: Adverse childhood experiences and their impact on health-harming behaviours in the Welsh adult population. Cardiff: Public Health Wales

Bovaird, T, Van Ryzin, G G, Loeffler, E and Parrado, S (2015) Activating citizens to participate in collective co-production of public services. *Journal of Social Policy* 44(1): 1-23

Bywaters, P, Scourfield, J, Jones, C, Sparks, T, Elliott, M, Hooper, J, ... and Daniel, B (2020) 'Child welfare inequalities in the four nations of the UK' *Journal of Social Work* 20(2): 193-215 doi:10.1177/1468017318793479

Butler, I (2011) Children's Policy in Wales. In Williams, C. (ed.) *Social Policy for Social Welfare Practice in a Devolved Wales, 2nd edition* Birmingham: BASW/Venture Press

Butler, I and Drakeford, M (2013, February) Children's rights as a policy framework in Wales. In The United Nations Convention on the Rights of the Child in Wales (pp9-20) Cardiff: University of Wales Press

Cameron, G, Coady, N and Adams, G R (eds.) (2007) *Moving Towards Positive Systems of Child and Family Welfare: Current Issues and Future Directions* Waterloo: Wilfrid Laurier University Press

Children's Commissioner for Wales (2018) *Policy Position: Adverse Childhood Experiences*. Retrieved from: www.childcomwales.org.uk/wp-content/uploads/2018/10/ACEs-Position-Paper-CCFW-Sally-Holland.pdf

Churchill, H and Sen, R (2016) 'Introduction: Intensive family support services: Politics, policy and practice across contexts' *Social Policy and Society* 15(2): 251–61 https://doi.org/10.1017/S1474746416000026

Diaz, C, Pert, H and Thomas, N P (2019) 'Independent Reviewing Officers' and social workers' perceptions of children's participation in Children in Care Reviews' *Journal of Children's Services* 14(3): 162-73

Featherstone, B, Morris, K and White, S (2014). 'A marriage made in hell: Early intervention meets child protection' *British Journal of Social Work* 44(7): 1735–49 https://doi.org/10.1093/bjsw/bct052

Hoffman, S (2019) 'The UN convention on the rights of the child, decentralisation and legislative integration: a case study from Wales' *The International Journal of Human Rights* 23(3): 374-91

Jones, R (2015a) 'The marketisation and privatisation of children's social work and child protection: integration or fragmentation?' *Journal of Integrated Care*, 23(6): 364-75

Jones, R (2015b) 'The end game: The marketisation and privatisation of children's social work and child protection' *Critical Social Policy* 35(4): 447–69 https://doi.org/10.1177/0261018315599333

Kellogg's (2014) *An Audit of School Breakfast Club Provision in the UK. A report by Kellogg's* Retrieved from www.kelloggs.co.uk/content/dam/newton/images/masterbrand/UK/R5_Kelloggs Breakfast Club Audit

Lyttleton-Smith, J, Elliott, M and Scourfield, J (2018) Supporting the Improvement Agenda in Welsh Children's Social Care. Research Report: Social Care Wales

Mitchell, E (2015) Social Services and Well-being (Wales) Act 2014: resulting differences for children's services in England and Wales. Practice Guidance. *Community Care Inform* [online] www.ccinform.co.uk/practice-guidance/key-practical-differences-english-welsh-childrens-services-result-social-services-well-wales-act-2014/ [accessed: 13.04.2020]

Moore, G, Murphy, S, Chaplin, K, Lyons, R, Atkinson, M and Moore, L (2014). Impacts of the Primary School Free Breakfast Initiative on socio-economic inequalities in breakfast consumption among 9-11-year-old schoolchildren in Wales. *Public Health Nutrition*, 17(6): 1280-89

Munro, E (2011) The Munro Review of Child Protection Final report: A child-centred system. Department for Education. London: The Stationery Office

Murphy S, Moore, G F, Tapper K, Lynch R, Clarke R, Raisanen L, Desousa C and Moore L (2011) 'Free healthy breakfasts in primary schools: A cluster randomised controlled trial of a policy intervention in Wales, UK' *Public Health Nutrition* 14(2): 219-26

National Assembly for Wales (2000) Children and Young People: A Framework for Partnership (Consultation Document). Retrieved from: http://dera.ioe.ac.uk/10502/1/q262a360_english1.pdf%3Flang%3Den

National Assembly for Wales (2011) Rights of Children and Young Persons (Wales) Measure, 2011. Retrieved from: www.legislation.gov.uk/mwa/2011/2/introduction/enacted

National Assembly for Wales (2018) Welsh Assembly Public Accounts Committee for Care-experienced Children and Young People: November 2018. Cardiff: National Assembly for Wales Commission

National Fostering Framework (2017) Communication Bulletin no.2: Phase Three 2017-18. Available at: www.thefosteringnetwork.org.uk/sites/www.fostering.net/files/content/nffcomsbulletin2.pdf

Norgrove, D (2011) Family justice review. Ministry of Justice. London: The Stationery Office

Pestoff, V, Brandsen, T and Verschuere, B (eds.) (2013) *New public governance, the third sector, and co-production* New York: Routledge

Pithouse, A (2011) Devolution and change since the Children Act 1989: New directions in Wales. Journal of Children's Services, 6(3): 172-85 https://doi.org/10.1108/17466661111176033

Public Health Wales and Co-production Wales (2015). Seeing is believing: co-production case studies from Wales, 104

Rees, O (2010) 'Dealing with individual cases: An essential role for national human rights institutions for children?' *The International Journal of Children's Rights*, 18(3): 417-36

Roberts, L, Maxwell, N, Palmer, C and Messenger, R (2018) CASCADE Briefing No.10: Evaluation of Reflect in Gwent. Cardiff: CASCADE Children's Social Care Research and Development Centre

Selwyn, J and Briheim-Crookall, L (2017) *Our Lives, Our Care: looked after chidren's views on their well-being*. Bristol: School for Policy Studies, University of Bristol

Smale, A (2016) *Rhondda Cynon Taf County Borough Council Cabinet: Childrens Commissioning Consortium (4cs)*. Rhondda Cynon Taf County Borough Council [online] www.rctcbc.gov.uk/EN/Council/CouncillorsCommitteesandMeetings/Meetings/Cabinet/2016/02/18/Reports/AgendaItem2ChildrensCommissioningConsortium.pdf [accessed: 15.04.2020]

Social Care Wales (2019) The Regulated Fostering Services (Service Providers and Responsible Individuals) (Wales) Regulations 2019. Available at: www.legislation.gov.uk/wsi/2019/169/made

StatsWales (2019a) https://statswales.gov.wales/Catalogue/Health-and-Social-Care/Social-Services/Childrens-Services/Children-Looked-After/childrenlookedafterat31march-by-localauthority-gender-age

StatsWales (2019b) https://statswales.gov.wales/Catalogue/Health-and-Social-Care/Social-Services/Childrens-Services/Children-in-Need/childreninneed-by-localauthority-agegroup

Thomas, C (2018) The Care Crisis Review: Factors contributing to national increases in numbers of looked after children and applications for care orders. London: Family Rights Group

Thomas, H, Lane, J, Lewis, S and Research, G-A (2018) Qualitative Research with Flying Start Families: Wave 3 report. Retrieved from https://gov.wales/docs/caecd/research/2018/180718-qualitative-research-flying-start-families-wave-3-en.pdf

United Nations (1989) United Nations Convention on the Rights of the Child. Retrieved from: www.unicef.org.uk/wp-content/uploads/2010/05/UNCRC_united_nations_convention_on_the_rights_of_the_child.pdf

Welsh Assembly Government (2004) *Children and Young People: Rights to Action*. Retrieved from www.assembly.wales/Committee%20Documents/HSS(2)-02-04%20Paper%201%20%20Children%20and%20Young%20People%20Rights%20to%20Action-04022004-14558/n000000000000000000000000016990-English.pdf

Welsh Assembly Government (2005) *A Fair Future for Our Children: The Strategy of the Welsh Assembly Government for Tackling Child Poverty*. Retrieved from: www.bristol.ac.uk/poverty/downloads/keyofficialdocuments/Fair%20Future%20Wales.pdf

Welsh Assembly Government (2010) *Children and Families (Wales) Measure, 2010*. Retrieved from: www.legislation.gov.uk/mwa/2010/1/section/19

Welsh Government (2011a) *Sustainable Social Services for Wales: A Framework for Action*. Cardiff: Welsh Government. Retrieved from: https://gov.wales/sites/default/files/publications/2019-06/sustainable-social-services-for-wales-a-framework-for-action.pdf

Welsh Government (2011b) Families First: Programme guidance, (October). Cardiff: Welsh Government. Retrieved from http://wales.gov.uk/docs/dhss/publications/110802ffprogguidance20en.pdf

Welsh Government (2012) Flying start: Strategic Guidance. Cardiff: Welsh Government. Retrieved from: https://gov.wales/flying-start-strategy-guidance-local-authorities

Welsh Government (2014a) *The Social Services & Well-being (Wales) Act 2014*. Cardiff: Welsh Government. Retrieved from: https://gov.wales/sites/default/files/publications/2019-05/social-services-and-well-being-wales-act-2014-the-essentials.pdf

Welsh Government (2014b) *Evaluation of the Integrated Family Support Service – Final Year 3 Report*. Cardiff: Welsh Government

Welsh Government (2015) *Free Breakfast in Primary Schools* [online]. Cardiff: Welsh Government. Available at: https://gov.wales/sites/default/files/publications/2018-03/free-breakfast-in-primary-schools.pdf

Welsh Government (2016) *Children and Young People's Participation in Wales ... Good Practice 2016*. Cardiff: Welsh Government. Available at: https://gov.wales/sites/default/files/publications/2019-06/good-practice-guide.pdf

Welsh Government (2017) *Families First: Programme Guidance*. Cardiff: Welsh Government. Retrieved from http://wales.gov.uk/docs/dhss/publications/110802ffprogguidance201en.pdf

Welsh Government (2019a) *Statistics and Research: Flying Start: Term 1 (April to August 2019)* [online]. Cardiff: Welsh Government. Available at: https://gov.wales/flying-start-term-1-april-august-2019

Welsh Government (2019b) *Improving Outcomes for Children Programme: Ministerial Advisory Group Annual Report 2019*. Cardiff: Welsh Government. Available at: https://gov.wales/sites/default/files/publications/2019-11/improving-outcomes-for-children-annual-report-2019_0.pdf

White, G and McCrindle, L (2010) *Interim Evaluation of Flying Start*. SQW Consulting Cardiff: Welsh Assembly Government Social Research

Williams J (2012) 'General legislative measures of implementation: individual claims, 'public officer's law' and a case study on the UNCRC in Wales' *The International Journal of Children's Rights* 20(2): 224-40

Williams, J (Ed.) (2013) *The United Nations convention on the rights of the child in Wales*. Cardiff: University of Wales Press

Young Wales (2018) *Children and Young People's National Participation Standards*. Available at: https://gov.wales/children-and-young-peoples-national-participation-standards

Chapter 12

Criminal Justice in Wales

Iolo Madoc-Jones and Karen Washington-Dyer

Introduction

In 2019 a Commission on Justice, which had been set up by the Welsh Government, recommended that justice matters should be devolved to and determined in Wales so that it aligned with the distinct and developing social policy emerging from Wales and the growing body of Welsh law. With this in mind, this chapter explores some features of Welsh devolution and how the Criminal Justice System is currently organised and delivered in Wales. The chapter then reviews the historical and evolving process of criminal justice devolution and whether the Criminal Justice System of England and Wales serves the democratic priorities and particular needs of the people of Wales. Using probation reforms and homelessness amongst prison leavers as exemplar issues, the 'jagged edge' (Wales Governance Centre, 2019) between criminal justice and social policy and practice in Wales is illustrated and the potential for further dragonisation (Edwards and Hughes, 2009) of criminal justice policy making and practice is explored. Several European countries e.g. Bulgaria, Romania, are looking to England and Wales for models of criminal justice practice (Canton, 2010). Moreover, devolution has become a key 'global trend' over recent decades (MacKinnon, 2015). The analysis presented in this chapter, therefore, will provide insight not only into criminal justice in Wales but factors that may influence how Criminal Justice Systems evolve and develop in other jurisdictions in Europe and beyond

Devolution

The constituent parts of the UK have always exhibited difference in policy and its implementation (Wallace, 2019). However, a peculiar feature of the UK at present is that while England continues to be governed by the UK Westminster Government, from 1999 onwards, devolution to various extents has enabled Welsh, Scottish and Northern Irish legislatures to pursue their own health, social care and housing priorities (Cairney, 2009). Whilst responsibility for overall economic policy is not devolved, priorities on devolved areas of responsibilities can be realised as legislatures spend block grants allocated to them through a mechanism known as the Barnett formula which, adjusted for population size and to some extent the need for public services, reflects spending levels in England (or England and Wales or Great Britain). The Welsh Assembly was initially the weakest of the three devolved legislatures, having power only to amend legislation from Westminster. However, The Wales Act 2017 moved Wales to a constitutional footing with Scotland so that the Assembly was assumed to have legislative competence unless an area of law was formally reserved to the UK Government.

The Criminal Justice System is commonly understood to comprise the police, prosecution, courts, and prison and probation services. Power over these agencies is devolved to the Governments of Scotland and Northern Ireland (Wallace, 2019). But this is not the case in Wales. Legislative responsibility for the constituent agencies of the Criminal Justice System is reserved to Westminster and policy is implemented under the oversight of the Attorney General (Crown Prosecution Service), Home Office (Police), Home Office and Her Majesty's Courts and Tribunal Service (Courts) and Ministry of Justice (via Her Majesty's Prison and Probation Service). This reflects a state of affairs in being since the legal system in Wales was the subject of unification with the system in England by The Statute of Rhuddlan in 1284 (Ross, 2005).

Over the last few years, however, and in a way that arguably reflects a growing maturity and confidence within political circles in Wales, the possibility for greater devolution of criminal justice to Wales has been explored. This has often been in tandem with calls for Wales to have its own legal system and judiciary so that the organisation of government in Wales more closely resembles the 'Westminster model' wherein the legislature, the executive and an independent judiciary provide a system for balancing the powers held by the state with the rights of the individual (Wales Governance Centre, 2019). Space precludes consideration in this chapter of the complex constitutional arguments for a separate Welsh legal jurisdiction and judiciary. But it is worth noting that in its absence, questions arise about democratic accountability in Wales.

The Commission on Devolution in Wales (Silk Commission), established by the UK Government, made recommendations in 2014 for devolving police and youth justice to Wales. Moreover it suggested that the possibility of devolving responsibility over prison and probation services should be explored. The Commission on Justice in Wales, then made further recommendations in 2019 for responsibility over some legal matters and the Criminal Justice System to be devolved to Wales. The rationale for such devolution rest primarily on the argument that the Criminal Justice System of England and Wales does not reflect the political priorities of Wales; does not meet the particular needs of the people of Wales; and moreover Welsh nationhood and civic identity is intimately linked to the Welsh executive exercising power over a high prestige area such as criminal justice.

The political priorities of Wales

Key classifications have emerged to compare different approaches to welfare provision. Esping-Andersen (1990) famously identified welfare regime types and this framework was subsequently developed to account for preferred models of criminal justice practice (Cavadino and Dignan, 2013). This was on the basis that the wider political, economic and welfare regime in which a Criminal Justice System sits produces a distinctive approach to understanding and then dealing with crime. Garland (2012) argues that whilst the criminal justice system may at times seem an independent system, it is part of a wider network of governance (Garland, 2012). In a similar vein Beckett and Western (2001:44) claim, "penal and social welfare institutions comprise a single policy regime aimed at the problems associated with deviance and marginality".

Cavadino and Dignan (2013) identify four main welfare and criminal justice regimes: Neo-liberal (USA, Australia, England), Social democratic (Sweden, Finland, Wales), conservative corporatist (Germany, France, Italy) and oriental corporatism (Japan). Here, for reasons that will become clear, the focus is on the first two types of welfare and criminal justice regimes. Whilst the likelihood that any country fits neatly into one welfare regime is low, systems blur into one another, and there is the potential that any sort of regime analysis can present societies in a static way (Barker, 2012), reference to welfare and justice regimes provide a foundation for understanding variations between countries, and in the case of Wales, tensions within one.

Consonant with a focus on the individual, neo-liberalism has emerged as the dominant political philosophy in the West and has been embraced as an orientating philosophy by successive governments in Westminster. Associated with neo-liberalism is the outsourcing of public service delivery and a reliance on competition to improve standards and drive down costs. In turn social order and cohesion is promoted not as a by-product of the sense of common citizenship associated with the welfare state, but through the exclusive operation of criminal justice and what Feeley and Simon (1994) refer to as an actuarial approach to justice. The actuarial approach assesses and categorises the risk of causing harm and deploys technologies of information-gathering and surveillance to monitor, control and at times exclude problem groups (Cowan *et al.*, 2001; Kemshall and Maguire, 2001). Social order and cohesion are further promoted through what Foucault (1991) termed 'governmentality'; the central feature of which is the state seeking to 'govern at a distance', or through proxies rather than directly (Garland, 2001). Also associated with neo-liberalism is that values and sentiments underpinning responsible self-government and morally desired behaviours are channelled into the public realm (Flint and Nixon, 2006). In this process, reliance on the state and criminality are constructed as the products of agency, immorality and personal failure rather than being attributable to structural causes (Dwyer *et al.*, 2014).

Conversely it has been widely argued that a more inclusive social democratic philosophy underscores the political and social landscape of Wales (Trumm, 2018). According to Cavadino and Dignan (2013) compared to neo-liberal regimes, social democratic regimes are more concerned with social cohesion and with equality of outcome than equality of opportunity. They are more committed to governing than governmentality and more sympathetic to the welfare state as opposed to the carceral state. To date there have been five elected assemblies in Wales (1999-2003; 2003-2007; 2007-2011; 2011-2016; 2016-) with Welsh Labour, albeit often in coalition, in power and thereby the Governing executive in each of them. Labour have also secured the most votes at every general election, including the most recent one in 2019, since 1922.

Consonant with social democratic sympathies, successive Welsh governments have largely rejected the neo-liberal concern with consumer choice and market forces in favour of citizen protection, public sector professionalism and universalism in service delivery. According to McKee *et al.* (2017:68) compared to Westminster Governments, Welsh Governments have traditionally held "vastly different interpretations of the causes and solutions to poverty and inequality, as well as the appropriate role and size of the state". During the term of the first Assembly, Labour also held power in Westminster but Rhodri Morgan, the Welsh First Minister, referred to "clear red water" between Welsh Labour and Westminster 'New' Labour (Moon, 2013). This was based on his belief that a more progressive and social democratic approach characterised Welsh Labour preferences. Since 2010 Conservative Governments have been in power in Westminster and policy divergence based on established fault lines between the right and left in UK politics have been evident. But ever since devolution was instigated it is argued successive Welsh Governments have pursued a more radical programme of social policy to address inequality than has been pursued in England including the abolition of prescription charges; opt-out system for organ donation; free public transport for the over sixties; cheaper tuition fees; no free schools and academies; dissenting from privatising parts of the NHS; pioneering preventative approaches to addressing health inequalities and homelessness (Brewster and Jones, 2019).

Whilst Fitzpatrick and Stephens (2014) and Barker (2012) have noted that social democratic welfare regimes are not necessarily less punitive in their response to people who offend, neo-liberal regime responses to crime are generally informed by individualistic explanations of the phenomenon whilst social democratic regimes draw inspiration from more structuralist accounts of crime. In turn neo-liberal regimes favour punitive approaches to crime whilst social democratic regimes favour penal welfarism and rehabilitation (Pratt, 2008). Galo and Kim (2016) find that suppressed punitiveness and lower incarceration rates are normally associated with political regimes associated with higher levels of welfare spending and greater economic equality.

In the context that no powers are devolved over criminal justice matters there are clearly limits on the extent to which Welsh Government is able to directly realise its own priorities in this area or adopt a whole system approach to tackling crime. For example, its ability to bare down on some criminogenic factors, like economic insecurity is limited. Whist the link between poverty and crime is not entirely clear, Tiratelli *et al.* (2020) have reported that as Universal Credit was rolled out as a new and less generous benefit system across the UK, so crime rates in those areas increased. Albeit rarely exercised, legislative responsibility over welfare payments is devolved to Northern Ireland. Subsequent to The Scotland Act 2016 a Social Security Agency for Scotland is being developed. Power over welfare benefit have never been devolved to Wales however. Rather responsibility for policy rests with the Department of Works and Pensions of the UK Government who, over the last ten years, have relentlessly pursued a policy of 'austerity' which has disproportionally impacted on some of the most vulnerable members of society.

However, as Connell *et al.* (2017) note, notwithstanding legal, institutional and financial constraints, Welsh Government has still been able to use its powers to realise distinctive social and criminal justice priorities in Wales. This is because a wide range of actors are involved in a policy interpretation process in devolved settings, including inter alia elected officials, political parties, bureaucrats/civil servants and pressure groups (Dolowitz and Marsh, 1996). The policy transfer literature identifies that 'cut and paste' transfers in which policy and practices are completely transferred from one setting to another are rare. Conversely, hybrid transfers, involving partial or piecemeal transfer of policy are much more common (Marsh and Sharman, 2009). Policies can mutate and be reconstituted in the process of moving (Peck, 2011) especially where there are considerable differences in the contexts involved (Park *et al.*, 2014).

One of the reasons Welsh Government has been able to realise its own criminal justice objectives in Wales is that delivery of criminal justice related outcomes often depends on complimentary or supportive activity in devolved areas of policy. Welsh Government may not be responsible for policing, prisons or probation policy, but it has responsibility for health, education, housing and substance use services delivered to prisoners and those under supervision in the community. So, for example, it has realised distinctive priorities for those who are drug dependant and in custody. Whilst opiate substitution treatment for prisoners who are dependent on illicit substances is available in English prisons, in Wales psychosocial and clinical support for the purposes of managing the symptoms of withdrawal is offered (HMIP, 2015). Moreover between 2001 and 2015 all prison leavers were automatically afforded priority need status for housing in Wales and became eligible for more assertive efforts to prevent homelessness on release from custody (Madoc-Jones *et al.*, 2018).

Welsh Government has exercised its discretion and used resources allocated to it to fund services that directly impact on the crime and criminal justice related outcomes. In 2017 and building on the accommodation provisions contained in The Housing (Wales) Act 2014 and the Social Services and Well-being (Wales) Act 2014, Welsh Government launched a range of policy and funding initiatives specifically aimed at ending youth homelessness especially amongst young people leaving custody. The Home Office part fund Policing in Wales through a grant which is additional to the Barnett settlement. When the police grant was cut by 19 per cent after 2010 to reflect austerity policies, Welsh Government allocated additional funding and allowed police precept/council tax rises as needed so that unlike in England, police numbers were protected (Commission on Justice in Wales, 2019). Welsh Government has also used its resources to support the appointment of additional Police Community Support Officers in each of the four Wales Police Service Areas (Welsh Government, 2019).

Criminal justice as an outcome also involves considerations over which Welsh Government does wield influence. A Minister for Social Justice and Local Government exists in Welsh Government who presides over a Community Safety Unit that promotes and funds Community Safety Partnerships. Despite no longer being in receipt of specific funding for such partnerships, Welsh Government has remained committed to funding such services, providing almost £50million in 2015-16 (Chambers, 2019). In relation to victims of crime, the Violence against Women, Domestic Abuse and Sexual Violence

(Wales) Act came into force in 2015. Along with the Social Services and Wellbeing Act 2014, it placed safeguarding 'adults at risk', including victims of crime, on a firmer statutory footing than in England requiring local authorities to work with criminal justice partners to prevent, protect and support victims.

By requiring agencies to work together, Welsh Government has also been able to bring its influence to bear on criminal justice practice in Wales. The Future Generations Act Wales, for example, required the establishment of Public Services Boards (PSBs) in each Local Authority. Chief Constables and representatives from other criminal justice agencies are invitees to these boards, arguably leading to some pressure for joint working to meet more locally determined, and Welsh Government influenced, priorities. In Wales Local Criminal Justice Boards, chaired by the local Police and Crime Commissioner, also report to an All Wales Criminal Justice Board. This further links police and the other criminal justice agencies to Welsh Government and it priorities.

The recent focus in policy circles on identifying and addressing the harms caused by 'adverse childhood experiences' are symptomatic of a greater interest in Wales than in England on targeting resources at some of the structural 'causes of crime' rather than just crime itself. The best documented example of policy 'dragonisation', however, concerns youth justice which, while a non-devolved policy domain, has been implemented less punitively in Wales than in England (Drakeford, 2010; Trumm, 2018). The term 'children first' is often used in Wales to reference 'an attitude of mind', where 'having offended' is understood as not the main element of a child's life (Drakeford, 2010:141). In Wales, the focus in terms of addressing youth crime has been on developing communities and systems on which a child depends (i.e. building social capital), rather than addressing the personal 'deficits' that led a young person to offend. This, it has been argued, is very different to the dominant approach taken in England where young offenders are responsibilised for their offending (Edwards and Hughes, 2009).

Particular criminal justice needs of Wales

As noted earlier, Welsh Government indirectly makes a financial contribution to criminal justice outcomes in Wales without having a say on policy. Moreover the terms of the devolution settlement in Wales is such that consent is required from Westminster when introducing policies in devolved areas that may impact on the justice system. However, the justification for devolving criminal justice to Wales is not only based on the potential for political misalignment between the criminal justice and social welfare arms of Welsh Government. It is also based on the argument that the existing system does not address the particular criminal justice needs of Wales.

A mix of non-devolved and devolved authorities, for example, are implicated in creating and implementing criminal justice policies and practice in Wales. As a result a complex multi-layered criminal justice system has been created which is difficult to penetrate and wherein responsibility for outcomes is fragmented and dispersed (Wales Governance Centre, 2019). The division of powers between England and Wales also makes cross border co-operation less easy. For instance, where an individual from England is received into custody, their NHS general practitioner record is transferred with them, but for prisoners from Wales it is more difficult for this to happen due to the absence of effective mechanisms to transfer records from NHS Wales to criminal justice partners in England. In 2019 the Commission on Justice noted there was good joint working on the ground in Wales to promote collaborative working. But this was, at times, in the absence of a coherent national strategy.

It is also argued that the needs of Welsh people are not met by a criminal justice system designed primarily to meet the geographic, demographic and cultural needs of people in England. The concentration of high levels of social need in some areas of Wales; the sparse population; the greater concentration of older people; the presence of fewer people in paid work and higher levels of chronic ill-health are perceived as lending themselves less well to some arrangements that may make sense in England. For example, court closures have rendered access to justice problematic for people in some rural Welsh communities. A policy focus on the threat of terrorism or gang crime may equally fail to address criminal justice priorities in many areas of Wales.

It is argued that Welsh prisoners and women prisoners are especially poorly served by existing criminal justice arrangements. In 2018 there were 4,704 Welsh people (based on home address) in custody, 37 per cent of whom were held in English jails (Jones, 2018). In many cases, therefore, Welsh prisoners are incarcerated at a distance from their home areas, compromising efforts at resettlement and keeping links with family and home communities. The situation in relation to women prisoners is especially acute, arising from the absence of a female prison in Wales and use being made of custody in cases where little risk of serious harm to others exists. A number of commentators have suggested new prison builds in Wales are not undertaken to meet the needs of Welsh people, but to house prisoners from England (Madoc-Jones *et al.*, 2016). The policy of locating prisoners from England in Wales results in health, education and substance misuse costs potentially falling on the Welsh Government.

Finally in Wales the ability to use the Welsh language is linked to issues of national identity and linguistic proficiency. A number of reports have drawn attention to the poor provision made for those who would prefer to use the Welsh language in the Criminal Justice System (Madoc-Jones and Parry, 2013; Welsh Language Commissioner, 2018; House of Commons, 2019) Feelings of being discriminated against arise particularly strongly where prisoners find themselves imprisoned in England where Welsh language resources are typically absent (Madoc-Jones, 2007).

Criminal justice and Welsh nationhood

A final argument for devolving responsibility for criminal justice matters is that Welsh nationhood and civic identity may be intimately linked to the Welsh executive exercising power over high prestige areas such as the legal and criminal justice systems. According to Day and Jones (2006), in response to globalisation, the significance of the nation-state has waned over recent decades and local ethnic identities have become re-activated.

In the UK this has led to resurgence in Welsh, Scottish, Irish, Cornish and English nationalism particularly among the young. According to Coupland *et al.* (2003) since the turn of the century a new more confident Welsh ethnic identity has begun to express itself, and being Welsh has come to be considered more fashionable by the young. More recently Bradbury and Andrews (2010:232) have argued that post devolution in Wales there has been a "trend of expanding Welshness and declining Britishness". In this context, devolution of criminal justice policy may be seen as central in the process of creating Wales. According to Billig (1995), the nation is recreated through the performance of a series of small scale acts. In *Banal Nationalism* (1995) he outlined his view that national identity is achieved through the completion of banal, routine, day to day activity such as the use of coins, stamps, flags, or the use of one language rather than another. Billig (1995) argued that as banal acts promote one conceptualisation of national identity, they oppress others. Thus Heller (2007) referred to the banal acts that suppress national identity as also micro-processes of symbolic domination. For Heller (2007) grand domination is supported by everyday micro actions of individuals and organisations, for example as when individuals engage with a Criminal Justice System for England and Wales as opposed to a distinctly Welsh system or are denied opportunities to use their language.

The jagged edge

Increasingly reference has been made to a 'jagged edge' being created in Wales as neo-liberal inspired criminal justice policies developed at Westminster collide with social democratic inspired social policy developed in Wales (Drakeford, 2010; Wales Governance Centre, 2019). In this section two examples of this 'jagged edge' are explored – the first focusing on probation reforms and practice, the second on policies and practices relating to the needs of prison leavers who face homelessness.

In 2015, the Westminster Government launched 'Transforming Rehabilitation', a programme to reform the management of offenders in England and Wales. This led to work that had previously been undertaken by the Probation Service with medium and lower risk offenders being outsourced to private 'community rehabilitation companies' (CRCs). CRCs were also contracted to undertake resettlement work at prisons. It is widely accepted that this was an ideologically driven revolution imposed by the then Conservative government despite widespread opposition and in the absence of any clear evidence it would improve the overall performance of the probation service. The ideology reflected a neo-liberal belief that competition for contracts to deliver services would lead to more effective, efficient and innovative services being delivered (Deering and Feilzer, 2019). Whilst the policy proved a disaster and is in the process of being reversed, it is hard to imagine that a Welsh Government responsible for criminal justice matters and focussed in terms of social policy on inclusion, rights, entitlements and social justice, would have approached reforms in this manner.

Neo-liberal sympathies do not simply influence how practice is structured. As Deering and Feilzer (2019) note, it influences the nature of the relationship between the probation officer and the supervisee and the values underpinning this relationship. As Peck (2013) argues, because neoliberalism represents a strategy of hollowing out of the state, it is associated with an expectancy of self-governance. It therefore supports criminal justice practices which are primarily focussed on the individual offender's moral failings. Conversely the kind of practice that is more consonant with social democratic tendencies would give greater consideration to the social circumstances that creates capacity or options to act in their own best interests. Criminal justice practice under such a banner would entail closer engagement with local communities, making a contribution to preventative social programmes with local people (including victims), developing the social networks of individuals involved in offending, and contributing to addressing factors associated with crime such as poverty, unstable accommodation/housing and discrimination (Vanstone, 2002).

CRCs were given responsibility for prisoner resettlement at the same time as the Welsh Government comprehensively reviewed its approach to supporting people at risk of, or experiencing, homelessness in Wales. From April 2015 onwards, Part 2 of The Housing (Wales) Act imposed new duties on local authorities to help prevent homelessness and help homeless people find accommodation. To this end the 'National Pathway for Homelessness Services to Children, Young People and Adults in the Secure Estate' was developed in Wales. The National Pathway sought to consolidate processes for providing services to prisoners with housing related needs and put in place systems for managing communication and relations between the agencies providing relevant services. Subsequent research into the operation of the pathway, however, suggests key elements were not implemented with any enthusiasm by the CRCs and this was partly because they were held accountable for different outcomes by the Westminster Government (Madoc-Jones *et al.*, 2018; Madoc-Jones *et al.*, 2020). As preventative policies were introduced to address homelessness in Wales, welfare policies were also being enacted in Westminster which inevitably made housing prison leavers who were homeless more difficult.

For example, linked to the Welfare Reform and Work Act 2012 the so called 'Bedroom Tax' was implemented so that welfare claimants had their housing benefit reduced by 14 per cent if they had one spare room and 25 per cent if they had two or more. As a result of both these developments the supply of one/two bedroomed rental properties, traditionally occupied by prison leavers, significantly atrophied. Further disincentivising landlords from offering accommodation to prison leavers, Single Accommodation Rates (SAR), introduced in 1996, were extended to include all persons under the age of 35 (Cooper, 2016). This limited housing welfare payments to a person under the age of 35, which prison leavers tend to be, to the average for a single person in shared accommodation in any particular local authority area. This reduced even further the number of properties prison leavers could afford to occupy. The Welsh Government, having no powers in these areas, had to accept these changes even though they clearly served to undermine its priorities for addressing homelessness and the needs of prison leavers in particular.

Conclusions

This chapter has explored the way criminal justice is organised and delivered in Wales. The arguments for greater devolution of the Criminal Justice System to Wales have been rehearsed and it has been noted that they are founded on the view that the Criminal Justice System of England and Wales does not reflect the political priorities of Wales; does not meets the particular needs of the people of Wales; and moreover Welsh nationhood and civic identity is intimately linked to the Welsh executive exercising power over a high prestige area such as criminal justice.

Criminal Justice practices take place within a wider ideological context. Carlen (2013: 1) argues that dominant neo-liberal political and populist ideologies on crime emanating from Westminster currently structure penal policy and practice around a punitive 'risk crazed governance' wherein the offending 'other' is extracted from their social context, largely perceived as the author of their own circumstances and responsible for changing themselves. Such a regime, it is argued, is at odds with the more social democratic tendencies and sympathies held in Wales and expressed, over the years, at the ballot boxes.

However, whether the population of Wales, as opposed to just some of its politicians, actively embrace social democratic sensitivities and yearn for a Criminal Justice System more sympathetic to penal welfarism is debatable. Some public opinion data suggests that social democratic sensitivities do resonate with the Welsh public (Scully and Jones, 2015). Conversely Trumm (2018) suggests that the decision of Welsh voters to reject membership of the European Union by 52.5 per cent to 47.5 per cent in 2016, is evidence that the electorate has begun to show a stronger desire for right of centre politics. The gains made by parties to the right of the political spectrum in Wales at the 2019 general election also suggests that the Welsh public may increasingly be less committed to social democratic principles than in the past and potentially, therefore, more aligned with punitive approaches to justice than has been suggested.

In 2009 Dingwall suggested that a less punitive approach to justice matters was being adopted in Wales than in England. He suggested that Criminal Statistics for England and Wales from 1996 to 2006 showed that compared to England, a lower proportion of people received an immediate custodial sentence in Wales. Moreover those that were sentenced to custody in England received longer terms of imprisonment. However, until very recently data on the operation of the Criminal Justice System in Wales has been hard to come by. This is because such data has been published on an all-England and Wales basis and disaggregation of the data has been problematic. More recently researchers at the Wales Governance Centre have made a significant contribution to this area, using Freedom of Information requests to reveal that while the criminological rhetoric in Wales might at times be different, claims for the existence of a more tolerant, fair and inclusive criminological approach should be treated with caution. Recent data suggests, for example, that courts in Wales are more punitive than anywhere else in Western Europe. In 2018 there were 150 Welsh prisoners per 100,000 people compared to a rate of 137 English prisoners per 100,000 of the population (Jones, 2019). This is despite the fact that police recorded crime in Wales was lower than England that year.

The Welsh Government's commitment to less punitive criminal justice policies may also be questioned. Over recent years it has voiced political support for a number of prison builds in Wales. Wales is currently home to the largest prison in the UK with proposals for building additional large prisons in Wales being developed.

Comparisons can be drawn between the criminal justice climate in Wales and in Scotland where a stronger commitment to policies generally associated with 'old' Labour and to reducing social inequality is also said to prevail (Mooney *et al.*, 2015). Scotland retained its own legal and justice system after the Act of Union in 1707 and subsequent to devolution. Nonetheless, Fitzpatrick and Stephens (2014) note there is evidence of punitive convergence between Scotland, and England & Wales because in both jurisdictions the prison population is high and on a similar upward trajectory. According to Mooney *et al.* (2015) a number of party political considerations arise in Scotland, that would also arise in Wales were criminal justice to be devolved, which would make pursuing a less punitive approach to crime and punishment politically dangerous. Since the 1990s the climate of popular punitiveness that has emanated from Westminster has rendered talk of rehabilitation synonymous with being 'soft on crime'. Moreover as Mooney *et al.* (2015) argues a reduced role for the Criminal Justice System in managing social problems would inevitably be associated with a greater role for the welfare state in managing these problems. Funding this would be problematic in the context that the economic priorities imposed from Westminster are around economic austerity and scaling back the welfare state. King and Maruna (2009) have explored the origins of punitiveness. They found it to be unrelated to the real threats of crime and to reflect non-crime related socio-economic anxieties and concerns. Bauman (2000) suggests that such anxieties and concerns are inevitable by-products of neo-liberal political economies. This is because of the flexibility to hire and fire employees required in a neo-liberal labour market. Accordingly a less punitive Criminal Justice System might depend on more than just devolving responsibilities for criminal justice matters. It may depend on a commitment to different socio-economic priorities and the opportunity to realise them.

Independence may be on the horizon for Scotland. In Wales, notwithstanding a greater number of people declaring themselves indy-curious, it is much further in the distance. It seems likely, however, that further devolution of the criminal justice system will follow. This is not least of all because of the practical challenges associated with delivering justice across two nations and legislatures; because such devolution already exists in Scotland and Northern Ireland and, more recently, there is increasing precedent set for such devolution as powers over policing have been devolved to PCCs and then extended to the Mayors of London and Manchester.

Finally it is worth noting that as this chapter goes to press, the UK is starting to adjust to a 'new normal' way of life following on from Covid-19. During the pandemic, and as different lockdown rules were imposed, enforced and then relaxed, it is arguably the case that many people in Wales were confronted with the fact that Wales and England have separate legislatures, that could impose and enforce different expectations, in a way that had not been the case in the past. The approach adopted by Welsh

Government was more stringent towards the lockdown and cautious towards relaxation than in England. Early indications are that this was popular amongst the electorate in Wales. Such positive experiences of Wales 'doing it differently' would be associated with greater support for further devolution of legal and criminal justice related powers to Wales in the future.

References

Barker, V (2012) 'Nordic exceptionalism revisited: Explaining the paradox of a Janus-faced penal regime' *Theoretical Criminology* 17(1): 5-25

Bauman, Z (2000) *Liquid Modernity*, Cambridge, Polity

Beckett, K and Western, B (2001) 'Governing social marginality: Welfare, incarceration, and the transformation of state policy' *Punishment and Society* 3(1): 43-59

Billig, M (1995) *Banal Nationalism*, London: Sage

Brewster, D and Jones, R (2019) 'Distinctly divergent or hanging onto English coat-tails? Drug policy in post-devolution Wales' *Criminology & Criminal Justice* 19(3): 364-81

Bradbury, J and Andrews, R (2010) 'State devolution and national identity: Continuity and change in the politics of Welshness and Britishness in Wales' *Parliamentary Quarterly*, 63 (2): 229-49

Cairney, P (2009) 'The role of ideas in policy transfer: the case of UK smoking bans since devolution' *Journal of European Public Policy* 16(3): 471-88

Canton, R (2010) 'Taking probation abroad' *European Probation Journal* 1(1): 66-78

Carlen, P (2013) Imaginary *Penalities.* London: Routledge

Cavadino, M and Dignan, J (2013) 'Political economy and penal systems' in Body-Gendrot, S, Hough, M, Kerzsi,K, Lévy,R and Snacken, S (eds) *The Routledge Handbook of European Criminology*. Abington, MA: Routledge, pp280-94

Chambers, S (2019) Evidence to the Commission on Justice in Wales. Available to view at https://gov.wales/sites/default/files/publications/2019-01/Submission%20to%20the%20Commission%20on%20Justice%20in%20Wales%20from%20Dr%20Sophie%20Chambers.pdf [Last Accessed 12.03.2020]

Commission on Justice in Wales (2019) *Justice in Wales for the People of Wales*. Cardiff: The Commission on Justice in Wales

Connell, A, Martin, S and St Denny, E (2017) 'How can subnational governments deliver their policy objectives in the age of austerity? Reshaping homelessness policy in Wales' *The Political Quarterly* 88(3): 443-51

Cooper, V (2016) 'It's all considered to be unacceptable behaviour Criminal justice practitioners' experience of statutory housing duty for (ex) offenders'. *Probation Journal*, Vol. 63(4): 433-45

Coupland, N, Bishop, H and Garrett, P (2003) 'Home truths: Globalisation and the iconising of Welsh in a Welsh-American newspaper' *Journal of Multilingual and Multicultural Development* 24(3): 153-75

Cowan, D, Pantazis, C and Gilroy, R (2001) 'Social housing as crime control: an examination of the role of housing management in policing sex offenders'. *Social & Legal Studies*, 10(4): 435-57

Day, G and Jones, D (2006) 'Civil society and the institutions of economic development' in Day, G, Dunkerley, D and Thompson, A (eds) *Civil Society in Wales: Politics, Policy and People*, Cardiff: University of Wales Press, pp39-64

Deering, J and Feilzer, M (2019) 'Hollowing out probation? The roots of Transforming Rehabilitation' *Probation Journal* 66(1): 8-24

Dingwall, G (2009) 'Resolution through devolution: Policing, youth justice and imprisonment in Wales', *Crimes and Misdemeanours: Deviance and the Law in Historical Perspective,* 3(1): 5-19

Dolowitz, D and Marsh, D (1996) 'Who learns what from whom: a review of the policy transfer literature', *Political Studies,* 44(2): 343-57

Drakeford, M (2010) 'Devolution and youth justice in Wales', *Criminology & Criminal Justice,* 10(2): 137-54

Dwyer, P, Bowpitt, G, Sundin, E and Weinstein, M (2014) 'Rights, responsibilities and refusals: Homelessness policy and the exclusion of single homeless people with complex needs'. *Critical Social Policy* 35(1): 1-21

Edwards, A and Hughes, G (2009) 'The preventive turn and the promotion of safer communities in England and Wales: Political inventiveness and governmental instabilities', in Crawford, A (ed.) *Crime Prevention in Europe: Comparative Perspectives,* Cullompton: Willan Publishing

Esping-Andersen, G (1990) *The Three Worlds of Welfare Capitalism*, Princeton, NJ: Princeton University Press

Feeley, M and Simon, J (1994) Actuarial justice: The emerging new criminal law. In Nelken, D (ed.) *The Futures of Criminology*, London: Sage Publication, pp173-74

Fitzpatrick, S and Stephens, M (2014) 'Welfare regimes, social values and homelessness: Comparing responses to marginalised groups in six European countries' *Housing Studies,* 29(2): 215-23

Flint, J and Nixon, J (2006) 'Governing neighbours: Anti-social behaviour orders and new forms of regulating conduct in the UK' *Urban Studies,* 43(5-6): 939-55

Foucault, M (1991). 'Governmentality' in Burchell, G, Gordon, C and Miller, P (eds.) *The Foucault Effect: Studies in Governmentality* Chicago, IL: University of Chicago Press, pp87–104

Gallo, C and Kim, M E (2016) Crime Policy and Welfare Policy. *Oxford Handbook Online.* Available to view at www.academia.edu/download/47744768/Gallo_and_Kim-2016-Crime_Policy_and_Welfare_Policy.pdf [Last accessed 12.03.2020]

Garland, D (2001) *The Culture of Control: Crime and Social Order in Contemporary Society.* Chicago: University of Chicago Press

Heller, M S (2007) *Linguistic Minorities and Modernity: A Sociolinguistic Ethnography*, London: Continuum

HMIP (2015) *Changing Patterns of Substance Misuse in Adult Prisons and Service Responses: A Thematic Review.* London: HM Inspectorate of Prisons

House of Commons (2019) *Prison Provision in Wales.* House of Commons: Welsh Affairs committee report

Jones, R (2018) Imprisonment in Wales: A breakdown by Local Authority (June 2018), Cardiff: Cardiff University. Available at: www.cardiff.ac.uk/__data/assets/pdf_file/0010/1286992/Imprisonment-in-Wales-A-Local-Authority-Breakdown-.pdf [Last accessed 12.03.2020]

Jones, R (2019) *Sentencing and Imprisonment in Wales 2018 Fact file.* Cardiff: Wales Governance Centre

Kemshall, H and Maguire, M (2001) 'Public protection, partnership and risk penality: The multi-agency risk management of sexual and violent offenders' *Punishment & Society,* 3(2): 237-64

King, A and Maruna, S (2009) 'Is a conservative just a liberal who has been mugged? Exploring the origins of punitive views' *Punishment & Society,* 11(2): 147-69

Madoc-Jones, I (2007) 'Welsh prisoners in English jails' *The Prison Service Journal,* No 169, pp28-37

Madoc-Jones, I and Parry ,O (2013) 'It's always English in the cop shop: Accounts of minority language use in the Criminal Justice System'. *The Howard Journal of Criminal Justice* 52(1): 91-107

Madoc-Jones, I, Hughes,C, Williams, E and Turley, J (2016) Big Prisons: Does Size Still Matter. *The Prison Service Journal* (lead article) No227: 4-11

Madoc-Jones, I, Hughes, C, Gorden, C, Dubberley, S, Washington-Dyer, K, Ahmed, A, Lockwood, K and Wilding, M (2018) 'Rethinking preventing homelessness amongst prison leavers' *European Journal of Probation* 10(3): 215-31

Madoc-Jones, I, Ahmed,A, Hughes, C, Gorden, C, Dubberley, D, Washington-Dyer, K, Lockwood, K and Wilding, M (2020) Imaginary prison prevention with prison leavers *Journal of Social Policy and Society* 19(1): 145-55

MacKinnon, D (2015) 'Devolution, state restructuring and policy divergence in the UK' *The Geographical Journal* 181(1): 47-56

Marsh, D and Sharman, J C (2009) 'Policy diffusion and policy transfer', *Policy Studies* 30(3): 269-88

McKee, K, Muir, J and Moore, T (2017) 'Housing policy in the UK: The importance of spatial nuance' *Housing Studies* 32(1): 60-72

Moon, DS (2013) 'Rhetoric and policy learning: On Rhodri Morgan's 'clear red water 'and 'made in Wales' health policies' *Public Policy and Administration*, 28(3): 306-23

Mooney, G, Croall, H, Munro, M and Scott, G (2015) 'Scottish criminal justice: Devolution, divergence and distinctiveness' *Criminology & Criminal Justice* 15(2): 205-24

Park, C, Wilding, M and Chung, C (2014) 'The importance of feedback: policy transfer, translation and the role of communication' *Policy Studies* 35(4): 397-412

Peck, J (2011) 'Geographies of policy: from transfer-diffusion to mobility-mutation' *Progress in Human Geography*, 35(6): 773-97

Peck, J (2013) 'Explaining (with) Neoliberalism' *Territory, Politics, Governance* 1(2): 132-57

Pratt, J (2008) 'Scandinavian exceptionalism in an era of penal excess Part I: The nature and roots of Scandinavian exceptionalism' *The British Journal of Criminology* 48(2): 119-37

Ross, D (2005) *Wales: History of a Nation* Lanark, Scotland: Geddes and Grosset

Scully, R and Jones, R W (2015) 'The public legitimacy of the national assembly for Wales' *The Journal of Legislative Studies* 21(4): 515-33

Tiratelli, M, Bradford, B and Yesberg, J (2020) The Political Economy of Crime: Did Universal Credit Increase Crime Rates? Available at: https://doi.org/10.31235/osf.io/e9ws8 [Last accessed 12.03.2020]

Trumm, S (2018) 'Representation in Wales: An empirical analysis of policy divisions between voters and candidates' *The British Journal of Politics and International Relations*, 20(2): 425-40

Vanstone, M (2002) *Understanding Community Penalties: Probation, Policy, and Social Change* Open University

Wales Governance Centre (2019) *Justice at the Jagged Edge* Cardiff: Wales Governance Centre

Wallace, J (2019) *Wellbeing and Devolution: Reframing the Role of Government in Scotland, Wales and Northern Ireland*. Switzerland AG: Springer Nature https://doi.org/10.1007/978-3-030-02230-3

Welsh Government (2019) Final Budget 2019-2020: Main expenditure group (MEG) allocations. January 2019. Cardiff: Welsh Government. Available at; https://gov.wales/sites/default/files/publications/2019-01/final-budget-2019-2020-restated-megs.pdf [Last accessed 12.03.2020]

Welsh Language Commissioner (2018) *The Welsh Language in Prisons A Review of the Rights and Experiences of Welsh Speaking Prisoners* Cardiff: Welsh Language Commissioner

Chapter 13
Adult Social Services
Jo Redcliffe

Introduction

This chapter focuses on the design and provision of social services care and support to adult citizens in Wales. The previous iteration of this chapter (Gwylim, 2011) noted how Wales has a reputation for innovation within the design and delivery of adult social care. The social demographics of Wales were examined, and important developments in the provision of social services to citizens since the creation of the Welsh Assembly in 1999 were charted. The chapter cast a critical eye over some of the ways in which policy makers attempted to design services to meet the diverse care and support needs of the population. Examples examined in 2011 include the *All Wales Strategy for the Development of Services for Mentally Handicapped People* (Welsh Office, 1983), a strategy that is regarded as a cornerstone in the recognition of the right of learning-disabled citizens to be treated as individuals and to live a life in their communities. The general erosion of confidence in the ability of institutions to provide acceptable care was noted and illustrated with reference to the mistreatment experienced by citizens resident in Ely Hospital in the 1960s (Department of Health and Social Security, 1969). The Disability Equality Scheme (WAG, 2006a) with its ultimate goal of inclusivity for all was examined, and the need for a National Strategy on Independent Living for Wales was identified. The National Assembly for Wales (NAW) 'Equity, Empowerment, Effectiveness, Efficiency' strategy, issued in 2001, and the 'National Service Framework for Mental Health' (WAG, 2005) were used to exemplify policy-makers' acknowledgment of social and economic factors in the maintenance of good health. Frameworks for older people were identified (WAG, 2003; WAG, 2006b) and the importance of citizen involvement was highlighted. The chapter concluded that effective joint working, particularly between social care and health services, would be a challenge for policymakers going forward.

This updated version examines the organisation and provision of adult services within a modern Wales with its population that is both growing and aging. We consider the grand challenge for policymakers, which is to ensure the availability of bespoke, accessible and collaborative care and support services that continue to meet the requirements of our steadily aging population within a climate of financial austerity. Contemporary demographic data is provided to illustrate both current and future trends. Dilemmas associated with the provision of care and support that is both universal and personal are considered. Legislation and policy are updated, and the focus of the chapter remains rooted in the care and support requirements of older and disabled citizens to reflect our distinctively Welsh focus.

The demography of Wales

Social care services must cater to the needs of the populations they serve. Welsh citizens aged over 18 received more than 122,415 social care and support services during 2018 (Social Care Wales, 2020). Wales is less ethnically diverse than other parts of the UK, with approximately 97 per cent of its citizens overall identifying as White. The statistics are consistent across the different age-ranges. People aged 65 and over comprise 20 per cent of the population of Wales, and 95 per cent of that group identify as White. People aged 16 to 64 years make up 62 per cent of the population, and 95 per cent of them identify as White. Children up to the age of 15 comprise 18 per cent of the population, with 94 per cent identifying as White (StatsWales, 2020). Like other industrial nations, Wales must tailor care services in order to meet the requirements of a population that is steadily aging within a climate of financial austerity (Tong *et al.*, 2018). With a quarter of the population aged over 50 years, and with forecasts projecting a continuing shift in demographics over the coming 20 years, this figure is expected to rise to over one million (Aging Well in Wales, 2019). The statistics relating to citizens aged 65 or over offer an even starker contrast, with forecasts of a 44 per cent increase in this age group, compared with an increase of just 6 per cent in the population overall (Welsh Government, 2015).

Similar trends are visible both nationally and internationally. The population of the United Kingdom (UK) is ageing at a substantial rate, resulting in an increase in the median age by 10 years (from 34 to 44) since 1950. From a global perspective, the median age is expected to increase by 18 years (from 26 to 41) by 2100 (Statista, 2020). However, while it is clear that this phenomenon is not unique to Wales, the effects are further compounded by our higher proportion of disabled citizens (26 per cent) as compared to other parts of the United Kingdom (Gwilym, 2011; Equality and Human Rights Commission, 2020). Old age is not in itself a disability, but most people will experience some form of illness during their lives (Priestly, 2003) and the prevalence of disability does increase with age. Across the UK, 45 per cent of citizens aged 65 or over are disabled as defined by the Equality Act (EA) 2010, in comparison with 19 per cent of working age citizens (Scope, 2020).

Indications of a significant increase in the number of Welsh citizens accessing social care and support services in the coming years suggest that social workers are likely to meet issues related to age and disability more frequently in their daily practice. The 'grand challenge' for social work occurs at a time of particular consequence, with the organisation of social care being characterised by austerity measures and higher thresholds (Baron and McLaughlin, 2017; Lubben *et al.*, 2018). The result is likely to be an increase in the number of citizens accessing generic services if they have their own funds, or informal services if not (Oliver, 2009; Oliver and Sapey, 2006; Oliver Sapey and Thomas, 2012). Simcock and Castle (2016) suggest that this practice brings increasing levels of inequality within an already imbalanced society. It is therefore imperative, and in everyone's interest, to ensure that social work practitioners in Wales are competent and confident to provide tailored support to citizens.

It is important to acknowledge that older disabled citizens comprise a heterogeneous group and have vastly different experiences, particularly citizens from Black Asian and Minority Ethnic (BAME) backgrounds. Therefore, using the terms is not an attempt to corral difference into narrow parameters, but a recognition of the existence of some similarities within general experiences of the labels (Hiranandani, 2005). It is worth pausing here to consider the contested nature of some of the terms that are common within the language of disability. This is critical because as Oliver (2004) and Shakespeare (2013) have identified, language can present us with dichotomies, and one's choice of language is a critical indicator of one's theoretical position. Our words have power, and the ways in which people construct meanings do influence their behaviours (Oliver and Barnes, 2012). Words can be used by the listener to generate positivity or to perpetuate negative stereotypes and barriers. For example, are people perceived to be disabled because of some sort of individualised biological deficit that should be addressed through medical intervention? Or, alternatively, is disability the result of the challenges associated with their impairment that emerge as a result of social oppression, dominant cultural discourse and barriers resulting from poorly designed environments? For clarity, the definition of disability used in this chapter is based on the presence of a congenital or acquired mental or physical impairment that has a substantial and long-term adverse effect on a citizens' ability to carry out typical day-to-day activities (EA, 2010). The term 'disability' is used to denote the socially constructed obstacles (Friedman and Owen, 2017) that can be experienced by people with impairments or conditions. Similarly, the term 'disabled citizens' illustrates the transfer of the concept of limitation away from the person to the society within which they exist (Ballan, Romanelli and Harper, 2011). This definition acknowledges both the impairment and the understanding that while the diagnosis of the citizen's condition/impairment may be constant, their experience of being disabled is dependent on the accessibility level of the environment they are in at the time (Snow, 2016).

Legislation and policy in Wales

Unlike the National Health Service (NHS), social services have never been universal, and our contemporary framework is the product of an evolution of care and support that started in an earlier age (Pumphrey and Pumphrey, 1961), prior even to the Elizabethan Poor Laws of the 16th Century that undertook to dispense aid to those in need. Ferguson (2016) urges us to look to the history of social work to identify issues that still retain relevance for contemporary practice. Harris (2008), cautions us against the over-simplification of events that are decidedly contextual, resulting in a mistaken view when gazed at through a historical telescope. However, Sloan, *et al.* (2018) recognise the importance of analysing social work history to identify blind spots, and suggest that examination of critical periods might uncover a more nuanced understanding of the current position. Cunningham and Cunningham (2012) agree and provide an example of this critical gaze. They suggest that, while a professionally-driven universalist approach to care and support may have fit the requirements of post-World War Two modernism, it failed to provide for citizens' diverse needs, particularly those of older and disabled citizens who ended-up being treated as passive recipients. A postmodernist approach was called for, one that takes account of diverse needs and reflects citizens' demands for more control over the care and support they receive.

The provision of social welfare in Wales is an activity that has generally been devolved from the UK Westminster Parliament, with Welsh Ministers taking a supervisory role and a duty of inspection. The Government of Wales Act 1998 granted competence through secondary legislation, and the updated 2006 version of the Act enhanced these legislative powers in relation to social welfare except for certain reservations. These reservations included the care or supervision of children under the Children Act 1989, powers and duties under the mental Capacity Act 2005, and social security schemes. Between 2007 and 2011 the National Assembly could legislate through the passing of Measures, including the Children and Families (Wales) Measure 2010, the Social Care Charges (Wales) Measure 2010 and the Carers Strategies (Wales) Measure 2010. The latter two of these Measures have now been repealed and replaced with the Social Services and Well-being (Wales) Act (SSWWA) 2014.

The Welsh response to criticisms of social care provision was to establish an Independent Commission on Social Services (ICSS), which in 2010 published its report into how the challenges of the next decade would be met. Priority areas of this review included the development of evidenced-based professional practice and the construction of inclusive, collaborative and integrated social services to meet the needs of all citizens. The review was premised on preserving early intervention and preventative services even in times of austerity in order to ensure the continuation of sustainable social services, sending a clear message that restricting delivery to core services only was considered an unpalatable option. Instead, it suggested that efficiencies could be achieved through more investment in Digital Inclusion Technology (for example, Telecare) and by taking action to shape the mixed economy of care in ways that encourage innovation and the development of self-directed support. Areas of improvement over recent years were noted, including a general increase in workforce qualification that emerged partly as a result of tighter regulation brought about by the Care Standards Act 2000. The report of the review (ICSS, 2010) identified the fundamental position of social services in the promotion of social inclusion and the protection of those at risk. The crucial role played by social services in connecting with allied services such as housing and transport when responding to areas of need that are layered and interconnected was acknowledged. The report recommended that Local Authorities should engage in more integrated strategic planning at the highest levels in order to provide joined-up services. Specific issues were identified related to consistency in the provision of services for citizens with learning disabilities, mental health issues and physical disabilities, for those transitioning from children to adult care, and for carers. The report also acknowledged the significance of robust pre- and post-qualifying training to provide practitioners with the requisite knowledge and skills to make informed decisions in often difficult situations. The influence of negative media coverage on encouraging risk adverse practice with an over reliance on process was noted. The report called for a culture-change in the provision of social services, a 'rebalance' which would value professional judgement and reflection while drawing on a sound evidence base (ICSS, 2010:8; Wilson and Kelly, 2010).

In addition to the ICSS report of 2010, the Welsh Government framework for social care services (WG, 2011) identified a number of challenges that impact on the provision of social work services, including increased expectations of citizens and the effects of changing demographics and economic hardship. The SSW(W) Act 2014 along with the Well-being of Future Generations (Wales) Act 2015 and 'Taking Wales Forward – The Programme for Government 2016-21' (WG, 2016) are key vehicles aimed at transforming the delivery of social care for a population that is both growing and ageing. The 2014 Act, which was fully implemented in April 2016, marked a significant step in the organisation and delivery of social care and support services. It outlined four underpinning principles, including the citizen having a voice and increased control of their care and support, prevention and early intervention, control of their well-being and an emphasis on co-production of services. These principles underscore the importance of quality social work that is sensitive and responsive to the requirements of citizens in contemporary society. It also represents a shift in perception of social workers from care managers to citizen-enablers, working with citizens in a more co-productive relationship (Symonds *et al.*, 2018). The Regulation and Inspection of Social Care (Wales) Act 2016 introduced a new regulatory regime for care and support services. It placed a duty on Social Care Wales to protect, promote and maintain the safety and well-being of Welsh citizens, in addition to its function as regulator of the practice and conduct of the social care workforce.

Practitioners in Wales are legally bound to deliver citizen-directed support as well as adhering to the concepts of personalisation and participation (Care and Social Services Inspectorate Wales, 2010; Independent Commission on Social Services in Wales, 2010; SSW(W) Act 2014). Policy direction encourages the delivery of citizen-directed support, with social workers acting as enablers (Rees and Raithby, 2012). However, the provision of services for adult citizens can be both fashioned and inhibited by the direction of social policy, and tensions may emerge as a result of a perceived mismatch between the traditional characteristics of the provision of social care and the emphasis on citizen-control brought about by the new legislation and policy (Clarke and Spafford, 2002). Symonds *et al.* (2018) suggest that the primary tension among both practitioners and citizens who receive services lay in achieving the delicate balance between citizen autonomy and professional judgement. Many researchers (Davis, 1993; Dominelli, 1994; Symonds, *et al.*, 2018) have identified this apprehension about institutional imbalance when attempting to both empower the wishes of the citizen and make decisions about the need for support. An ill-judged approach risks the citizen becoming an obligated, yet reluctant, receiver of services that have been prescribed for them (Cunningham and Cunningham, 2012). Davis (1993) has delineated how, in this context, the profession holds all the cards. These tensions are heightened during times of austerity when service delivery is affected by financial constraint (Symonds *et al.*, 2018). In respect of disability particularly, policies have been accused of failing to support citizens in their attempts to achieve access to the full range of rights that are available to the majority (Oliver *et al.*, 2012). As pointed out by Soldatic and Meekosha (2012), the position of disabled people in society is somewhat dependent on the whims of contemporary policy makers. For example, the boundaries of the category (ies) of people defined as unable to work as a result of their disability (ies) are regularly adjusted by the UK government in order to align with contemporary political concerns (Oliver and Barnes, 2012).

While universalistic social policy strategies have been rejected in favour of more emancipatory postmodern tactics, the principle of personalisation has itself faced censure. Critics suggest that this represents a step too far towards an even harsher and ultimately marginalising model (Cunningham and Cunningham, 2012). Within a system characterised by increasingly slashed budgets, eligibility criteria for care and support services must be tightened even in this era of co-production (Symonds *et al.*, 2018). Other concerns include that this is merely a rhetoric of empowerment which ignores the role of power relations and will result in state intervention only when the harshest thresholds have been met, leaving most social care to be provided by the community itself (Oliver, 2009; Oliver and Sapey, 2006; Oliver *et al.*, 2012). From feminist, antiracist or anti-disablist perspectives, this may be viewed as hegemonic practice designed to perpetuate the stereotyping of those perceived to be subordinate within a rhetoric of citizenship that serves to continue to deprive them of a true voice (Dominelli, 2002; Carey, 2009). Symmonds *et al.* (2018) concur and suggest that, despite the intention, personalised approaches risk viewing challenges at an individual level and therefore fail to address the wider political role of structural inequality.

The following three sections of this chapter examine the most recent legislative and policy developments relating to three groups of citizens in Wales: older citizens, disabled citizens and learning-disabled citizens. It is important to pause here and remember that while groups of citizens in Wales may share some characteristics each citizen is an individual with distinct support needs and this is of particular significance for citizens from BAME backgrounds. As Gwilym (2011) noted, despite social care in Wales being organised into groups, there should be no one size fits all approach that attempts to bulldoze citizens into metaphorical furrows defined by service area (Harris and Roulstone, 2011). Similarly, when taking a person-centred approach, we must avoid individualising issues in a manner that locates the 'blame' within the citizen themselves and ignores broader social issues that may serve to reinforce inequality (Oliver and Barnes, 2012).

Older citizens

Aging is a serious matter. Many citizens experience changes in physical and mental health as they age, with decreased mobility and stamina levels leading to greater dependence on others and an increased risk of isolation (Blaschke *et al.*, 2009). While the population is aging and developing increasing care and support needs, a growing number of citizens are remaining in their own homes and receiving care and support from a combination of different agencies (Tong *et al.*, 2018). It is essential to acknowledge that older adults may find the contemporary adult services mixed economy of care a challenging landscape to navigate and within which to make decisions regarding their support requirements (Ward and Barnes, 2016). Effective partnerships are required to enable the delivery of enduring and efficient care and support within environments that are constantly changing. The previous version of this chapter identified the driving forward of collaborative working between social care and health services as a propriety of the Welsh Assembly following establishment in 1999 (Gwilym, 2011). It also described the Care Programme Approach and the Unified Assessment Process as two examples of joint working processes aimed at streamlining processes between social care and health. The significance afforded to collaborative approaches is reflected in more recent legislation and policy direction. The SSW(W) Act 2014, the Well-being of Future Generations (Wales) Act 2015, 'Taking Wales Forward – The Programme for Government 2016-21' (WG, 2016) and the 'Strategy for Older People in Wales 2013-2023' (WG, 2013) all highlight the importance of social, economic, environmental and cultural well-being in a time of austerity. They also require public services including social care, health, education, housing and the voluntary and private sectors to work together to deliver joined-up community-based services that promote well-being. 'Prosperity for All' is the strategy by which the Welsh Government (2017) details its four main commitments as the development of a prosperous and secure economy, the improvement of citizens' health and well-being, the encouragement of education and ambition, and the reinforcement of united and connected communities.

It is vital to recognise that individual factors can affect citizens' access to support. Research on the experiences of BAME citizens as they age remains limited and requires more sustained attention (Zubair and Norris, 2015), but it is clear that the presence of societal challenges including inequality and exclusion can affect access to support and treatment. Matsuoka (2015) has identified how older citizens can be more susceptible to mental health issues than their younger peers due to them experiencing a series of losses including their family/friends, work and functional ability. This may be exacerbated in BAME citizens who experience racism in addition to facing additional culturally specific losses, for example language, support and respect. According to The Mental Health Foundation (2020), citizens with Black, African, Caribbean or Black British backgrounds are more likely than citizens with White backgrounds to experience mental illness and in 2017/18 were four times more likely to be detained under the Mental Health Act 1983. This has led to calls for culturally appropriate interventions and treatments to address systemic cultural imperialism by responding to the needs of older people from a range of ethnic backgrounds, including language (translation, literacy), faith and religion, diet and gender-specific services. Going forward it is imperative that researchers and policy makers pay attention to wider aspects of ageing among BAME citizens by recognising both the existence of cultural diversity between different ethnic groups and the layered nature of social inequality, in a manner that does not pathologise but instead acknowledges the positive elements of ethnicity as a valuable protective resource for citizens (Zubair and Norris, 2015).

Another factor that can affect access to social support is sexuality. Willis (2017:111) has written about the 'shadow of invisibility' that encompasses members of the Lesbian, Gay, Bisexual, Transgender, Queer/Questioning and Intersex (LGBTQI) community, particularly older male citizens who lived through the era of criminalisation pre 1967 when they received no legal protection. Research by the Welsh Government (2014) identified barriers of individual perceptions, abuse and culture that may be faced by LGBTQI citizens in Wales when attempting to access residential or nursing care services in Wales that have been created with heterosexual citizens in mind. The continued existence of these individual, cultural and structural barriers are echoed by Willis, *et al.* (2016; 2017), in their research into the role of sexual well-being in the experiences of older LGBTQI citizens in long-term care facilities in Wales. They advocate that there is a key role for social workers who provide support to adult citizens to promote acceptance of inclusive sexual well-being and to lobby for more policy and legislative direction.

Citizens with physical disabilities

The discipline of social policy has long been acknowledged as an essential component of social work (Cunningham and Cunningham, 2012). Despite this, contemporary social work has itself been criticised for remaining depoliticised due to its reluctance to challenge political dimensions of education, practice and research that reinforce inequality and do not sit comfortably with its acknowledged values and ideals (Reisch and Jani, 2012). Cunningham and Cunningham (2012) highlight a systematic failure by UK health and social care services to adequately meet the needs of adult citizens, instead exacerbating exclusion and marginalisation. This is particularly visible, the same authors argue, in the support offered to disabled citizens, who grew increasingly dissatisfied with the professionally driven form of welfare services. This dissatisfaction spurred a social movement that introduced the social model of disability as an alternative to the individual and often medicalised perspectives that prevailed (Union of the Physically Impaired Against Segregation, 1976).

When considering the impact of the social model, it is essential to note that it was used by Oliver (1983) specifically to help his social work students gain a better understanding of the lives of people with physical, intellectual or sensory impairments. He did this by severing the causal link between impairment and disability (Roulstone and Morgan, 2011). Reframing the perceived problem of disability as 'disablism' encouraged movement away from a focus on individual deficit to understanding it to be a form of oppression that is similar to other forms including racism, sexism and ageism. This was to bring about a different, more emancipatory approach to working with disabled people (French and Swaine, 2012; Oliver *et al.*, 2012). The social model has been unarguably embraced by social work, and according to the social work regulator, it has received formal recognition in Welsh social work education and practice

(Care Council for Wales, 2003). Despite this recognition, Soldatic and Meekosha (2012) have identified how the professional discretion of social workers is sometimes impaired through convoluted interactions of legislation, policy and structural issues. Social workers, in their attempts to make decisions that accommodate both the citizens they serve and the policies that guide them, may be left feeling ineffective within environments that become increasingly challenging because of austerity (Symonds *et al.*, 2018).

The 2019 Welsh Government consultation 'Action on disability: the right to independent living' aims to replace the 'Framework for Independent Living' (WG, 2013) and to improve the independence of citizens by making it easier for them to access integrated advice and support. The success of collaborative working depends on the development of good interpersonal relationships and practices including the identification of mutual goals, shared accountability and clear lines of responsibility (Frey, *et al.*, 2006). Achieving partnership between agencies that may have very different organisational structures typically requires changes to be made to established patterns of working. Without change, it is possible for collaboration to impede rather than generate effectiveness. Oliver and Barnes (2012) have highlighted how the concerns of social workers can sometimes be trumped by those of other professions, particularly the medical sector. Weiss, *et al.* (2010) researched partnership approaches within community health, and their findings suggest that dissatisfaction is likely to occur within systems that are closed and unsupportive of inclusivity, dialogue and disagreement from all members.

Citizens with learning disabilities

The UK government identified elements of what we now refer to as person-centred and relational practice as priorities for the provision of social support to citizens with learning disabilities as early as the 1970s. The Chronically Sick and Disabled Persons Act 1970 required local authorities to provide a range of services to disabled people. In 1971 came the publication of a White Paper that emphasised the importance of home life for citizens with learning disabilities, and the opportunity to make lasting attachments (Department of Health, 1971). The All Wales Mental Handicap Strategy 1983 was, despite its name, hailed as a forward-thinking blueprint that would change the delivery of services from traditional institutional forms to the community, a principle echoed by the NHS and Community Care Act 1990. However despite these legislative and policy steers, the conclusions of the report into the Winterbourne View scandal (Transforming Care and Commissioning Steering Group, 2014) suggested that still thousands of UK citizens with learning disabilities remained inappropriately in hospital when, with the right support, they could live in communities. As Goodley and Runswick-Cole (2014) have pointed out, process-driven care management procedures have continued to be prioritised, resulting in social justice sometimes getting lost within risk-adverse practices. Accordingly, the British Association of Social Workers (BASW, 2020) has launched a timely research project to investigate how to improve the social care support offered to older citizens with learning disabilities and their carers. The aim of the research is to develop strategies that ensure the research has a direct impact on practice, and the emphasis on relationship-based practice resonates with particular relevance during the Covid-19 pandemic.

An example of the weight afforded by the Welsh Government to integrated approaches to care and support is found in the Learning Disability Improving Lives programme (WG, 2018). This programme estimates that there are approximately 15,000 adult citizens with learning disabilities known to social services in Wales, with potentially at least 60,000 not known. It suggests that advances in health care means that many premature babies now survive with physical or learning disabilities, and citizens with learning disabilities are living longer than before and as a result develop more complex needs as they age. Additionally, it acknowledges well-being as a key aim, with community integration and joint working cited as essential themes for improving citizens' lives. The programme (WG, 2018:3) also identifies the continuing challenges of delivering integrated and collaborative services, quoting terminology including 'fight' and 'battle' to describe how some citizens report feeling when attempting to access services. The programme calls for recognition and action regarding the right of citizens with learning disabilities to have career paths, employment opportunities and access to education, all of which are closely linked to the need for adequate transport links. Pugh and Cheers (2010) have identified how citizens from minority (in all respects) communities in rural locations can become lost and therefore less likely to receive support that addresses their needs. They explain that the high visibility of general daily life in rural communities plus the assumption of homogeneity can result in differences being masked in order to avoid discrimination and social othering – in other words, a desire 'not to make a fuss' (Pugh and Cheers, 2010:95). As acknowledged by Fenge and Jones (2011), the concept of the rural idyll may in fact conceal citizens from marginalised groups, resulting in poor access to support services, poverty, marginalisation, stigma and stress.

A further fundamental challenge of contemporary support is the enhancement of well-being through delivery of education that specifically addresses personal and sexual relations. This is echoed by Lee and Fenge (2016), who explored the link between well-being and sexuality. Their findings indicate that the sensitivity of the topic combined with a lack of guidance can hinder the provision of evidence-based support within an aspect of human life that they term to be one of the most profound. Failing to acknowledge a learning-disabled citizen's sexual identity, or viewing the display of sexual behaviour as deviant, risky or problematic, has been described as a denial of 'sexual citizenship' (Lee and Fenge, 2016:2264). Turner and Crane (2016:2300) concur, and their research identifies how the sexuality of learning-disabled people has been denied through institutionalism and the dominance of the medical model. They are inspired to perceive acceptance of the 'sexual voice' of learning-disabled citizens as an issue of power, self-determination, human rights and social justice. They suggest that social care providers have a role because the development of a sexual voice falls within the remit of advocating for self-determination. Social work educators are perceived to have a role in influencing both students and qualified practitioners to practice in ways that improve practice competency. Furthermore, Turner and Crane (2016) appeal for the sexuality of learning-disabled citizens to be awarded the same consideration as that of other marginalised citizens, including the LGBTQI community.

Conclusions – A way forward?

Contemporary practice that is characterised by the compliant discharge of a narrow range of statutory approved duties and an unconvincing adherence to the social model is insufficient, and it has been proposed that for social work to continue as a profession with something to offer citizens (particularly older and disabled citizens) then a significant shift in attitudes is required (Oliver, 2004; Cousin, 2006; Lymbery and Postle, 2007; Morgan, 2012; Sloane *et al.*, 2018). Long-established structures and practices should be altered significantly in order to appropriately address the social model (Harris and Roulstone, 2011; Rees and Raithby, 2012). Ferguson (2016) predicts three potential outcomes for the profession. Firstly, echoing Harris and Roulstone (2011), there is a possibility that social work as a profession with something to offer our specific population could become redundant or disappear altogether, defeated by funding cuts and tighter eligibility criteria. The second suggests the continuation of social work as a governmental tool for the promotion of social content, rather than as a profession with a set of distinct values and principles of social justice. However, Ferguson's option three is more optimistic. The suggestion is that the global economic recession represents a pinch point that has sparked new mindsets, resulting in a new wave of radical thinking about what social work can offer. This new radical mindset is illustrated by Ioakimidis (2011) as being apparent in Southern Europe, particularly in Hungary and Slovenia. In the UK, this is represented by the Social Work Action Network (SWAN) which emerged in opposition to the perception of social work as a business overly concerned with profitability instead of citizens' needs.

The further development of 'what works' research is key in the identification and application of best practices. Recent growth in the requirement for social workers to be conversant with scientific reasoning at complex levels in their everyday practice highlights the importance of evidence based practice as one of a number of different types of knowledge used by practitioners to inform their professional decision-making (D'Cruz and Jones, 2004). Perceived as part of a profession-wide long-awaited maturation process, this suggests a way by which social work can gain legitimacy and credibility in its contributions to society that goes beyond adherence to a strong set of values (Sheldon, 1998, in D'Cruz and Jones, 2004). Part of this process is alignment of the link between the generation of unbiased research knowledge and policy (and by default practice) development, with a strong focus on outcomes. It cannot be disputed that in order to work with citizens from a best practice position we must all be aware of how different interventions perform, but evidence-based practice from a positivist stance is not the only source of this knowledge. De Jong, Schout and Abma (2015) have proposed that it is not possible to control all factors in certain social work situations, and that in general the samples under study are too small, thereby rendering the making of generalised conclusions challenging. Khoury (2019) suggests that evidence-based practice is too often defined by uniformity based on standardisation, and that the definition of evidence should be opened-up to include the lived experience, reflection, doubt and curiosity. The demand for social work research which is characterised by both methodological rigor and relevance to practice is part of a wider call to arms in order to locate the profession in a more 'creative and transformative' evidence enriched location (Shaw, 2011:609).

An analysis of the development of social work with adult citizens in Wales may be best summed up by Jones (2014:485) as representing both 'the best of times' and 'the worst of times'. Social work with BAME, LGBTQI, disabled and older citizens is on the radar but requires our further attention. As our population grows, ages and diversifies, intersectionality (how different forms of oppression interact and impact on our daily lives) becomes more important and requires our active acknowledgement and action (GOV.UK, 2020). Our adherence to the social model requires examination of discriminatory barriers including economic inequality. The Global Agenda for Social Work and Social Development (the International Federation of Social Workers (IFSW), the International Association of Schools of Social Work (IASSW) and the International Council on Social Welfare (ICSW), 2012) represent an attempt to address inequalities that have emerged as the result of globalisation. In the United States of America (USA) the National Association of Social Workers (2017) mandate that social workers pay particular attention to the needs of people living in poverty. In the UK the BASW Code of Ethics requires social workers to ensure that the resources at their disposal are distributed fairly, according to need (BASW, 2014). However, examination of USA and UK social work curricula reveal that social workers receive little economics education, and it is generally acknowledged to be a neglected area (Wolfsohn and Michaeli, 2014). Its absence appears to be at odds with the professional requirement for social workers to engage in practice with citizens who are often financially vulnerable and who may themselves lack the financial knowledge and skills to undertake basic 'book balancing' exercises (Fenge, 2012). It also fails to align with the current economic climate which is characterised by austerity and the reduction of state services resulting from the tightening of eligibility criteria (Garett, 2007). Increases in life expectancy mean that resources need to be carefully planned so that they last through longer periods. Garrett (2007:517) has warned us to beware of the ideological 'rhetoric of re-enchantment' which has emerged from the austere climate. This rhetoric claims to be empowered to not only reduce bureaucracy within a profession notorious for it, but in addition to liberate social workers to creatively work with citizens in the spirit of well-being, co-production and mutuality emphasised by contemporary legislative and policy direction. Evans *et al.* (2011) advise that what social work requires is adherence to a sustainable approach within which the ability to recognise and assess available resources leads to a targeted social work response with the overall aim of alleviating socio/economic exclusion. Incorporation of economic literacy into social work education of social workers in Wales will benefit social workers and the citizens they work with (Wolfsohn and Michaeli, 2014). Citizens who receive services and those who do not meet ever-tightening eligibility criteria are both more likely to face economic hardship, and the challenge for policy makers now and in the future is the creation of a robust policy response to address it. The challenge for practitioners is to recognise our collective responsibility and take action to ensure that we exert an influence and are not simply subjected to the future direction of social work practice.

References

Aging Well in Wales (2019) *State of The Nation: An Overview of Growing Older in Wales* www.olderpeoplewales.com/Libraries/Uploads/State_of_the_Nation_e_-_online.sflb.ashx

Ballan, M, Romanelli, M and Harper, J (2011) 'The Social Model: a lens for counselling transgender individuals with disabilities' *Journal of Gay and Lesbian Mental Health* 15(3): 260-80

Baron, S and McLaughlin, H (2017) 'Grand Challenges: a way forward for social work?' *Social Work Education* 36(1): 1-5

Blaschke, C, Freddolino, P and Mullen, E (2009) 'Ageing and technology: a review of the research literature' *British Journal of Social Work*, 39(4): 641-56. doi: 10.1093/bjsw/bcp025

British Association of Social Workers (2014) *The Code of Ethics for Social Work* Birmingham: BASW. Available at www.basw.co.uk/about-basw/code-ethics

British Association of Social Workers (2020) *Research launched to investigate how to improve support for older people with learning disabilities and carers* Birmingham: BASW. www.basw.co.uk/media/news/ 2020/jul/research-launched-investigate-how-improve-support-older-people-learning

Care and Social Services Inspectorate Wales (2010) *Improving Care and Social Services in Wales: Chief Inspector's Annual Report 2009-2010* Cardiff: Care and Social Services Inspectorate Wales

Care Council for Wales (2003) *Approval and visiting of degree courses in social work (Wales) Rules* Cardiff: Care Council for Wales

Carey, M (2009) 'Critical commentary: happy shopper? The problem with service user and carer participation' *British Journal of Social Work* 39(1): 179-88

Chronically Sick and Disabled Persons Act 1970. Available at: www.legislation.gov.uk/ukpga/1970/44/contents

Clark, H and Spafford, J (2002) 'Adapting to the culture of user control?' *Social Work Education*, 21(2): 247-57

Cousin, G (2006) 'An introduction to threshold concepts' *Planet,* 17(1) pp4-5 DOI: 10.11120/plan.2006.00170004

Cunningham, J and Cunningham, S (2012) *Social Policy and Social Work: An Introduction* London: Sage

Davies, R (1993) 'The crafting of good clients' in Swain, J, Finkelstein, V, French, S and Oliver, M (eds.) *Disabling Barriers - Enabling Environments* London: Sage, pp205-05

D'Cruz, H and Jones, M (2004) *Social Work Research: Ethical and Political Concepts* London: Sage

De Jong, G, Schout, G and Abma, T (2015) 'Examining the effects of family group conferencing with randomised controlled trials: The golden standard?', *British Journal of Social Work*, 45(5): 1623-9 https://doi.org/10.1093/bjsw/bcv027

Department of Health (1971) *Better services for the mentally handicapped*. London: Her Majesty's Stationery Office [Online] http://filestore.nationalarchives.gov.uk/pdfs/small/cab-129-157-cp-61.pdf

Department of Health and Social Security (1969) *Report of the Committee of Inquiry into Allegations of Ill – Treatment of Patients and other irregularities at the Ely Hospital, Cardiff* Available at: www.sochealth.co.uk/national-health-service/democracy-involvement-and-accountability-in-health/complaints-regulation-and-enquries/report-of-the-committee-of-inquiry-into-allegations-of-ill-treatment-of-patients-and-other-irregularities-at-the-ely-hospital-cardiff-1969

Dominelli, L (1994) 'Deprofessionalizing social work: anti-oppressive practice, competencies and postmodernism' *British Journal of Social Work* 26(2): 153-75

Dominelli, L (2002) *Feminist Social Work Theory and Practice* Basingstoke: Palgrave

Equality and Human Rights Commission (2020) *Disabled people in Wales: Housing Crisis* Available at: www.equalityhumanrights.com/en/our-work/news/disabled-people-wales-housing-crisis

Evans, S, Hills, S and Orme, J (2011) 'Doing more for less? developing sustainable systems of social care in the context of climate change and public spending cuts' *British Journal of Social Work* 42(4): 744-64 https://doi.org/10.1093/bjsw/bcr108

Fenge, L (2012) 'Economic well-being and ageing: the need for financial education for social workers' *Social Work Education* 31(4): 498-511

Fenge, L and Jones, K (2011) 'Gay and Pleasant Land? Exploring Sexuality, Ageing and Rurality in a Multi-Method, Performative Project' *British Journal of Social Work* 42(2): 300-17 doi: 10.1093/bjsw/bcr058

Ferguson, I (2016) 'Hope over fear: Social work education towards 2025' *European Journal of Social Work* 20(3): 322-32 www.tandfonline.com/doi/full/10.1080/13691457.2016.1189402

French, S and Swaine, J (2012) *Working with Disabled People in Policy and Practice* Basingstoke: Palgrave Macmillan

Frey, B, Lohmeier, J, Lee, S and Tollefson, N (2006) 'Measuring collaboration among grant partners' *American Journal of Evaluation* 27(3): 383-92

Friedman, C and Owen, A (2017) 'Defining disability: Understandings of and attitudes towards ableism and disability' *Disability Studies Quarterly* 37(1)

Garrett, P (2007) 'Re-enchanting social work? The emerging 'spirit' of social work in an age of economic crisis' *British Journal of Social Work* 44(3): 503-21 https://doi.org/10.1093/bjsw/bcs146

Goodley, D and Runswick-Cole, K (2014) 'Becoming dishuman: thinking about the human through dis/ability' *Discourse: Studies in the Cultural Politics of Education* 37(1): 1-15 DOI: 10.1080/01596306.2014.930021

GOV.UK (2020) *Why Intersectionality Matters for Social Work Practice in Adult Services.* https://socialworkwithadults.blog.gov.uk/2020/01/31/why-intersectionality-matters-for-social-work-practice-in-adult-services

Gwilym, H (2011) 'Social Services for adults in Wales' in Gwilym, H and Williams, C (eds.) *Social Policy for Social Welfare Practice in a Devolved Wales* 2nd Ed. Birmingham: BASW

International Federation of Social Workers (2000) *Definition of Social Work* www.ifsw.org/what-is-social-work/global-definition-of-social-work

Harris, J (2008) 'State Social Work: Constructing the Present from Moments in the Past' *British Journal of Social Work* 38(4): 662-79 https://doi.org/10.1093/bjsw/bcn024

Harris, J and Roulstone, A (2011) *Disability, Policy and Professional Practice* Sage: London

Hiranandani, V (2005) 'Towards a critical theory of disability in social work' *Critical Social Work* 6(1): 1-14

Independent Commission on Social Services in Wales (2010) *From Vision to Action. The Report of the Independent Commission on Social Services in Wales.* https://gov.wales/sites/default/files/publications/2019-06/from-vision-to-action-the-report-of-the-independent-commission-on-social-services-in-wales.pdf

Ioakimidis, V (2011) 'Welfare under warfare: The Greek struggle for emancipatory social welfare' in Lavalette, M & Ioakimidis, V (eds.) *Social work in Extremis* Bristol: Policy Press pp115-32

Jones, R (2014) 'The Best of Times, The Worst of Times: Social Work and its Moment' *British Journal of Social Work*, 44(3): 485-502 https://doi.org/10.1093/bjsw/bcs157

Khoury, E (2019) 'A Response to the Notion of Avoidable Ignorance in Critiques of Evidence-Based Practice' *British Journal of Social Work* 49(6): 1677–81 https://doi.org/10.1093/bjsw/bcz032

Lee, S & Fenge, L (2016) 'Sexual well-being and physical disability' *British Journal of Social Work* 46(8): 2263-81 https://doi.org/10.1093/bjsw/bcw107

Lubben, J, Barth, R, Fong, R, Flynn, M, Sherraden, M and Uehara, E (2018) 'Introduction' in R Fong, J Lubben and R Barth (eds.) *Grand Challenges for Social Work and Society* Oxford: Oxford University Press, pp1-17

Lymbery M and Postle, K (2007) 'Social work in challenging times' in M Lymbery & K Postle (eds.) *Social Work: A Companion to Learning* London: Sage, pp3-21

Matsuoka, A (2015) 'Ethnic/Racial Minority Older Adults and Recovery: Integrating Stories of Resilience and Hope in Social Work' *British Journal of Social Work* 45 (Issue suppl_1) pp i135–i152. doi: 10.1093/bjsw/bcv120

Mental Health Foundation (2020) *Black, Asian and Minority Ethnic Communities* Available at: www.mentalhealth.org.uk/a-to-z/b/black-asian-and-minority-ethnic-bame-communities

Morgan, H (2012) 'The social model of disability as a threshold concept: troublesome knowledge and liminal spaces in social work education' *Social Work Education* 31(2): 215-26

National Assembly for Wales (2001) *Equity, Empowerment, Effectiveness, Efficiency: Strategy Document* Cardiff, NAW

National Association of Social Workers (2017) *Code of Ethics of the National Association of Social Workers* www.socialworkers.org/About/Ethics/Code-of-Ethics

National Health Service and Community Care Act 1990. Available at www.legislation.gov.uk/ukpga/1990/19/contents

Oliver, M (1983) *Social Work and Disabled People* Basingstoke: Macmillan

Oliver, M (2004) 'The social model in action: if I had a hammer' in Marnes, C and Mercer, G (eds.) *Implementing the Social Model Of Disability: Theory and Research* Leeds: The Disability Press, pp18-31

Oliver, M (2009) *Understanding Disability: From Theory to Practice* (2nd Ed.) London: Palgrave Macmillan

Oliver, M and Barnes, C (2012) *The New Politics of Disablement* Basingstoke: Palgrave Macmillan

Oliver, M and Sapey, B (2006) *Social Work with Disabled People* (3rd Ed.) Basingstoke: Palgrave Macmillan

Oliver, M, Sapey, B and Thomas, P (2012) *Social Work with Disabled People* (4th Ed.) Basingstoke: Palgrave Macmillan

Priestley, M (2003) *Disability: A life course approach*. Cambridge: Polity Press

Pugh, R and Cheers, B (2010) *Rural Social Work: An International Perspective*, Bristol, Policy Press

Pumphrey, R and Pumphrey, M (1961) *The Heritage of American Social Work: Readings In Its Philosophical And Institutional Development* London, Columbia University Press

Rees, J and Raithby, M (2012) 'Increasingly strange bedfellows? An examination of the inclusion of disability issues in university- and agency-based social work education in a Welsh context' *Social Work Education* 3(2): 184-201

Reisch, M and Jani, J (2012) 'The new politics of social work practice: understanding context to promote change *British Journal of Social Work* 2(6): 1132-150

Roulstone, A. & Morgan, H. (2011) 'Neo-Liberal Individualism or Self-Directed Support: Are We All Speaking the Same Language on Modernising Adult Social Care?', Social Policy and Society, 8(3): 333-345.

Scope (2020) Disability Facts and Figures. https://www.scope.org.uk/media/disability-facts-figures

Simcock, P and Castle, R (2016) Social Work and Disability, Cambridge: Polity Press

Shakespeare, T (2013) *Disability Rights and Wrongs Revisited* Oxon, Routledge

Shaw, I (2011) 'Innovation and the practice of social work research' British Journal of Social Work 41(4): 609-24

Sheldon, B (1998) 'Social work practice in the 21st century' *Research in Social Work Practice* 8(5): 577-88

Sloane, H, David, K, Davies, ., Stamper, D and Woodward, S (2018) 'Cultural history analysis and professional humility: historical context and social work practice' *Social Work Education* 37(8): 1015-27

Snow, K. (2016) 'People first language', Disability is Natural Newsletter https://nebula.wsimg.com/1c1af57f9319dbf909ec52462367fa88?AccessKeyId=9D6F6082FE5EE52C3DC6&disposition=0&alloworigin=1#page=2

Soldiac, K & Meekosha, H (2012) 'The place of disgust: disability, class and gender in spaces of workfare' *Societies* 3(3): 139-56

Social Care Wales (2020) *Adults: Care and Support Services* Available at www.socialcaredata.wales/IAS/themes/adults/adultsreceivingcareandsupport/tabular?viewId=2212&geoId=1&subsetId=

Statista (2020) *Mid-year population estimate of the United Kingdom in 2018, by age group* www.statista.com/topics/3811/british-demography-2017/#dossierSummary__chapter3

StatsWales (2020) *Ethnicity by age* https://statswales.gov.wales/Catalogue/Equality-and-Diversity/Ethnicity/ethnicity-by-age

Symonds, J, Williams, V, Miles, C, Steel, M and Porter, S (2018) 'The social care practitioner as assessor: people, relationships and professional judgement' *British Journal of Social Work* 48(7): 1910-28

Tong, C, Franke, C, Larcombe, K and Gould, J (2018) 'Fostering inter-agency collaboration for the delivery of community-based services for older adults' *British Journal of Social Work* 48(2): 390-411

Transforming Care and Commissioning Steering Group (2014) *Winterbourne View – Time for Change.* www.england.nhs.uk/wp-content/uploads/2014/11/transforming-commissioning-services.pdf

Turner, G and Crane, B (2016) 'Sexually silenced no more, adults with learning disabilities speak up: a call to action for social work to frame sexual voice as a social justice issue' *British Journal of Social Work* 46(8): 2300-17

Union of the physically impaired against segregation (1976) *Fundamental Principles of Disability* London, UPIAS

Ward, L and Barnes, M (2016) 'Transforming Practice with Older People through an Ethic of Care', *British Journal of Social Work*, 46(4): 906-22. doi: 10.1093/bjsw/bcv029

Weiss, E, Taber, S, Breslau, E, Lillie, S and Li, Y (2010) 'The role of leadership and management in six southern public health partnerships: a study of member involvement and satisfaction'. *Health education & Behaviour : the Official Publication of the Society for Public Health Education* 37(6): 737-52

Welsh Assembly Government (2003) *Strategy for Older people in Wales.* Cardiff, WAG

Welsh Assembly Government (2005) *Raising the Standard: The Revised Adult Mental Health National Service Framework and an Action Plan for Wales* www.wales.nhs.uk/documents/WebsiteEnglishNSFandActionPlan.pdf

Welsh Assembly Government (2006a) *Welsh Assembly Government Disability Scheme* www.assembly.wales/meeting%20agenda%20documents/supporting%20document%20-%20welsh%20assembly%20government%20disability%20equality%20scheme-29112006-44881/bus-chamber-e728ace14cb397ba3f3fd58c6405a874-english.pdf

Welsh Assembly Government (2006b) Framework for Older People Cardiff: Welsh Assembly Government

Welsh Government (WG) (2011) *Sustainable Social Services for Wales: A Framework for Action.* Cardiff: Welsh Government. www.wales.nhs.uk/sitesplus/documents/829/WAG%20-%20Sustainable%20Social%20Services%20for%20Wales%202011.pdf

Welsh Government (2013) *The Strategy for Older People in Wales 2013-2023.* Cardiff: Welsh Government. https://gov.wales/sites/default/files/publications/2019-06/strategy-for-older-people-in-wales-2013-2023-delivery-plan.pdf

Welsh Government (2014) *Barriers faced by Lesbian, Gay, Bisexual and Transgender People in Accessing Domestic Abuse, Stalking and Harassment, and Sexual Violence Services.* Cardiff: Welsh Government. https://gov.wales/sites/default/files/statistics-and-research/2019-07/140604-barriers-faced-lgbt-accessing-domestic-abuse-services-summary-en.pdf

Welsh Government (2015) *National Level Population Estimates.* Cardiff: Welsh Government. https://statswales.gov.wales/Catalogue/Population-and-Migration/Population/Estimates/nationallevelpopulationestimates-by-year-age-ukcountry

Welsh Government (2016) *Taking Wales Forward 2016-2021.* Cardiff: Welsh Government. https://gov.wales/sites/default/files/publications/2017-08/taking-wales-forward.pdf

Welsh Government (2017) *Prosperity for All: The National strategy. Taking Wales Forward.* Cardiff: Welsh Government. https://gov.wales/sites/default/files/publications/2017-10/prosperity-for-all-the-national-strategy.pdf

Welsh Government (2018) *Learning Disability Improving Lives Programme.* Cardiff: Welsh Government. https://gov.wales/sites/default/files/publications/2019-02/improving-lives-programme-cab%2817-18%2937.pdf

Welsh Government (2019) *Action on Disability: The right to independent living.* Cardiff: Welsh Government. https://gov.wales/action-disability-right-independent-living

Welsh Office (1983) *All Wales Strategy for the Development of Services for Mentally Handicapped People* Cardiff: HMSO

Willis, P (2017) 'Queer, Visible, Present: The Visibility of Older LGB Adults in Long-Term Care Environments' *Housing, Care and Support*, 20(3): 110-20

Willis, P, Raithby, M, Maegusuku-Hewett, T and Miles, P (2016) 'Swimming upstream: the provision of inclusive care to older lesbian, gay and bisexual (LGB) adults in residential and nursing environments in Wales' *Ageing & Society* 36(2): 282-306

Willis, P, Raithby, M, Maegusuku-Hewett, T and Miles, P (2017) 'Everyday advocates' for inclusive care: perspectives on enhancing the provision of long-term care services for older lesbian, gay and bisexual adults in Wales' *British Journal of Social Work*, 47(1): 409-26

Wilson, G and Kelly, B (2010) 'Evaluating the effectiveness of Social work education' *British Journal of Social Work* 40(8): 2431-49 https://doi.org/10.1093/bjsw/bcq019

Wolfsohn, R and Michaeli, D (2014) 'Financial Social Work'. In C Franklin (ed.) *Encyclopaedia of Social Work* Washington, DC, and New York: NASW Press and Oxford University Press. doi:10.1093/acrefore/9780199975839.013.923

Washington, DC, and New York: NASW Press and Oxford University Press. doi:10.1093/acrefore/9780199975839.013.923

Zubair, M, and Norris, M (2015) 'Perspectives on ageing, later life and ethnicity: ageing research in ethnic minority contexts' *Ageing and Society* 35(5): 897-916 doi:10.1017/S0144686X14001536